Turning Point: Zionism and Reform Judaism

BROWN JUDAIC STUDIES

Edited by

Jacob Neusner
Wendell S. Dietrich, Ernest S. Frerichs,
Sumner B. Twiss, Alan Zuckerman

Number 12

Turning Point: Zionism and Reform Judaism

by Howard R. Greenstein

Turning Point: Zionism and Reform Judaism

by

Howard R. Greenstein

Scholars Press

Distributed by
SCHOLARS PRESS
101 Salem Street
P.O. Box 2268
Chico, California 95927

Turning Point: Zionism and Reform Judaism

by Howard R. Greenstein

Library of Congress Cataloging in Publication Data

Greenstein, Howard R.
Turning point: Zionism and reform Judaism.

(Brown Judaic studies ; no. 12)
Bibliography: p.
1. Reform Judaism–United States–History–20th century. 2. Zionism and Judaism. I. Title. II. Series.
BM197.G72 296.3'877 81-8996
ISBN 0-89130-512-2 (pbk) AACR2

Printed in the United States of America
1 2 3 4 5
Edwards Brothers, Inc.
Ann Arbor, Michigan 48104

To

CARL HERMANN VOSS

lover of Israel and all peoples

TABLE OF CONTENTS

ACKNOWLEDGEMENTS. ix

INTRODUCTION. 1

CHAPTERS

1. THE PRELUDE TO THE COLUMBUS PLATFORM 9

2. THE JEWISH ARMY CONTROVERSY AND THE RISE OF THE AMERICAN COUNCIL FOR JUDAISM 33

3. THE HOUSTON CONTROVERSY. 51

4. ADVOCATES AND ADVERSARIES: THE INNER CONFLICT OVER ZIONISM. 73

5. DEBATE OVER THE AMERICAN JEWISH CONFERENCE 101

SUMMARY AND CONCLUSIONS. 127

NOTES 135

BIBLIOGRAPHY. 163

APPENDICES

A. THE STUDENT BODY -- TODAY AND YESTERDAY. 173

B. RESOLUTION ADOPTED AT INFORMAL MEETING OF RABBIS, 30 NOVEMBER 1943 AND APPROVED BY THE UAHC AT ITS BIENNIAL COUNCIL MEETING, 3-6 MARCH 1946 177

C. RESOLUTION ADOPTED BY THE EXECUTIVE BOARD OF THE UNION OF AMERICAN HEBREW CONGREGATIONS AT CHICAGO, SATURDAY, JUNE 5, 1948 179

D. REPLY TO RESOLUTION OF TRIBUTE TO THE STATE OF ISRAEL FROM THE EXECUTIVE BOARD OF THE UAHC. 181

INDEX 183

ACKNOWLEDGEMENTS

This book would never have materialized without the initial inspiration of Dr. Zvi Ankori, former Melton Professor of Jewish History, and Dr. Robert Chazan, who succeeded him in that same chair, during the period of my graduate studies at the Ohio State University from 1969 to 1973. I am most thankful to them both for helping me to develop and refine the subject of this study in my own mind.

In gathering the source materials for this effort, I am especially grateful to Dr. Jacob Radar Marcus, Director of the American Jewish Archives, and to Dr. Stanley Chyet, his former associate, for providing me with complete access to all pertinent archival materials and guiding me in locating previously unpublished documents. I deeply appreciate as well the very generous and gracious assistance of Ms. Miriam Leikind, former Librarian of the Abba Hillel Silver Archives at the Temple in Cleveland, Ohio, for responding to all my requests for information from that collection.

Most particularly, do I wish to thank my very dearest friend and colleague, the Rev. Dr. Carl Hermann Voss, whose literary skill and encyclopedic knowledge of the history of Zionism aided me immeasurably in the organization of the final manuscript, and to whom I dedicate this volume.

I am grateful to Ms. Virginia Bass for typing this manuscript in preparation for its publication and to Mrs. Deborah Schlackman for assisting me in the tedious task of indexing and proof-reading the final product.

Above and beyond all else, I am forever indebted to my family for their patience, encouragement and unbounded love. I refer specifically to my wife, Lenore, who was, is and forever will be the turning point of my life, and to my children, Lisa, Micah and Karen in whom I find the fulfillment of my fondest dreams.

INTRODUCTION

The roots of the conflict between Zionism and Reform Judaism actually originated in the aftermath of the French Revolution. The ideas of liberty, equality and fraternity shattered the foundations of monarchies which had existed in Europe for centuries. With the Declaration of the Rights of Man, thousands of Jews envisioned the imminent arrival of the Messianic Age and actively solicited support for a program of Liberal Judaism which would divest Jewish life of its parochial features and emphasize instead those moral principles on which all men could and inevitably would unite. They proclaimed an abiding faith in the redemption of the Jewish people and all peoples through the democratic process, and they lived by that faith. Many of them even believed that Judaism properly conceived and practiced, would eventually destroy itself, because a world of peace and harmony would no longer require the Jewish people as the special envoys of moral truth.

The early leaders of Reform Judaism in Germany and later in America were not only liberals intellectually. They were firm believers in the political Messianism which proclaimed the imminent brotherhood of all men. They joined their political liberalism to their spiritual liberalism and declared that Reform Judaism was not only a religion for the liberated mind of the new day, but it was now and forever anti-nationalist. Whereas traditional Judaism had temporarily suspended all laws depending upon residence in Israel for their fulfillment, Reform completely abrogated them. It rejected all laws pertaining to the priests and Levites and declared instead that all Jews were a "kingdom of priests and a holy people" and that the obligations for moral purity applied to every Jew with equal responsibility.

The Reform prayerbook eliminated references to "Galut" (Exile) or to a Messiah who would miraculously restore world Jewry to the land of Israel and rebuild the Temple in Jerusalem. It eliminated all prayers referring to "Shivat Zion" (a return to Zion), since Reform Judaism insisted that the mission of Judaism required the active participation of Jews in all lands of the Diaspora. They regarded the nationalist period of Jewish life as only a temporary stage in the evolutionary development of Judaism which existed only to prepare the Jewish people for the opportunity of service to all mankind.

At the time of the Pittsburgh Platform in 1885, Reform Judaism could have or had already become the religion of the majority of American Jews. The climate of social liberalism and the birth of the Social Gospel in American Protestantism made Reform Judaism and its emphasis on prophetic moralities extremely palatable to large numbers of Jews who welcomed as few differences as possible between them and their non-Jewish neighbors. By the end of the 19th Century, the majority of congregations in the United States were in fact affiliated with the national synagogue body of Reform Judaism, the Union of American Hebrew Congregations (UAHC).

When the tide of Jewish immigration to America shifted from its source in Germany to sources in Eastern Europe, the Reform movement began to suffer from a numerical decline. East European immigrants at first did not join, and certainly did not establish any Reform Temples. It was not the liberalism of the Reform synagogue which discouraged them. Many of them were extremely daring in their political and social ideologies and would have found considerable reinforcement in Reform synagogues. What alienated them from Reform Judaism more than anything else was its repudiation of Jewish nationhood. The immigrants from Eastern Europe had been oppressed as a people and uprooted as a people, regardless of their religious beliefs. Experience had taught them that what really mattered was not how they worshipped, but who they were. Their experience would not permit them to deny their identity as a people, and they were convinced that those who did deny that reality were either fools or dreamers. These new immigrants were not all Jewish Nationalists, but all of them acknowledged the reality and the primacy of Jewish peoplehood.

Jewish Nationalists did not share the enthusiasm of Reform Jews for the promise of the Emancipation. The prospect of complete freedom for the Jew, in their estimation, was and remained a Messianic hope and not a reality. The oppression, persecution and suffering, which they had endured, convinced them that ordinary safeguards for human liberty did not include Jews. The only assurance of creative Jewish survival, they claimed, rested on the principle of self-determination for the Jewish people. Only if the Jewish people enjoyed the same conditions of sovereignty and independence as other people, only if they could achieve a "normal" existence, could they expect to live fully as free men. Such conditions required a nation of their own. Any other alternative was a hopeless enterprise, doomed to inevitable disaster. The emergence of modern Zionism under the leadership of Theodore Herzl began with this proposition as its premise. For fifty years following the first Basel Conference, the Zionist movement labored to achieve the fulfillment of its dream, the reestablishment of Jewish sovereignty in the land of Palestine.

Zionism elicited substantial support in lands where the problem of Jewish "homelessness" was an oppressive reality. The Jews of Eastern Europe, who suffered repeated waves of persecution under Polish and Russian monarchs, appreciated the implications of Herzl's analysis for their own safety and security. The Jews of Western Europe, however, most of whom were still reaping the harvest of Emancipation, mixing freely with non-Jews in political, social and economic life, could not believe that they were strangers on their own soil.

For the founders of American Reform Judaism especially, the question of "homelessness" was preposterous. They were convinced that Jews were more at home here in the young, vibrant, promising and prosperous democracy of America than they could have possibly been anywhere else in the world, including Western Europe. Jews were not primarily a nation. They were a religious community. Their major task was not the restoration of a sovereign, secular state, but the dissemination of prophetic ideals of justice, truth, love, brotherhood and peace. The leaders of American Reform Judaism considered themselves the spokesmen and fore-runners of a new age of universal understanding and good will, a world devoid of all the old hatreds and prejudices.

American Reform was essentially an attempt by likeminded, religiously oriented Jews to meet this prospect of a new age by shaping their belief and practice according to the requirements of reason and individual conscience. It rested upon the premise that religion, no less than all other human disciplines, is evolutionary and cannot claim any monopoly on truth or knowledge. In addition, religious truth could transcend but not contradict the rules of rational thought. The principal task, as the founders of Reform understood it, was to develop the ability to distinguish the essential, "eternal" realities from the changing form.

The major controversy in Reform circles centered on the extent of change that was necessary. Without the authority of divine revelation, Reform Judaism confronted the problem of democratic authority. The only basis for truth, in the absence of any supernatural source, was a consensus of individual, human minds. The Reform position implied that just as it was impossible in the modern world of politics to return to the rule of kings or feudal barons, so was it equally impossible in religion to assume that the word of God was the foundation for religious practice. The new scientific method required a new rationale for claims to knowledge.

In the context of Reform Judaism, the quality which distinguished the Jewish people from all others, was not its ritual peculiarities, but its prophetic mission to become a "light unto the nations." The founders of Reform conceived of that function in almost exclusively ethical terms. If Israel was in any way a "chosen people," it was a matter of their special responsibility as the spokesmen for humanity. By their words and their performance, they were charged to insist that the management of human affairs must be subject to the rule of justice and mercy. The major task of the Jewish community was to labor actively toward the fulfillment of the Messianic promise of peace, brotherhood and righteousness among all men.

The collision between Zionist claims of Jewish "homelessness" and the Reform emphasis on the prophetic and religious priorities for modern Judaism was immediate and inevitable. Each assumed a different concept of Jewish peoplehood and faith and each attached a different meaning to the significance of Jewish history and experience. Each also appealed to a different segment of the Jewish community. Reform Judaism emerged out of the emancipation of Western Europe, especially, in Germany. Zionism arose out of the kind of repressive conditions which prevailed in Eastern Europe.

Although the ideology of early Reform Judaism was clearly anti-Zionist, not all Reform Jews were. Some of the earliest Reform Rabbis in America were ardent Zionists. More importantly, the range of support and opposition to Zionism was extremely broad and complex. Between those few who endorsed Zionist goals, and the many who loathed any reference to Zion, was a substantial conglomeration, with considerably ambivalent attitudes towards Jewish nationalism. In some circles, the opposition was based primarily upon a resistance to the political aspects and ideology of Zionism and not to the colonization of Palestine, particularly as a refuge for oppressed Jews. These adversaries objected only to the proposed plan for a Jewish state, the Zionist concept of a separate Jewish nation, and to such an alternative as a solution for Jewish suffering and oppression. They opposed "political" Zionism, the establishment of an independent commonwealth, but not what they called "practical" Zionism, or the resettlement of Jews in Palestine.

In addition to these "practical" Zionists, concerned about Palestine only as a haven of refuge, were those who followed in the footsteps of Ahad Ha'am, one of the earliest and best known essayists on cultural Zionism. They envisioned a Jewish presence on their cultural Zionism. They envisioned a Jewish presence on their ancient soil as a source of profound spiritual inspiration and enrichment. They endorsed a concept of Palestine as at least mercaz ruchani - the spiritual center of world Jewry. They hoped, as did Ahad Ha'am, that the cultural influence of a small but creative nucleus in Palestine would consolidate all Jews everywhere. They shared Ahad Ha'am's position that a return to Palestine was basically a manifestation of Jewish peoplehood expressed through the revival of Jewish culture. The first item on the agenda of world Jewry must be a solution to the problem of Judaism, not of immigration.

Many Reform moderates on Zionism also took comfort in Ahad Ha'am's awareness of the political complications of Jewish settlement in Palestine. Palestine was simply not a vacuum. He warned repeatedly that it was occupied and ruled by other people whose national interests were also inseparable from the land; and concluded that existing historical conditions were hardly encouraging for the prospect of massive Jewish immigration. At least, it was not a likely development for the foreseeable future. Such an analysis met with warm approval in many Reform communities.

It is important then, in tracing the conflict between Zionism and Reform Judaism, to recognize the various degrees and kinds of opposition and support. There were many gradations; and, even within a particular stance, consistency was often a rare viture. Reform Jews and others qualified their endorsement of Zionism by describing themselves as "political Zionists," "cultural Zionists," "spiritual Zionists," "non-Zionists" or simply "anti-Zionists." Essentially, however, few Reform Jews objected to programs which would permit Jews to go to Palestine, to build up their homes, to cultivate the Hebrew language, to practice Judaism, to produce art, literature and music in a Jewish environment and to live useful, creative lives there as Jews. The overwhelming opposition to Zionism in Reform Judaism was directed against the objective of the Zionist movement to establish an independent, political Jewish state in Palestine. That was the heart of the conflict - not the question of relief and rescue, of immigration, of settlement, of reconstruction, of philanthropic and spiritual support for special Palestine projects. The heart of the conflict was the establishment of a third Jewish commonwealth.

Whatever the range of gradations may have been in Reform Judaism on the subject of Zionism, the movement has unquestionably traveled an enormous distance in the course of almost a hundred years. Few if any other issues in Reform Judaism ever elicited the passion and furor which Zionism produced. Dr. David Philipson, as late as 1929, could declare that "Palestine represents for us an outgrown phase of Jewish historical experience. Back to Palestine is not our rallying cry . . . . To those of us who are Jews in religion and Americans in nationality, political Zionism is anathema."

That position is remote from that which Roland B. Gittelsohn articulated as President of the Central Conference of American Rabbis (CCAR) in 1970 when he declared that "we (Reform Jews) shall use our influence, wherever and whenever we can, to persaude the world that its own survival and integrity are irrevocably linked with those of Israel. We shall do all this not as a gesture of philanthropy, but because we know how imperative the survival of Israel is for the enhancement and vitality of our own Judaism."

The beginnings of reconciliation between the opposing camps, of course, coincided with the inception of the conflict itself. From the very first announcement of the Zionist program at the Basel Conference in 1897, there were forces at work within the Reform movement which sought to bridge the distance between both ideologies. The major focus of the work that follows, however, concentrates primarily on the period from the passage of the Columbus Platform in 1937 to the establishment of the State of Israel in 1948.

The period under examination was chosen for several considerations. First, it is the most recent but the least understood period in the entire history of transition in Reform Judaism on this issue. The earlier periods have been studied previously, but this crucial juncture of little more than a decade has not yet been carefully examined. Secondly, the Columbus Platform is frequently considered the culmination of the transformation in Reform Judaism on Zionism. Anything which followed that Platform was regarded as anti-climatic. The plank on Palestine repudiated the anti-nationalist statements of the Pittsburgh Platform which signaled for many Zionist sympathizers in Reform Judaism the decisive victory for Zionism. The evidence cited in the following pages suggests that subsequent events were hardly insignificant, but rather were crucial to the ultimate position of liberal Judaism.

In addition, many of those who participated in the decisions of this period are still living, and their personal observations helped considerably to substantiate the reports and records of this decisive juncture. Indeed, the information on this issue was much more plentiful and accessible for this more recent interval than for earlier ones. The terminal point in 1948 was chosen because all debate which followed that date was purely academic. The actual existence of the State of Israel terminated all the controversy about its necessity or merits.

Most of the source material for this study derived from memoirs, correspondence of the major participants, and from the official records and reports of meetings which included discussions and decisions bearing on the subject of Zionism. In addition, numerous articles, periodicals and newspaper accounts provided helpful insights into the nature of the issue and its ramifications. Especially valuable were the personal interviews which the author was able to arrange with several key figures in the controversy, including Maurice N. Eisendrath, Abraham J. Feldman, James G. Heller, Arthur J. Lelyveld, Jacob R. Marcus, Mortimer May, Samuel Wohl. The author also benefited from personal correspondence with others who also participated actively, such as Philip Bernstein, Sidney Brooks, Leon Feuer, Robert I. Kahn, Morris S. Lazaron, Julian Morgenstern, Jacob Rudin and Hyman Judah Schachtel.

Most of the materials which contributed to this study were secured or obtained on loan from the American Jewish Archives in Cincinnati, the Abba Hillel Silver Archives in Cleveland, the Library of the Union of American Hebrew Congregations in New York and the Library of the Hebrew Union College - Jewish Institute of Religion in Cincinnati. The author is especially indebted to the Director of the American Jewish Archives, Dr. Jacob R. Marcus and his Associate, Dr. Stanley F. Chyet and to the librarian of the Abba Hillel Silver Archives, Ms. Miriam Leikind, for their generous and invaluable assistance in locating and explaining the information available in their files on this subject.

One area which the author attempted to explore but for which specific material is extremely scanty was the domain of congregational activity. Temple bulletins of the period mention very little if anything at all about support or opposition to Zionism. A congregation occasionally invited a speaker to present his position on the issue, but there was little evidence of any public reaction.

The following study embraces as much material as could be obtained in an effort to understand the historical perspective of the controversy over Zionism in Reform Judaism and the dynamics of the realities which transformed the movement from staunch opposition to ardent support. To comprehend the way in which Reform Judaism changed so radically on this issue is to comprehend the dimensions of its most serious challenge of almost a century.

CHAPTER 1
THE PRELUDE TO THE COLUMBUS PLATFORM

Any discussion of Reform Judaism and Zionism requires some preliminary understanding of the nature of Reform Judaism. Reform Judaism is not a monolithic structure. The movement is not regulated by any binding source of authority. Its position on Zionism or any other issue must be extracted from a wide range of statements and decisions by professional spokesmen, lay leaders and active participants. What complicates the matter even further is the existence of three major component organizations in the movement, each of which is related to, but independent of, the others.

In order of their establishment, the organizational structure of Reform Judaism consists of its lay body, The Union of American Hebrew Congregations, its seminary, the Hebrew Union College-Jewish Institute of Religion, and its rabbinical arm, the Central Conference of American Rabbis. The College-Institute and the Union presently receive financial support from a single fund-raising apparatus, but during the period under examination, each of those institutions operated with a substantial measure of independence, both financial and ideological. In discussing, therefore, the position of "Reform Judaism" it is largely a matter of extracting particular postures from each of its major institutions and their spokesmen and attempting to construct out of that material some features of general consensus.[1]

It is a major thesis of this study that the controversy over Zionism did not reach its zenith with the passage of the Columbus Platform in 1937.[2] It was unquestionably a turning point in the reassessment of the merits of Jewish nationalism in Reform circles, but it also sowed the seeds of further discord which would not produce complete support for Jewish nationalism until the re-establistment of a Jewish state in Palestine in 1948.

Understanding the events which followed the Columbus Platform requires first an understanding of the events which preceded it. That is the purpose of this chapter which can be reached most fruitfully by analyzing the earlier debates over Zionism from the perspective of the three major institutions in Reform Jewish life, the Conference, the College and the Union of American Hebrew Congregations.

This attempt to define the significance of the pre-Columbus period is not intended to be an exhaustive one. Studies of earlier Reform attitudes toward Zionism have received extensive treatment elsewhere.[3] This analysis is designed only to recapitulate the highlights and major developments in Reform Judaism on the subject of Zionism prior to the Columbus Platform as a helpful prerequisite for better understanding the turbulent period following the adoption of the Platform until the re-establishment of the Jewish state in 1948. It is a story which sounded only the opening volleys to one of the most bitter and divisive conflicts in the history of American Reform Judaism.

The story begins with Isaac Mayer Wise, the major spokesman and organizing genius of the early Reform movement in America. Wise was a bitter adversary of Zionism from its very inception, because, he charged, it was incompatible with the aims of liberal Judaism. The major vehicle of his opposition was the Anglo-Jewish weekly newspaper which he published, The American Israelite. The pages of the Israelite were constantly filled with a barrage of condemnations of what Wise called "Ziomania."[4] Aside from his ideological opposition,[5] Wise was convinced that the whole Zionist scheme was impractical and even dangerous.[6]

He did not limit his denunciations to the newspaper. Following the close of the first Zionist Conference in Basle in 1897, Wise unloaded a blistering article on the subject in the Hebrew Union College Journal.[7] He opened with a magnanimous concession that to support "this extended Benai Berith association chiefly for the benefit of Russian, Polish and Roumanian coreligionists" was a highly commendable gesture "like the dispensation of alms in any form."[8] So far as Wise was concerned, the only redeeming feature of Zionism was the opportunity it afforded for wealthy "Western Jews" to rescue their less fortunate brethren in Eastern Europe from poverty, persecution and even death. He praised philanthropists like the Baron deRothschild, who harbored grave misgivings about the wisdom of Jewish emigration to Palestine but supported it nonetheless in an effort to relieve the distress of afflicted Jews.

Wise was most annoyed, however, when "those Zionists came to whip us again into the dark corners of isolation . . ."[9] In his view the claim to Jewish nationhood was entirely unwarranted, because it had not existed for nearly 2000 years. Zionism was simply the product of romantic, misguided nostalgia at best and would only "brand us fossils and mummies, fit subjects for the museum . . . No normal man can believe that we Jews leave the great nations of culture, power and abundant prosperity in which we form an integral element, to form a ridiculous miniature State in dried-up Palestine; nor did Hertzl or Nordau ever believe it. They evidently . . . had this in view, to expose the Jewisn communities as foolish and sentimental phantasts; and in this they succeeded well to a large extent . . . . We can never identify ourselves with Zionism."[10]

Since Wise was also the founder of the Hebrew Union College as well as a virulent anti-Zionist, it is not difficult to understand why this seminary for Reform rabbis did not look favorably upon Jewish nationalism for many years. That condition however also posed a strange paradox. While the College remained a bitter adversary of Zionism under the influence of Wise and his immediate successors, it was the first of the three major institutions in Reform Judaism to evidence a transition. The Hebrew Union College was clearly sympathetic to Zionism long before either the CCAR or the UAHC had made any accommodation. That development deserves some detailed explanation.

Admittedly, the College faculty had always included an occasional Zionist, but such scholars were conspicuous by their lonely distinction. One of the most popular and distinguished was Professor Casper Levias, an early Zionist spokesman and advocate. Levias had been unexpectedly called upon in 1899 to defend Zionism before the annual meeting of the Central Conference of American Rabbis. Being unprepared for any effective presentation, he declined the invitation but promised to provide a manuscript on the subject for publication in the next issue of the CCAR Yearbook. The Conference, however, rejected his request which explains why Levias released it for publication in the H.U.C. Journal.[11] The article was a most thoughtful and perceptive presentation of the argument for Zionism, but it stirred barely a ripple in a sea of antagonism at H.U.C.[12]

In those early days at the College, one of the major objections to the Zionist program was an ideological one. Support for Jewish settlement in Palestine was altogether different from support of Jewish political sovereignty. This was a distinction with which the CCAR and the Union would also inevitably wrestle, but the struggle at the College began much earlier and terminated much sooner. Very likely the controversy erupted there first for the same reason that ideological debates usually begin in the academic community. The world of ideas is their primary concern and investigation of ideas its primary pursuit. Conventional wisdom is subject to continuous reassessment.

Until at least the announcement of the Balfour Declaration in 1917, a substantial majority of students and faculty at H.U.C. agreed that the emphasis on nationalism as the principal solution to anti-Semitism was incompatible with the exuberant optimism of the Pittsburgh Platform which anticipated and wlecomed a new world order founded on brotherhood, peace, and justice for all men, irrespective of their cultural or political differences.[13] The creative role of the Jewish people in this effort was indisputable, but a Jewish state was not.

Perhaps the best evidence for the adverse climate for Zionism prevailing at the College in these early years derives from three episodes, each of which directly involved the president of the Hebrew Union College, Dr. Kaufmann Kohler. Kohler was a militant anti-Zionist, although some would contend that he mellowed on the subject in his twilight years.[14] However he may have changed at the end, his presidency was marked by repeated attempts to resist any Zionist influence at the Reform seminary. The first incident involved the dismissal of Professor Levias in 1905. Kohler informed the Board of Governors that Levias was "no teacher such as we need, outside of his grammar."[15] To replace him, Kohler recommended the appointment of Max Margolis whom he described as "a scholar of note . . . thoroughly imbued with the spirit of Reform Judaism, who is no Zionist and not a one-sided man . . . ."[16]

Following this decision, Kohler sparked a major controversy two years later with a recommendation for further dismissals, including Margolis whom he had nominated earlier to succeed Levias. Max Margolis had undergone a complete ideological reversal from extreme universalism to Jewish nationalism and had set himself to agitating against the basic ideas of Reform Judaism as represented by the College and championed by Dr. Kohler.[17] Two other professors had associated themselves with him. One of them, Henry Malter, was by temperament unable to adjust to American Judaism and was particularly resentful of the atmosphere and spirit that prevailed at H.U.C. The third party was Max Schloessinger who joined his other two colleagues in creating unrest among the students and challenging the position of the President. According to David Philipson, all three men submitted their resignations expecting them to be rejected.[18] Instead, they were accepted. Despite denials there was very likely a question of Lehrenfreiheit involved, or that support for Zionism was a major consideration in the dismissal of all three professors.[19] Even Kohler himself replied to protest from students and alumni that academic freedom is proper only in a secular university but not in a theological seminary which is dedicated to the teaching of certain definite doctrines.[20]

The third and final incident demonstrating the prevailing mood at the College on this issue involved a speaking invitation to Horace Kallen in 1915. The student body invited Professor Kallen to deliver an address to a College audience on the subject of Zionism. Kallen was a member of the faculty at the University of Wisconsin; and, when Louis Brandeis became President of the Provisional Executive Committee for General Zionist Affairs, Kallen rallied to the support of the Zionist program.[21] The invitation from the students met with an indignant response from the President. Kohler actually cancelled Kallen's scheduled appearance which in turn produced a storm of protest from the student body.[22] The student officers appealed to Rabbi Stephen Wise, who immediately left New York for Cincinnati to arrange a conference on the subject with Kohler and student representatives. As a result of that meeting, a new policy on community affairs provided that any Jew would be permitted to speak on Zionism at the Hebrew Union College. That concession which Kohler yielded very reluctantly was a most significant achievement for Zionist supporters.

The fact that the subject of Zionism was no longer at least officially taboo made it easier for students and faculty to voice their honest convictions on the issue. Although some students had always defended the merits of Jewish nationalism privately, now they felt safer doing so publicly. Shortly following the Kallen episode, a rabbinical student delivered a sermon in the chapel at H.U.C. endorsing Zionism as an asset to Reform Judaism. The student was James Heller, no newcomer to the Zionist philosophy. His father, Max Heller, ranked among the earliest and staunchest advocates of the Zionist program, and James had been conditioned at an early age to the merits of Jewish nationalism. As a student and later as a rabbi and President of the CCAR, he mobilized every ounce of strength toward achieving the goal of Jewish statehood which had motivated so much of his father's career.

Heller's sermon is too lengthy to reproduce in its entirety here, but it was a masterful exercise in reason and oratorical skill.[23] He argued essentially that all human behavior and ideals are the reflection of the particular human spirit, and that Jewish ideals are therefore the reflection of the Jewish spirit. Such a spirit, he continued, must be embodied in some existing structure in order to achieve any lasting results.[24] He cited specific episodes in Jewish history as evidence for that thesis.[25] He submitted that the universal mission of the Jewish people could be fulfilled only by the restoration of its nationhood.[26] He cited the Biblical prophets themselves as fervent nationalists as well as universalists. "What right have we," he concluded, "to accept the prophets' ideals of justice, righteousness and the knowledge of God--and call them our superiors in spiritual insight--and to refuse recognition of their belief in the mission of the Jewish nation?"[27]

Heller may have persuaded a few listeners that Sabbath morning, but Kohler was not one of them. He saved his rebuttal for the opening exercises of the College on October 14, 1916. This time, however, Kohler's rebuttal was significantly different in character. For the first time in public forum, his tone was defensive in quality. He spoke of the "perversity" and "degeneracy" of the present generation, and confessed a failure to understand how informed and knowledgable Jews could be Zionists.[28] He could only explain the phenomenon by charging that "ignorance and irreligion are at the bottom of the whole movement of political nationalism."[29]

The transition at the College gathered rapid momentum with the formal announcement of the Balfour Declaration in 1917. Arthur James Balfour, the Foreign Secretary of Great Britain, addressed his statement to Lord Rothschild assuring him that "his Majesty's government views with favor the establishment in Palestine of a national home for the Jewish people, and will use their best endeavors to facilitate the achievement of this object, it being clearly understood that nothing shall be done which may prejudice the civil and religious rights of existing non-Jewish communities in Palestine, or the rights and political status enjoyed by Jews in any other country."

Following the announcement of this official British policy, the Allied Powers charged Great Britain with the Mandate for Palestine at their meeting in April, 1920, at San Remo, Italy. The League of Nations subsequently confirmed the Mandate on July 24, 1922 and invested Great Britain with complete responsibility for providing the favorable conditions that would provide for the establishment of a national Jewish home. In 1922, President Warren G. Harding signed a Joint Congressional Resolution expressing the approval of the United States for the terms of the Balfour Declaration, and by the close of that same year, a total of fifty-two governments had endorsed the Declaration which embodied the basic political aims of the Zionist movement.[30] Modern Zionism had won the most convincing victory in its short history.

That victory triggered a considerable shift in support for Zionism at the College, especially among the students. Students began publising articles explaining the rationale for their "conversion" to Zionism.[31] Far from presenting them with a conflict in their rabbinic careers, they envisioned the establishment of a Jewish state as a goal and aim which would itself fortify Judaism with new vitality and enthusiasm. In 1928 the College awarded an honorary degree of Doctor of Hebrew Letters to Chaim Weizmann, then President of the World Zionist Organization.

Responding to the reorganization of the Jewish Agency for Palestine in 1929, an editorial in the Hebrew Union College Monthly applauded the representatives of "all religious, cultural and economic strata in American Jewish life" who "have accepted at Zurich the principle of joint and open action in the cultural and economic rehabilitation of Palestine."[32] The editorial urged the Agency to act rapidly and vigorously on this principle and concluded with a resounding affirmation that "many of us at the Hebrew Union College regard the Jewish Agency as a magnificent constructive endeavor, bound to imbue the rickety ideal of Kelal Yisrael with new strength and destined to transform the communities of the Diaspora in countless ways."

Several students also registered a vigorous protest in 1929 over a substantial number of failures on the qualifying examinations for the Bachelor of Hebrew Letters degree. They objected to procedures which "let a student stroll serenely through the classrooms for four or five years and then to chop off his head.[33] It expressed the hope, however, that such students might be "the last victims of a transition which the College is undergoing."

It was clearly evident at the College that this "transition" included a growing tendency to replace the classical humanist approach with a more concentrated Hebraic one. Notwithstanding the contributions of early American Reform rabbis to the emphasis on prophetic ideals and the use of the vernacular in all synagogue affairs, they were still, for this new generation of younger colleagues, "the inevitable products of the Seventies and Eighties, decades in which Reform Judaism provided eloquent periods but no living realities."[34] Such changes in curriculum evidently signalled a shift toward a more traditionalist approach among the faculty as well as the students, since such decisions were not controlled by the student body.

The increasing concern for more traditional elements in Reform ideology, of which ahavath Zion was certainly one, manifested itself in a variety of ways. Objections were raised to the use of the term "minister" in Reform circles instead of "rabbi."[35] Comparisons were drawn between the lethargy of young people in Temple affairs in contrast to the "incredible resurgence of interest among young people in Zionist organizations."[36] The rabbinic faculty was summoned to "the task of Judaizing the students of the Hebrew Union College," specifying provision for courses in such areas as emigration, Zionism, and international philantropic work.[37] The students even criticized themselves for rejecting Orthodox elements in the liturgy without specifying the superior merit of their alternatives. Opposition to Orthodoxy was evidently a major proposition of many sermons with defense of Reform as the corollary. The discontent with "classical Reform" reached its peak with an angry allegation that "the reform movement consists conspicuously of empty utterances and time-worn platitudes; it must return to a more concretely Jewish point of view. The emotional appeal of orthodox Judaism must be instilled into the reform movement."[38]

This "transition" process from an emphasis on universal morality to an emphasis on traditional norms received almost an official endorsement from the students in a major statement on "Jewish Studies and Jewishness."[39] Specifically, the statement included a request for certain changes in curriculum which would provide for new courses in Yiddish literature, current Jewish literature, modern Jewish problems, psychology of religion and even the creation of a whole department in comparative religion.

The nature of these proposed innovations were in themselves sufficient to raise eyebrows among many Reform laymen and even some rabbis, especially an offering in Yiddish literature. Even more remarkable, however, was the explanation for such proposals. A representative segment of Reform rabbinic students now declared that adequate preparation should equip them not only for an intellectual appreciation of Judaism, but for an emotional fulfillment as well. Reason alone was insufficient for true insight into the nature of man and his world. Truth encompassed the heart as well as the mind. Such a perspective would have elicited a sharp rebuttal from Kaufmann Kohler, but apparently the new President, Julian Morgenstern, did not debate the issue at all. Morgenstern was by no means sympathetic to Zionism, as will be amply demonstrated elsewhere; but, unlike Kohler, he was willing to permit faculty and students to follow their own direction.[40]

For a seminary that began with unquestioned allegiance to "Wissenschaft des Judentums," with absolute confidence in the rule of reason and wholesale rejection of non-rational impulses, including the emotive components of Jewish ritual and ceremony, such a declaration implied a substantial shift in practice and ideology. The lofty idealism of the early Reformers had yielded to a quest for rootedness. There was more interest than ever before in reclaiming the past before redeeming the future. There was a renewed search for ideas and institutions that would build new attachments to Jewish history and culture. Zionism afforded an effective means toward that end and became a natural outlet for all the enthusiasm generated by a paramount concern for Jewish problems.

The final and most convincing verification of this transformation emerged out of a survey by one of the senior students, D. Max Eichorn.[41] The survey compared the attitudes of rabbis who had been students in 1900 with the existing student body in 1930. The results helped considerably to explain why changes in attitude toward Zionism began and ended first at the Hebrew Union College before they visibly affected either the Central Conference of American Rabbis or the Union of American Hebrew Congregations. First, it was clear that by 1930 the overwhelming majority of students were the second generation of East European immigrant stock. While students of West European parentage were decreasing in number, students of East European parentage were increasing. The rapid rise of mixed parentage (East European and West European) indicated that the old animosities and dichotomies between the two communities were obviously diminishing.

By 1930 the total attitude toward East European Jews had undergone a transformation. While many students in 1900 looked upon them largely as social service recipients, students in 1930 regarded them as the preservers of Judaism in America. One student in 1930 described the East European Jew as "the saving remnant who set ablaze the modern Jewish renaissance with a spark from the fire within. His spiritual stiff-neckedness preserved him as a Jew and has made possible the continuance of Jewish ideals. He made Zionism possible, he revived Hebrew, he saved the Jewish group from spiritual extinction."[42] Whereas East European Jews had once been a source of embarrassment they had become by 1930 a romantic model of Jewish excellence.

Another factor which accelerated the change in attitude toward Zionism was the steady influx of traditional elements. Although there was a growing feeling that Yiddish could not long survive in the modern world (an attitude formulated before the advent of the Holocaust), most students declared themselves overwhelmingly receptive to Yiddish in 1930. Far greater numbers of them were able to read and speak the language than was the case in 1900.

The pendulum had also shifted on the issue of ritual and ceremony. A pronounced bias in favor of eliminating ceremony from Judaism in 1900 had dwindled to practically nothing in 1930. Indeed, to the contrary, the reassessment had produced an increasing demand for more ceremonialism.

Finally, the concept of the rabbinate had changed. The students of 1930 were far less concerned with oratory and prophetic Judaism than with Jewish scholarship and Jewish values. In evaluating the qualifications of his classmates for service in the rabbinate, one student expressed high regard for their intellectual competence but added that "many of them are not well-fitted for the ministry . . . because of lack of common sense and sympathy for the Jewish people, their needs and troubles."[43] The changing self-image could also be attributed to the fact that with the shift in immigration patterns in the early twentieth century, fewer students were coming to the College from Reform homes, as Orthodox and Conservative Judaism began to mobilize substantial followings of their own.

This was the emotional and intellectual baggage which the rabbinic leadership of Reform Judaism would bring to the issue of Zionism on the eve of its fiercest struggle both within and outside the ranks of the Reform movement. Their commitment to Zionism was not conditioned by the desperate plight of European Jewry, which was not at all yet apparent. Neither could they be classified as Zionists because of their poverty and desperate struggle for upward socio-economic mobility, a charge which anti-Zionist Reformers had so often invoked to dismiss the credibility of the Zionist cause. These pro-Zionist rabbinic students came from far more prosperous families than their predecessors. They were Zionists as a result of their prescription for improving the quality of Jewish life. Zionism was for them a key to Jewish survival and regeneration in the Diaspora. That conviction would become a decisive factor in reshaping the attitude of the entire movement toward the concept of Jewish nationhood.

****

This rapid transformation on the Zionist question at the Hebrew Union College did not affect leading laymen of the Union of American Hebrew Congregations nearly as much as it did the future Reform rabbis of America. In fact, there was enormous distance between the two groups. The UAHC never voiced even one word of support for Jewish settlement in Palestine until 1923.[44] That the lay leadership of Reform Judaism would endorse any effort to rebuild Palestine was itself a notable achievement, but what made this action especially significant was the approval of such a resolution despite its rejection by the Resolutions Committee.[45]

Until this period Reform laymen rested their position entirely on the terms of the Pittsburgh Platform of 1885. The Platform itself included eight major planks, proclaiming in Kaufmann Kohler's terms "what Judaism is and what Reform Judaism means and aims at."[46] The fifth plank of the Platform embodied an outright rejection of any attempt to restore an independent Jewish commonwealth. It declared that "we consider ourselves no longer a nation but a religious community, and therefore expect neither a return to Palestine . . . nor the restoration of any of the laws concerning the Jewish state."

Zionism, as a political movement of Jewish nationalism, was a weak adversary at this time. The major storm signals for Reform Judaism were originating not from Europe but from the Lower East Side of New York City as a result of the massive waves of immigration from Eastern Europe. The major segment of the resident American Jewish community in the late 19th century was of Germanic origin and descent. These "German Jews" were already highly acculturated and acclimated to American society and extremely anxious to prove in substance and style that their approach to Judaism was most compatible with American principles of freedom and democracy. Even in Europe their attachments to Judaism had been almost exclusively religious; and they participated in national affairs in the spirit of liberty, equality and brotherhood.

The new Jewish immigrants arrived from an entirely different environment. Far less universal in their culture and social relationships, they came from relatively self-contained Jewish communities. They were much less "westernized" and, by secular standards, extremely ignorant, not only strangers to the non-Jewish world but scornful of it and very suspicious. Judaism for them was not simply a matter of faith; it encompassed every conceivable activity in their lives. It dictated what they should eat and wear, what they should learn and teach, what they should approve and reject. It determined where and how they should organize their entire existence. That some Jews, like those they found in America, could be Jewish only in religious terms, and Reform no less, was entirely incomprehensible to them.

Consequently, the well-acclimated, successful, highly-cultured resident German Jew was most reluctant to welcome his impoverished, ignorant, parochial and cowering cousin from Eastern Europe. In truth, the feeling was mutual. They not only resented each other; they rejected each other.

Part of the cultural heritage the new immigrant brought with them, resented and rejected by German Reform Jewry, was their philosophy of Jewish socialism and Jewish nationalism which envisioned the future of the Jewish community as a single, integrated, autonomous unity, self-sufficient and independent of non-Jewish society. Polish and Russian Jews were among the early disciples of such pre-Zionist movements as Bilu and Chovevay Zion. They embraced a mentality of "clannishness" which was wholly alien and repugnant to American German-Jews.[47]

Few features of the Pittsburgh Platform received such overwhelming endorsement as did the opposition to Jewish nationalism.[48] In the report of the discussions which followed the presentation of the Platform in Pittsburgh, the assembled rabbis debated portions of almost every paragraph except that dealing with Zionism.[49] They argued over propositions involving revelation, resurrection, the role of ritual and cermony, and Messianism, but not over the question of Jewish nationalism. The conversation on that subject was apparently not considered sufficiently significant even to record. Zionism received a resounding defeat.

Leading Reform laymen were among the most vigorous spokesmen for an unprecedented age of peace, justice, and brotherhood the dawn of which, in their view, was imminent. A considerable measure of their optimism about the future may be attributed to the mood of the times. Reform Judaism achieved a position of commanding leadership in the American Jewish community in what was probably the most dynamic period of growth and expansion in American history. Enormous improvements in transportation and communication, the constant movement westward, the rapid rise of big business and giant corporations, the incredibly rapid accumulation of wealth and increase in the money supply, and the steady improvement in political stability all produced a climate of "manifest destiny" which implied for most Americans that their nation would dominate the future destinies of mankind.

Coupled with this political and economic enthusiasm was an equal uncertainty about the prospects for social improvement. Problems of ignorance, poverty, disease, prejudice and discrimination were no longer consigned to the realm of the "inevitable." Several visible signs of public concern were emerging, not the least of which was the Protestant Social Gospel. Liberal rabbis were influenced in no small measure by the zeal of ministers like Washington Gladden who insisted that all economic questions were essentially spiritual ones, since spiritual matters suffused all compartments of everyday life.[50] The language of the early Reformers in projecting the hope of the future was not far removed from phrases like "the enthusiasm of concerned Christians for the improvement of social morality."[51] Publications like The Dawn,[52] experimental communities like The Christian Commonwealth Colony,[53] and especially measurable results such as the assult of Tammany Hall by the Rev. Charles Parkhurst[54] all contributed to a growing confidence that mankind was on the threshold of a new era of moral excellence.

This "dawn of a new world" also presumed an uncompromising devotion to the rule of reason. In philosophy, it was the emerging period of logical positivism and pragmatism under the major influence of creative minds like William James and John Dewey. Man, in this view, was capable of achieving any excellence, so long as he followed the laws of logic and rationality. The same principles of science and technology that had transformed the world of business and industry could also be applied as instruments to improve the social welfare of the nation. Emotion and feeling were unreliable regulators, because they were too "subjective." Reason was the supreme criterion, because it was "objective," and more informative about reality.

In this total social context, any program of parochial concern was inadmissible. A movement to divorce Jews from the rest of the world and to reconstitute them as a separate, political entity was considered hopelessly archaic and obsolete. It was believed that nationalism of all kinds would one day yield to a universal community of mankind and the responsible and knowledgeable citizen would realize it was his task to raze, not strengthen, the political sovereignties which divide men. That Jews, the heirs of prophetic universalism, should encourage and advocate a return to sovereignty and a retreat from reason for the sake of unfounded emotion and feeling was intolerable to devotees of the Pittsburgh Platform. Simply stated, their opposition to Zionism stemmed substantially from this general mood of the times.

That position did not change significantly for several decades. Zionism could always claim a segment of its support from Reform ranks and at times even recruited its leadership from major spokesmen for Reform Judaism. Nonetheless, the prevailing attitude in the Reform community, especially among laymen, was decidedly anti-Zionist.

That the UAHC agreed in 1923, despite the adverse recommendation of its Resolutions Committee, to endorse the principle of Jewish settlement in Palestine may be explained by the divided response to the Balfour Declaration among prominent Reform Jews. The lack of unanimity among them was the first evidence that some Reform laymen might be persuaded to change direction on the Zionist Question.

Rabbi Henry Berkowitz circulated a petition for which he solicited signatures to protest Zionist claims at the peace conference in Versailles and which would be presented to President Woodrow Wilson when he left for Paris in 1919. The petition acknowledged sympathy for Zionist efforts "to secure for Jews at present living in lands of oppression a refuge in Palestine or elsewhere" but the petition rejected "the demand of the Zionists for the reorganization of Jews as a national unit to whom now or in the future territorial sovereignty in Palestine shall be committed."[55]

The petition was actually more significant in light of those who did not sign than of those who did. The nonsigners included Felix Adler, the founder of the Ethical Culture movement, Maurice Bloomfield, professor at Johns Hopkins University, J. Walter Freiberg, President of the UAHC, Louis Marshall, President of the American Jewish Committee and Julius Rosenwald, President of Sears Roebuck and Co. Dr. Solomon Solis-Cohen, a well known Philadelphia physician, considered the anti-Zionist statement "ill-advised and incorrect and very likely to injure all Jews, both Zionists and non-Zionists." He urged Berkowitz to reconsider his action. Rabbi Louis Wolsey, a prominent anti-Zionist, was distressed over the conspicuous absence of several names from the petition and complained that it proved to him that "some of our Jewish laymen have no backbone."

Probably the most encouraging endorsement came from Oscar Strauss who opposed the petition by explaining that "not only as a Jew but pre-eminently as an American, I am strongly in favor of having Palestine made a land of freedom, so as to enable oppressed Jews in other lands to return to their historic homeland."

These faint stirrings of some internal adjustments developed an added dimension in 1927 when the 30th Council of the UAHC expressed "its sincere sympathy with those Jewish brethren and others in Central and Eastern Europe who are suffering from the political and economic consequences of the War" and declared that it "heartily endorses the humanitarian efforts for spiritual and educational development and for agricultural settlements in Russia, Poland and Palestine . . ."[56] This time, unlike the 1923 resolution, the Resolutions Committee had recommended adoption of the statement submitted to the delegates.

One of the most prominent laymen who deplored the rigid opposition to Jewish settlement in Palestine was Louis Marshall. Marshall was never a major voice in the councils of Reform Judaism, but he belonged to a Reform congregation for almost sixty years and knew intimately many of the leading personalities in the Reform Movement.[57] Even though he himself was not actively involved in the operations of the UAHC, Marshall claimed many friends who were; and his own attitude was at least symbolic of a growing segment of Reform leadership.

Marshall had helped to spearhead an economic assistance program for Palestine through the union of non-Zionist forces under his direction together with the Zionist supporters of Chaim Weizmann. Marshall explained that his support of economic assistance to Palestine did not imply any commitment to Zionism; in fact, he specifically disavowed any allegiance of that kind.[58] He was solely concerned with the philantrophic endeavor of aiding a Jewish community which he believed would not mature into statehood for many years to come, if ever.[59] He could not envision any inconsistency between belief in Palestine and Reform Judaism.

If any change was evident at all within the Reform lay leadership prior to the Columbus Platform (1937), it amounted to little more than a concession to cooperate in the spiritual, cultural, economic and social renewal of a Jewish homeland in Palestine which had already been sanctioned by the international community anyway. At the same time, however, they clearly underscored their continuing opposition to all Zionist political activity intended to achieve an independent Jewish state. Without sacrificing the spirit of the Pittsburgh Platform entirely, a number of leading laymen were seeking some accommodation with the glowing victory of Zionism following World War I. Later on, of course, the impending disaster of European Jewry would make that accommodation much more urgent. Still, whatever flexibility was emerging was motivated primarily as an attempt to avoid any alliance with the political ambitions of thoroughly committed Zionists by transforming the return to Palestine into an extended religious and cultural project.

In the years preceding the Columbus Platform, the issue of Jewish nationalism both at the College and in the UAHC was primarily one of words. Even at that level, the debate was fairly moderate. Feelings ran high at the Hebrew Union College; but after Kaufmann Kohler's retirement, endorsement of Zionism emerged rather quickly and completely. Within the UAHC, the transformation had just barely begun; it would not end until the actual re-establishment of the Jewish state. On the threshold of the Columbus Platform, Zionist supporters were so relatively few that the question had not yet even reached major proportions.

Only in the Central Conference of American Rabbis did the controversy over Zionism engender widespread conflict. There the actual battle had begun, and from there it would eventually engulf the entire movement. The first serious challenge affecting performance as well as principles was the celebrated Hatikvah Controversy which erupted at the CCAR convention in 1931. The Conference was preparing to publish its Union Hymnal, a collection of liturgical music for use in all Reform synagogues. One of the most heated quarrels centered about the inclusion of Hatikvah as one of the selections.

The Zionist sympathizers urged inclusion of Hatikvah as evidence of affirmation of Zionist goals for the future of Palestine. The Zionist opposition in the Conference urged its deletion for precisely the same reasons. Most of the veteran members of the CCAR were fairly conspicuous in their positions on Zionism. The real question was the problem of where the newer, younger men stood on this issue.

The Reform rabbis finally voted 54 to 41 in favor of retaining Hatikvah in the Union Hymnal. That victory should not be misunderstood as the result of a Zionist majority in the Conference. It could be attributed considerably to several men who supported the measure but who still remained inactive in relation to Zionism. Julian Morgenstern was among those non-Zionists who voted for inclusion, but he felt constrained to "explain" his vote was due to the fact that he felt it unethical to abrogate the decision of the 1930 convention which had originally approved the inclusion of the hymn.[60]

Louis Witt, another non-Zionist, also voted favorably on the question of the basis that "this hymn (is) expressive not so much of this or that 'ism' as of the indestructible hope of my people, of their yearning not for Zionism, but for Zion."[61] A considerable segment of non-Zionist rabbis thus agreed to include Hatikvah in their liturgical repertoire both out of consideration for the growing sympathy of many of their colleagues for Zionism as well as their own commitment to the principle of Jewish peoplehood, regardless of its association with nationalism.

In 1935 a remarkable document was published, entitled Rabbis of America to Labor Palestine. It was a statement by 241 Reform rabbis, all members of the CCAR, in which they urged and pledged support for Histadruth and the League for Labor Palestine.[62] The special significance of the document was cited by Rabbi Stephen S. Wise in an introduction to the declaration in which he considered it an expression of sympathy for the concept of the Jewish National Home.

The signers of the Labor Zionist statement represented more than half of the total membership of the CCAR.[63] Again, such support, like that for the inclusion of the Hatikvah in the Union Hymnal, did not necessarily imply that the majority of Reform rabbis were now Zionists. Many had signed more out of admiration for the social idealism of Histadruth than for the program of the Zionist movement. Still, the balance of forces was slowly shifting in favor of the Zionist camp, so that by 1935, the Conference was able to ratify its first official departure on the subject of Jewish nationalism since the formulation of the Pittsburgh Platform. The CCAR approved a resolution that would later become a target of fierce controversy. It adopted a position of official neutrality on the issue of Zionism.

The famous Neutrality Resolution stated that "acceptance or rejection of the Zionist program should be left to the determination of individual members"; that the CCAR "takes no stand on the subject of Zionism," but "will continue to cooperate in the upbuilding of Palestine, and in the economic, cultural and spiritual tasks confronting the growing and evolving Jewish community there."[64]

The Zionists in the Conference considered this statement a major triumph. The opposition understood it at most as a "cease-and-desist" order to the Zionist activists. In truth, many of the anti-Zionists were deeply distressed with this decision of the Conference; David Philipson described himself as "heartsick" over what he called the actions of "rabbinical politicians."[65]

Philipson and other anti-Zionists may have been disappointed over the changing mood in Zionism, but they should not have been surprised. Both the rabbinate and the congregations were the recipients of increasing Zionist strength occasioned by the affiliation of new members who were deeply rooted in East European traditions or were the products of traditional chederyeshiva education. In a survey among forty-three Reform congregations located in the largest centers of Jewish population in 1931, the report indicated that about equal proportions of Temple members were of German parentage and East European origin. In addition, most of the pulpits were occupied by the sons of Orthodox immigrants, and in many instances, those of East European extraction were providing a "fine and well-deserved lay leadership."[66] Most significant of all, it was apparent that, in this new group, "a love of Zion was active in its tent, and much of the Zionism which flourishes in our country has sprung from the midst of its affection."[67]

It is not true, of course, that all Jews of East European origins were ardent Zionists. Many of them were vigorous opponents, while some of the staunchest advocates were the product of classical Reform education. Nonetheless, a more traditional East European influx was definitely exercising a powerful influence. Further evidence of that impact was apparent in a report of seventy-eight replies to a CCAR questionnaire (approximately a 20% response from the total membership) in which two questions related to Zionism. In reply to the question, "Is the trend toward placing less emphasis on Judaism as a cult and more emphasis on Judaism as a civilization, i.e., identifying it with all the activities and relations of life?", fifty rabbis answered "yes," and only fifteen said "no." To the question, "Is the trend toward becoming more Zionistic?", forty-six members answered "yes" while twenty-seven said "no."[68]

The changing attitude in the Reform rabbinate was only reinforced by evidence that Reform laymen were beginning to change if ever so slightly. A survey reported by the UAHC in 1931 reported that "despite the traditional opposition of Reform Judaism to Zionism in the past, we find one member of every five families enrolled in the Zionist Organization of America or Hadassah."[69] The findings revealed that Reform affiliation with Zionist organizations was now no smaller than the proportional membership of Reform families in YMHA and YMHA institutions. It should be remembered that these realities were evidenced in 1931, long before the Zionist Organization of America reached its maximum momentum.[70] The impact of traditional views was beginning to soften a once-unified and rigid opposition even among ordinary Reform laymen.

In addition to the changing composition of Reform Jewry, a major consideration which prompted many to re-examine their sympathies for the Zionist cause was the rise of the Third Reich in Germany and the Nazi persecution of Jews throughout Europe. The Hitler terror severely jolted the ideology of the anti-Zionists and affected the deliberations of the UAHC as early as 1933. In that year, the Union affirmed a lengthy resolution on the urgency of "Sympathizing With German Jews and Expressing Confidence in the U.S. Government's Attitude."[71] The statement deplored the treatment of German Jews as well as the failure of the German people to condemn such outrageous assults upon human decency. Nonetheless, it refused to abandon its abiding optimism in the ultimate vindication of their fellow-Jews in this tragic episode.

At the next Biennial Convention two years later, the plight of German Jewry had become sufficiently desperate to elicit from American Reform Jews the most urgent demand for effective relief on behalf of the victims. The Union announced that since the last meeting of the national body, Reform Jews "have not contented themselves with words, but . . . have zealously carried out their pledge of aid and succor to alleviate the suffering of the oppressed."[72] It acknowledged that the crisis had seriously worsened and that the task of relief was increasingly more formidable.

Reform Jews had often proclaimed their support for American interests even at the expense of particular Jewish concerns. It is important to note then that in the new resolution, Reform laymen declared that as "loyal Americans" they were "mindful of the problems which confront those who must determine our national policy." Nonetheless, they still summoned the conscience of the world community to condemn and continue to combat, as a blight upon civilization, the barbarity that seeks to deny to worthy Jews . . . all that is cherished in life." They pledged an unending and unconditional battle to win the support of humanity "until this great world wrong shall be righted."

At the very same time, in March, 1935, the UAHC endorsed the efforts of the Jewish Agency in upbuilding Palestine.[73] In light of the approaching catastrophe in Europe, it was clearly evident that the entire Reform movement was evolving a deeper appreciation for the role of Palestine in any program of relief and rescue. The Nazi tyranny was becoming eroding to the optimism on which the calmer, simpler world of the 19th century had relied.

Those most concerned with and most aware of the distance between ideology and reality were rabbis. It was they more than scholars and students, and certainly laymen, whose task it was to explain the application of ideas to conduct. They more than others realized how dysfunctional the Pittsburgh Platform had already become, and it is therefore reasonable to expect that the effort to reformulate Reform Judaism thought should begin within the CCAR. In 1932 Rabbi Barnett Brickner delivered the Conference Sermon and suggested that the time had arrived for "a reform of Reform Judaism," especially in its attitude toward Zionism. Assessing the pronouncements of the early Reformers, he observed that "history has proved that they exaggerated the hope for the immediate messianic cosmopolitanism which they associated with political emancipation."[74]

In his President's Message of 1933, Morris Newfield expressed profound indignation and heartache over the reports concerning Nazi persecution of German Jews. Newfield acknowledged the wide range of sentiment on the wisdom of emigration to Palestine, but he pleaded for at least a measure of compromise from all sides in order to salvage some portion of European Jewry.[75] The Conference by no means supported the view of its President unanimously. Samuel

Goldenson, an avowed anti-Zionist, unhappily conceded the growing strength of the Zionist cause and declared he could not "remember a time when there were such divisions in our ranks."[76]

On the eve of the fiftieth anniversary of the Pittsburgh Platform, Abraham Feldman urged his colleagues to reassess the merits of Zionism. Feldman insisted categorically that "in 1885 Palestine did not occupy the place in Jewish life which it occupies today." He declared that the hour had arrived for a "new statement, a new declaration of principles," one that would "recognize and reassert the spiritual and ethnic Gemeinschaft of Israel and take sympathetic cognizance of the Palestine that is being rebuilt . . ."[77]

In response to Feldman's appeal, the Resolutions Committee recommended a symposium for the following year (1935) to reexamine the Pittsburgh Platform with a view toward reformulating the philosophy and practices of Reform Judaism. The machinery was thus set in motion for the eventual document that would result in the Columbus Platform of 1937.

The symposium in 1935 consisted primarily of several papers presented on the three major concepts of God, Torah and Israel. The presentations on the subject of Israel were delivered by Abba Hillel Silver, a young, vigorous protagonist for a Jewish state, and Samuel Schulman, an able, veteran opponent of Zionism. Both men articulated their positions with rare eloquence and thoroughgoing scholarship.[78] Their confrontation produced in many respects the high water mark of the Zionist debate in Reform circles and unquestionably contributed to the Neutrality Resolution cited above.

The 1935 symposium also led to the appointment of a committee composed of Samuel Cohon, James Heller, Felix Levy, David Philipson, Max Raisin and Abba Hillel Silver to draft a new set of "Guiding Principles." Four of the six committee members were avowed Zionists, and one was favorably disposed. Only David Philipson was a determined dissenter.

It is ironic that as often as it has been quoted, the Columbus Platform never occasioned any fierce debate on any of its planks, with the possible exception of the statement on Zionism. The first report of the committee at the 1936 meeting was received with little discussion at all.[79] The official endorsement in 1937 likewise passed with relatively little comment.[80]

Less than half the membership of the CCAR registered for the convention in Columbus, Ohio in 1937 at the Winding Hollow Country Club. The morning session ended in a motion to refrain from adopting any platform at that time. The vote resulted in a tie of 81 in favor and 81 against. The Conference President, Felix Levy, chose to cast his deciding ballot by defeating the resolution. The meeting then broke for lunch to resume consideration of the motion at the afternoon session.

The afternoon session found only 110 rabbis gathered to debate the platform. According to one personal report, one-fifth of the registered rabbis deserted the conference hall for the golf course.[81] Leaders on both sides met each other on the first tee. Another motion to postpone adoption of the platform lost by a vote of 48 to 50. The platform then carried by only one vote and became the new "Guiding Principles of Reform Judaism."

The crucial section on "Israel" reflected the language of the Neutrality Resolution in 1935, declaring in its full text, that Judaism:

> . . . is the soul of which Israel is the body, Living in all parts of the world, Israel has been held together by the ties of a common history, and above all, by the heritage of faith. Though we recognize in the group-loyalty of Jews who have become estranged from our religious tradition, a bond which still unites them with us, we maintain that it is by its religion and for its religion that the Jewish people has lived. The non-Jew who accepts our faith is welcome as a full member of the Jewish community.
>
> In all lands where our people live, they assume and seek to share loyally the full duties and responsibilities of citizenship and to create seats of Jewish knowledge and religion. In the rehabilitation of Palestine, the land hallowed by memories and hopes, we behold the promise of renewed life for many of our brethren. We affirm the obligation of all Jewry to aid in its upbuilding as a Jewish homeland by endeavoring to make it not only a haven of refuge for the oppressed but also a center of Jewish culture and spiritual life.
>
> Throughout the ages it has been Israel's mission to witness to the Divine in the face of every form of paganism and materialism. We regard it as our historic task to cooperate with all men in the establishment of the Kingdom of God, of universal brotherhood, justice, truth and peace on earth. This is our Messianic goal.

This definitive statement on the role of Palestine in Jewish life by no means settled the issue of Jewish nationalism in Reform Judaism. To be sure, the mood and philosophy had changed substantially since the time of the Pittsburgh Platform, but the Zionist opposition had by no means surrendered their cause. Indeed, for many of them, the battle had only begun.

Columbus was a major milestone in the changing posture of Reform Judaism toward Zionism, but it was not the final judgment on the matter or even the most decisive. In the first place, so far as the total movement was concerned, the Columbus Platform was a statement by, for and of rabbis. Laymen did not consider themselves bound by this rabbinic decision. In fact, Zionism as a political movement was not even debated in any official forum by the UAHC until 1943 over the question of the Union's participation in the American Jewish Conference.

The Columbus Platform was not even the final authority on the subject in Reform rabbinic circles. The majority of the CCAR was still in the non-Zionist camp.[82] The number of men present when the final vote was taken on the Zionist plank represented but a fraction of the total Conference membership. The victory was virtually a *coup d'etat* on the part of the Zionist minority which very carefully and skillfully engineered the proceedings to ensure that their viewpoint would prevail.

Finally, the conflicts and controversies that followed the Columbus Platform also demonstrated that the issue was not at all resolved by 1937. The Jewish Army controversy, the emergence of the American Council for Judaism, the Houston controversy and other quarrels all occurred in the next six years. Rather than having settled the question, it might be argued that the new Guiding Principles set the stage for the most bitter period of all in the battle over Zionism. The non-Zionist rabbis never forgot and never fully recovered from the manner in which they were outmaneuvered on the floor of the Conference in 1937.

Whatever transitions occurred in the attitude of the Reform movement toward Zionism during this earlier period followed an opposite course of development from the one which had launched Reform Judaism in its infancy. The movement at the outset, in the early nineteenth century, had been the creation of laymen who sought to accommodate their Jewish observance with the new demands and opportunities of the secular world. Their professional religious leadership formulated an ideology in response to the changes in practice that already existed. The process began with laymen and ended with rabbis.

The controversy over Zionism reversed that direction. Here the transition began with rabbis or rabbinical students and ended with laymen. Actually, it was more complicated than that. Had changing realities been the only variable, one could have expected the same sequence of support for Zionism as for the entire movement in its infancy. The existence of several other considerations help to explain the different pattern on this issue.

First, the influx of East European Jews into the ranks of Reform Judaism was bound to affect the seminary and the rabbinate before the lay organizations. In the space of three to five years the entire complexion of the Hebrew Union College would change. Within five to ten years, a considerable number of these graduates would exercise substantial influence in the voting patterns of the CCAR. It would take far more than five to ten years for laymen with similar attitudes to achieve dominant positions of leadership in their own local congregations, no less the national lay governing body of Reform Judaism. Rabbis and rabbinical students with Zionist sympathies were far more visible and vocal in their convictions than their laymen could have been. Indeed, Zionism could be a very lonely cause for a Reform Jew to champion until a rabbi filled the pulpit who then served as a catalyst and support for the concept of Jewish nationalism.

Related to this consideration, but somewhat different in focus, is a recognition that the Zionist debate was essentially a conflict between older and younger Reform Jews, lay and rabbinic. With few exceptions, the faculty at the Hebrew Union College was decidedly unresponsive to Zionist aspirations. The ensuing struggles over the issue there usually found the student body stressing concern for Jewish peoplehood and the administration defending universalism against the evils of nationalism. Within the CCAR, too, the Zionist movement usually enjoyed far greater support from the younger rabbis than from their older colleagues. Again, there were exceptions including such Zionist spokesmen as James Heller, Abba Hillel Silver and Stephen S. Wise; but the fact remains that the Conference did not begin to reconsider the question of Jewish nationalism until the impact and influence of its younger constituency made it possible and necessary.

This phrase, "the generation gap," also helps to explain the very slow and gradual shift within the UAHC. The young Zionist-minded rabbis could find very few age peers in the leadership circles of the Union even as late as the establishment of the State of Israel. The UAHC Board of Directors consisted of individuals who were raised in homes and congregations in which Zionism was anathema. These laymen would hardly be expected to champion the cause for a national Jewish homeland in Palestine. Their ideology would not permit it.

With reference to ideology, it is evident that with the exception of occasional episodes in the years prior to the Balfour Declaration, the question was never really one of support for or against Jewish settlement in Palestine. Even the UAHC, as early as the period of the Balfour Declaration, affirmed its endorsement of efforts to rebuild the spiritual and cultural foundations of Jewish life in Palestine. Those who opposed Zionism feared that it would ultimately weaken the religious component of Jewish identity. Those who supported Zionism were convinced that the land was inseparable from the faith. Few Reform rabbis or laymen ever denied the desirability of a flourishing community of Jewish culture in Palestine. What many did reject was the concept of an independent, non-religious, secular Jewish state in the Middle East or anywhere else. In terms of this distinction, the anti-Zionists usually understood their opposition better than the Zionists understood theirs.

Notwithstanding the differences in ideology, the decisive consideration was still the flow of events and not of ideas. The Balfour Declaration was perhaps only the opening volley in the onslaught of circumstances which demolished the ideology of the Pittsburgh Platform, but as the changing composition of the movement increased, as anti-Semitism in America and Nazi terror in Germany blazed across the front pages, as immigration virtually ceased and harbors of refuge sharply dropped, the reassessment of Jewish nationalism gathered momentum. By 1937 it was a major issue for American Reform Judaism but by no means resolved. The process by which it did reach its conclusion is the subject of the pages that follow.

CHAPTER 2
THE JEWISH ARMY CONTROVERSY AND THE RISE OF THE AMERICAN COUNCIL FOR JUDAISM

After the Columbus Platform was ratified by the CCAR in 1937, it was by no means certain that Reform Judaism would endorse and support the efforts for the re-establishment of a Jewish state. It was clear that the spiritual climate, at least in rabbinic circles, was definitely dominated by more traditional influences of all kinds, but the deepest and stormiest agitation over Zionism was yet to come.[83] Until 1942 it appeared that Reform had made its peace with the Zionist question rather smoothly and quietly. That was a conclusion which rested largely upon the period of strange silence that had settled over the movement after the Columbus meeting.

The CCAR convention of 1941 even suggested that perhaps the transition was now complete, that the victory had been won without even a battle. Anti-Zionism was associated with the older members of the Conference whose influence was waning and who inevitably, if not already, would find themselves hopelessly out-numbered. The crowning evidence for this shift to tradition was seen in the election of an ardent Zionist, James G. Heller, to the presidency of the Conference and to a readily accepted resolution calling for a genuinely representative and comprehensive Jewish Council to act for American Jews on all matters affecting their vital interests.[84]

In 1942, however, the CCAR endorsed the formation of a Jewish Army in Palestine, a decision which infuriated the anti-Zionists in the Conference. By that action, the Conference had approved more than another resolution. It had actually passed the corner of reconciliation with the anti-Zionist members of the CCAR.

The festering resentment among anti-Zionist rabbis of the CCAR over the efforts of Zionist colleagues to establish Jewish nationalism as a component of Reform ideology cannot be explained as a consequence of any single cause. The rupture between the two groups was the result of accumulated grievances which had begun several years earlier. The Jewish Army controversy was simply the proverbial straw that broke the back of the anti-Zionist camel.

In 1939 Great Britain issued a restrictive and repressive White Paper on Palestine confirming the worst fears of world Zionist leaders. The British declared that they would limit immigration to Palestine to 15,000 Jews per year for a period of five years. Such an arrangement would allow a total immigration of only 75,000 Jewish refugees among the millions fleeing the terror of Nazi Europe. In addition, the White Paper postponed any plans for a projected Jewish state indefinitely, at least for the next ten years. Further Jewish immigration would not be allowed without the approval of the majority in Palestine (the Arabs).

The terms of this British document galvanized widespread protest among American Jews, regardless of their views on political Zionism. Even as outspoken an anti-Zionist as Rabbi Morris S. Lazaron, who eventually would become one of the founding fathers and future leaders of the American Council for Judaism, urged American Jews to make the best of a bad situation, and, while explaining his own "non-Zionistic" approach to the Palestine problem, expressed deep regret and concern over what he considered to be a most unfair policy.[85]

In March 1940, the British issued a second White Paper, this time restricting the sale of land in Palestine to Jews. Again, Jews everywhere registered a vigorous protest but to no avail. Great Britain had effectively blocked every avenue by which Jews could establish a national identity in Palestine.

In July of that year one further attempt was made to gain recognition for the _Yishuv_ (Jewish settlement) in Palestine. Agitation began for the formation of a Jewish Army in Palestine; and at the convention of the Zionist Organization of America that year, a resolution was passed urging Great Britain to arm the Jews of Palestine as a special force in defense of their homeland.[86]

The shattering impact of the White Papers, coupled with the vision of a Jewish fighting unit, apparently ignited the imagination of some American Jewish leaders. Rabbi James Heller, President of the CCAR, reportedly stated that Reform Judaism was no longer anti-Zionist; to the contrary, it was now fully committed to unite with all Jews in working for Palestine.[87]

By "fully committed," Heller meant complete support for Zionist efforts on all fronts. He elaborated upon his understanding of the Conference position on the eve of the American Jewish Conference less than a year later by urging, as President of the CCAR, "a united program in regard to post-war rehabilitation in Europe, and in respect to the setting-up of a Commonwealth in Palestine with large-scale immigration under Jewish auspices. I, for one, feel confident that this is the will of the overwhelming majority of American Jews, and I want it to be expressed in no uncertain terms in the American Jewish Conference."[88] Heller further urged the CCAR to form a Committee on Palestine to cooperate with all agencies trying to make it a Jewish homeland. He wanted to "put the force of the liberal rabbinate behind the beneficient and creative work of Zionism."[89]

By the end of 1941, Louis Lipsky had declared that "the Jew had a right to defend his free homeland in Palestine."[90] Chaim Weizmann explained that, in view of Hitler's specific indictment against the Jewish people, "the Jews desire to serve under their own name and flag."[91] The Jewish Army question had become a white-hot issue inside and outside Zionist circles. Support for the idea had reached a fever pitch among Zionists for whom it was a last-ditch effort to salvage some formal recognition of their legitimacy. For anti-Zionists, it was a wholly repugnant political subterfuge.

The argument supporting the creation of a Jewish fighting force rested basically upon four considerations.[92] First, the advocates contended that Jews wanted the right of self-defense. They especially deserved that recognition inasmuch as they had been singled out for purposes of persecution and destruction.

Secondly, the advocates supported a Jewish Army as a force similar in status to units representing free France or free Belgium. They rested the analogy on the terms of the British Mandate which regarded a Jewish national home as a recognized political entity.

The third consideration was a repudiation of British procrastination. Zionists charged that England had failed to deliver on her most sacred commitments. They claimed that in September, 1940, Churchill had promised that Jews could organize their own army in Palestine to fight alongside British troops but under their own Jewish flag. In March, 1941, the Colonial Secretary delayed that development because of what he termed "technical difficulties," and on October 15, Great Britain openly retracted and canceled its original promise.

Finally, the idea of a Jewish Army received support from Jews who pleaded for the same right as other nations conquered by the Nazis who formed national defense forces under British jurisdiction. A sizable number of American Jews strove zealously to win recognition of a Jewish contribution to the Allied victory in Europe.

The Central Conference of American Rabbis met in Cincinnati in 1942, from February 24 to March 1, and the question of a Jewish Army occupied center stage. Thirty-three Reform rabbis submitted a resolution calling upon their colleagues to approve "the demand that the Jewish population of Palestine be given the privilege of establishing a military force which will fight under its own banner on the side of the democracies, under allied command, to defend its own land and the Near East to the end that the victory of democracy may be hastened everywhere."[93] This was the original resolution submitted to the Resolutions Committee.[94]

The Committee on Resolutions rejected the wording of this statement and offered a much milder substitute instead, one which avoided reference to a separate Jewish fighting unit and any assumptions about Jewish political sovereignty in Palestine. Their recommendation declared that "the CCAR is in complete sympathy with the demand of the Jews of Palestine that they be given the opportunity to fight in defense of their homeland on the side of the democracies."[95]

The ensuing discussion was heated and impassioned with several requests not only to table the motion but to expunge the entire discussion from the record. The basic positions of the discussants split into four directions. One segment argued in favor of a Jewish Army, because it would strengthen democratic countries engaged in this global struggle. Another group supported it, simply because they believed the Jews of Palestine deserved such recognition just as much as any other victimized nationality under the Nazis. Another group resisted any endorsement because they feared the implications such action would suggest for support of the entire political Zionist program. Finally, a fourth segment argued against it, not out of opposition to the Zionist movement, but out of concern for the well-being of the CCAR and the irreparable damage it could inflict on that body.

Louis Wolsey declared that "I do not believe that the Conference, a religious organization, should take any action on this subject,"[96] to which Philip Bookstaber retorted, "The survival of a people is of as much importance as the survival of our religion."[97]

Maurice Eisendrath, on the eve of his appointment as President of the UAHC, rose to add that "I think I have seen more real religion, more real appreciation of social justice and moral righteousness in the labor colonies of Palestine than I have seen as a consequence of much of our work as rabbis . . . . I urge the adoption of a resolution with teeth in it on this question. We are seeking to protect spiritual and religious values in America even though regretfully by force -- let us grant the same right to our brethren in Palestine."[98]

Finally, Phillip Bernstein stated the naked political realities of the situation by reminding his colleagues that "peace is not made on the basis of abstract justice or pleas to the world's conscience. Peace reflects the contributions that the peoples make to victory in the war. Whether the Jews will emerge from this war helpless and defenseless, or whether they will emerge strong, vigorous and hopeful will depend in no small measure on whether the Palestinian and stateless Jews will have the right to fight for their rights and human freedom in a Jewish Army under the Allied command."[99]

The opposition, however, was by no means intimidated by this barrage of rhetoric from the Zionist "heavy artillery." It was Solomon B. Freehof, one of the most highly-respected members of the Conference and a principal mediator between both factions in the Zionist controversy, who sensed the growing hostility and rigidity on both sides and proposed that the whole discussion, including all resolutions, be stricken from the Conference records.

Freehof therefore moved to table the resolution, but his motion lost by a vote of 45 to 51.[100] At this point, the sequence of events becomes somewhat confusing. The anti-Zionists claimed that Heller, as the presiding officer, very shrewdly manipulated passage of the original resolution drafted by Zionist colleagues, which was a much stronger version than the substitute resolution offered by the Resolutions Committee. They insisted that Barnett Brickner had moved to send the resolution on the floor, which was the milder version, back to the Resolutions Committee for further consideration. Heller, they continued, then declared that the motion was "to substitute the original motion (the statement supporting the creation of a separate Jewish fighting force) for the substitute (the resolution of the Committee)," Heller then supposedly asked Brickner whether "this form is satisfactory to you," to which Brickner reportedly answered that he could not determine, since he was not on the Resolutions Committee and "I don't know what the original resolution was." Heller presumably then called for a vote on the original resolution, and the CCAR approved by a vote of 64 to 38 a statement calling for the formation of a Jewish Army.[101]

Heller's account of the record indicates that the presentation of the mild version by the Resolutions Committee was <u>followed</u> by a further motion to substitute for the Committee report a stronger resolution which would favor a "Jewish fighting-force, based in Palestine." The ensuing discussion then revealed that a similar resolution had already been in the hands of the Resolution Committee but was rejected. Heller then insisted that the feeling was expressed repeatedly that the "substitute" motion called for should not be that of the Resolutions Committee but the original resolution which the Committee had rejected but which this new motion now resurrected. "All that I did," Heller explained, "was to inquire of the mover of the resolution whether this was his intention, and thereafter to put the motion in this form." He added further that "the stenographic record shows that I went out of my way to make all this perfectly clear, when several 'points of order' were raised."[102]

It is difficult to determine on the basis of available documents what actually transpired at this critical Conference session. The original stenographic record to which Heller refers cannot be located.[103] The Conference Yearbooks do not include any information which supports the reported conversation between Brickner and Heller, according to the anti-Zionist sources, nor do they confirm Heller's reference to any motion which followed the report of the Resolutions Committee. The anti-Zionists complained that only 102 members even voted on this issue out of 300 who had registered for the convention. Heller, however, quickly pointed out, and properly so, that the actual registration was 236, and that even the Neutrality Resolution of 1935 which the anti-Zionists considered inviolate had carried by a vote of only 81 to 25, a total of 106 votes out of 182 men who attended the Chicago convention.

In any event, passage of the Jewish Army resolution remained an open wound in the hearts of those rabbis who rejected the concept of Jewish nationalism. They refused to accept the margin of Zionist victory as sufficient support for a statement on behalf of the entire CCAR. For them the battle had only begun.

They were not the only Reform Jews who were distressed by the Conference action. Immediately following the CCAR convention, the UAHC Board of Trustees met in Cincinnati and registered very strenuous objections to the Jewish Army resolution. Members of the Board confided their lack of confidence in the quality of rabbinic leadership as evidenced by their actions. As one trustee observed, "Many of the resolutions adopted were not only unwise, they were idiotic."[104] Other Board members suggested that the UAHC and not the CCAR should function as the spokesman for American Reform Jews, and they urged that "we ought to be unrestrained in the strength and wording of a type of resolution that we offer . . . ."[105]

Adolph Rosenberg, chairman of the Board, was more moderate in his response and attempted to soften the retaliation which at least a segment of UAHC leadership was anxious to inflict. The resolution finally adopted by the Board was extremely mild and formulated only as a reaffirmation of Jewish loyalty to America should the question of dual allegiance ever emerge in conjunction with the creation of a Jewish Army.[106]

One of the earliest public statements of opposition to the CCAR resolution appeared in the Philadelphia Jewish Exponent on March 20, 1942. Sixty-three rabbis had announced jointly that American Jewry was sharply divided on the question of a Jewish Army and that the recent action of the CCAR on that issue should in no way be interpreted as the will of the Reform movement, no less of the total American Jewish community. Many, they claimed, were confident that such a unit would only inflame misunderstandings and lead to further friction in Palestine. In opposition to the establishment of a separate force, these rabbis urged all Palestinians to arm under the British flag and to put aside temporarily their individual interests and concentrate on winning the war. This proposal was hauntingly similar to the resolution which the CCAR Resolutions Committee had presented but which had failed.[107]

The following week 350 rabbis representing all three major segments of American Jewry published a rejoinder to that statement which included, among other items, an enthusiastic endorsement for the creation of a Jewish Army. Stephen S. Wise stated specifically in a preface that the proposal of the sixty-three rabbis published earlier was directly contrary to the publicly expressed view of their own respective rabbinic organizations. Wise further discredited the "minority report" by citing widespread support from both Jewish and Christian leaders in the United States for the formation of a Jewish Army.

The pro-Zionist rabbis were not alone in their indignation. Such a devoted Zionist and Reform lay leader as Mortimer May voiced his deep distress over the rancor and opposition.[108] The emerging conflict even prompted a response from ordinary laymen like one who wrote to his rabbi, Barnett R. Brickner, that "if these 62[109] rabbis had deliberately set out to harm the cause of Jews in America and the rest of the world, they certainly could not have chosen a better way to do it than by issuing such a statement."[110]

On April 16, 1942, Rabbi Louis Wolsey sent an invitation to all non-Zionist rabbis for a meeting in Atlantic City on June 9-10.[111] The purpose of the meeting was to arrange a forum for discussion of the entire situation regarding the CCAR's position on Zionism. This general invitation had resulted from a series of preliminary gatherings at which he presided and included colleagues from the most concerned dissident faction.[112]

That series had begun on March 24 in Wolsey's office in Philadelphia where he explored the alternatives for action with William H. Fineshriber, Eugene J. Sack, David Wice, Abraham Shusterman and Samuel Sandmel.[113] That initial meeting led to a second conference on March 30 and to still another on April 6, by which time the attendance had grown to twenty-four.[114] The participants all agreed that the magnitude of the crisis warranted a general meeting of all like-minded men in Atlantic City. Out of the 160 invitations that were issued to all those who would conceivably endorse the purpose of such a conference, forty-five replied favorably. That number amounted to a little more than 10% of the total membership of the CCAR.

The anticipated conference in Atlantic City and its aftermath started a flurry of correspondence between Heller and Wolsey. As late as May 11, Solomon B. Freehof arranged a meeting in Pittsburgh composed of Heller, Samuel Goldenson, Louis Wolsey and himself in a final effort to reach some compromise. Heller declared he would agree to seek a reaffirmation of the Neutrality Resolution of 1935 from the Conference at its next convention and to make that ratification an established by-law of the CCAR which would preclude any future efforts to change it.

The proposal was an inviting one to Wolsey and Goldenson, but after polling their supporters, they decided that the price of peace was too high. In return for his concession, Heller had called upon them to cancel the Atlantic City meeting and, in effect, to abandon any orangized opposition. Wolsey and Goldenson declared they would accept Heller's proposal only if he also agreed to recommend that the Jewish Army resolution be expunged from the official minutes of the Conference. Heller absolutely refused.[115]

At this delicate juncture in negotiations, Heller's refusal may have been a fatal tactical error. Had he agreed to seek a complete repudiation of the Army resolution, he would have forced a cancellation of the Atlantic City meeting. That development might have completely aborted the birth of the American Council for Judaism. The anti-Zionist agitation may have remained entirely within the deliberations of the CCAR itself, and the final stage of reconciliation with Jewish nationalism in Reform Judaism might have arrived much earlier than it did.

The Heller-Wolsey correspondence is extremely valuable for the candid manner in which it illuminated the high emotional pitch as well as the rationale of the opposing sides. In a series of letters circulated to all their colleagues but really intended for each other, Heller and the Wolsey forces recited their respective positions in considerable detail. Wolsey's major complaint was that the Jewish Army resolution was a clear violation of the neutrality agreement reached in 1935. The official endorsement of a Jewish fighting force was, in his view, a deliberate attempt to ignore the convictions of non-Zionist colleagues. Heller replied that non-Zionist colleagues were far less considerate of their opposition in the Conference when they were in command. In fact, Heller insisted, he would refuse to resort to that kind of tactics by which "anti-Zionism had been rammed down the throats of Zionists for many years, with more than a little cruelty and exultation."[116]

The Wolsey camp, however, attributed the passage of the Army resolution to more than shifting attitudes in the Conference. They charged that Heller had master-minded and engineered the whole procedure as presiding officer. Convinced of that manipulation, Wolsey could not accept any explanations from Heller to the contrary. Indeed, Wolsey repeatedly substantiated his charges with reference to Heller's association with an advertisement in the New York Times proclaiming and urging support for the Zionist program, including the creation of a Jewish Army.[117] Heller replied that his name had been attached without his knowledge or permission but his disclaimer was less than convincing.

Heller was clearly distraught over this sharp cleavage in the Conference and constantly reiterated his abiding concern and affection both for his colleagues and their association. He was deeply troubled over the impending split and was searching desperately for some way to resolve a dilemma which pitched his convictions about Zionism against his personal friendships. He repeatedly stressed that his major goal was simply to avoid a complete rupture and division within the ranks of the CCAR. "I foresee," Heller warned, "a long period of a widening breach, driven not merely through the Conference, but through the Union and College too." Even after the American Council for Judaism had emerged, he confessed to his colleagues that "this whole thing has hurt me more than I can tell you . . . I cannot understand the reasons for this whole outbreak. I love the Conference. Its members are my dear friends. And I cherish genuine admiration for them."[118]

Heller further argued that whatever differences may separate them, there was never any reason for any minority position within the Conference to organize and campaign outside the available structure of the association. Such a procedure would only weaken and eventually destroy the authority and influence of the Reform rabbinate in general and the CCAR in particular. The dissidents strongly disagreed. Wolsey contended that an organized opposition remained the only recourse for his group. Any disruption of the Conference procedures or any potential threat to its existence would result not from the creation of any formal anti-Zionist organization, but from its absence. Wolsey even rejected a proposal for a special session of the CCAR to deal specifically with this problem, because "the stentorian oratory of extremism on both sides would only lash emotions into unhappy conditions and disagreements, and we believe that such a session would cause more harm than good." Wolsey assured all his colleagues, however, that independent action did not imply secession from the CCAR. So far as the Conference was concerned, he insisted that, no less than Heller, he and his "like-minded men" had "rendered it loving service, and we believe in it, and we do not, we will not secede from it, and we will not permit our determination to meet as free men to impeach our intention to give it continued faithful and loyal service and participation."[119]

Still, without questioning their sincerity, Heller contended that the anti-Zionist faction did not fully realize themselves the disastrous consequences which would result from their decision. In the earlier stages of their deliberations, Heller declared, it may have been possible to argue that the Zionist opposition was simply being misled and was unaware of the magnitude of its contemplated organization. After they realized the potential dangers involved, however, it was clearly irresponsible to deny any intention of provoking an irreversible schism. Heller likened such a position to a situation in which one might "take a loaded pistol in your hand, have someone tell you it is loaded, point it at someone's head, pull the trigger, and then contend that you had no idea that it might kill him."[120]

Finally, Heller castigated the action of the Zionist opposition as a clear violation of democratic procedure. In his view, the Conference by-laws fully protected the interests of the minority and provided ample forum for debate and dissent. The projected formation of the American Council for Judaism was nothing less than a recourse to blatant pressure tactics and outright disregard for the principles of orderly democratic process and persuasion.

Wolsey, in reply, leveled the same charge at Heller. It was the Conference itself, as a result of his manipulation, which had thwarted the democratic process. Not only did Wolsey resent what he felt was an ideological stampede over the convictions of many colleagues; but, even more significant, he submitted that the Conference had ignored the sentiments of the overwhelming majority of Reform laymen on this matter. The American Council for Judaism was their only instrument, he asserted, "to defend a point of view which has wide acceptance among us -- indeed which represents the dominant convictions of the vast majority of Reform Jews in the United States."[121]

In spite of their determined resistance, the anti-Zionist faction was still willing, as late as May, 1942, to propose to Heller the appointment of a special Conference committee which would seek reconciliation and which would include Zionists and non-Zionists in equal representation. Among their purposes would be a concerted effort to achieve some accord on appropriate procedures for "the practical reconstruction of Palestine."[122] Wolsey emphasized his high regard and personal esteem for Heller, assured him that "we approach your efforts for peace with complete respect, and we appreciate deeply the amicable spirit of the negotiations we have had together" and even commended him for having "served in a greatly difficult position with dignity, sincerity and tact. . . ."[123] Heller did not respond to that overture, which may have amounted to an additional tactical error, and the special committee never materialized.

On June 1, 1942, the non-Zionist rabbis convened in Atlantic City and organized the association which subsequently became the American Council for Judaism. On June 2, the founders of this organization also issued a statement of principles which declared in part that ". . . realizing the dearness of Palestine and its importance in relieving world problems, (the Council) members will render unstinted aid to all Jews in their economic, cultural and spiritual endeavors there. But . . . (we) cannot support the political emphasis in the Zionist program which diverts attention from the historical Jewish role as a religious community and which confuses people as to the nature of Judaism."[124]

The reaction to the events in Atlantic City was swift and furious. Stephen S. Wise wrote to Heller that ". . . I do not want to take this lying down from a little group of malcontents, who ought to be ashamed of themselves, and who, I am sorry to see, included such men as Shusterman whose support of this is a desecration of the memory of Ed Israel.[125] I am glad for his sake and for our own, that Jonah (Wise?) has not joined them nor David P. Philipson nor Sammy S. (Schulman?). It is a lamentably weak little clan, isn't it?"

The rift in Reform ranks became a matter of public knowledge, much to the embarrassment of the Zionists in Reform Judaism. The Independent Jewish News Service reported that "with the objective of splitting all of American Jewish life, war has been pledged on

Zionism and on all institutions sympathetic to that program with the wealth of influential Jews and the power even of irreligious Jews mobilized in order to smash every gain the Zionist movement has made in the United States and Palestine in forty years."[126]

The founders of the Council received less than polite consideration from their Zionist CCAR colleagues. One even claimed sufficient support for his proposal that "all these traitors should be driven out from the important positions they now occupy. Jonah Wise must not be allowed to exploit the J.D.C. and use it against Palestine. . . . Public opinion, Jewish and non-Jewish, is with us, and if we are sufficiently militant, we will succeed in eliminating these traitors from their important positions of influence which they use against Zion and against Jewry."[127]

The "coup de grace" of repudiation appeared in the forum of a declaration entitled, "Zionism -- An Affirmation of Judaism," signed by 757 Orthodox, Conservative and Reform rabbis.[128] Circulated primarily under the direction of Stephen S. Wise, Abba Hillel Silver, James Heller, Philip Bernstein, Joshua Loth Liebman and Barnett Brickner, the document charged that the non-Zionist statement "comes as a cruel blow" and that opposition to the restoration of a Jewish homeland at such a critical hour has been "unwise and unkind." The signatories rejected the Council's attack upon the "political" aspects of Zionism by declaring that "there can be little hope of opening the doors of Palestine for Jewish immigration after the war without effective political action."[129]

An official call to disband the American Council for Judaism highlighted the CCAR convention in June, 1943. Heller, in the second year of his Presidency, recommended that in charting the future course of the Council, ". . . there is only one good solution: namely, for it to disband, for its members to continue to agitate for their point of view within the framework of existing organizations, to advance it as strongly as they can in the Central Conference of American Rabbis, and from their own pulpits; but to cease constituting an organization which, in my opinion, is bound to become an antagonist of the Union and the Conference."[130]

It proved impossible to deal exhaustively with the issue during the regularly scheduled time period of the Conference. It was necessary to convene a special session of the convention after the regular session had formally adjourned. The special meeting was not recorded in any official minutes, but it did approve two decisive resolutions. The first affirmed that there was "no essential incompatibility between Reform Judaism and Zionism, no reason why those of its members who give allegiance to Zionism should not have the right to regard themselves as fully within the spirit and purpose of Reform Judaism."[131]

In the second resolution, the CCAR deplored the American Council for Judaism whose "continued existence would become a growing threat to our fellowship" since it "was founded by members of the CCAR for the purpose of combatting Zionism." This conclusion was substantially incorrect. The Council originated, as will be explained in greater detail below, not as an anti-Zionist weapon but as a reaffirmation of the basic precepts of earlier Reform Judaism. Nonetheless, having been shocked by the rise of this organization . . .," the Conference overwhelmingly voted "in the spirit of amity" to "urge our colleagues of the American Council for Judaism to terminate this organization."[132]

The American Council for Judaism refused to disappear quietly, but its original ideological moorings slowly and gradually eroded. Within one year after the Atlantic City meeting, the Council was weakened considerably. A bitter controversy erupted between a virulent anti-Zionist faction and another segment genuinely devoted to its concept of the religious dimension in American Jewish life. In addition, by 1943, the majority of members in the Council were already laymen. Very few signatories of the Atlantic City statement remained. By August, 1943, only twenty-six rabbis still retained membership. With the re-establishment of the State of Israel in 1948, the debate became academic; and the American Council for Judaism appealed almost exclusively to that small circle who refused to support the political claims of sovereignty by the Jewish state.[133]

The Zionist attack upon its opposition was certainly not without legitimate cause, but it was also a very clear case of verbal annihilation. The urgent plight of world Jewry could explain the anger and impatience evidenced by the Zionist camp, but it certainly did not require the merciless barrage of invective which they unleashed on their adversaries. The Zionist dissenters had specifically endorsed from the outset "the high place that that country (Palestine) holds in Jewish history and consciousness," and had encouraged support for "the revival of cultural interests in that ancient land and the notable achievements of the Jewish settlers in its rehabilitation."[134] However misguided this minority may have been about the political realities in the Middle East, they did not repudiate the role of Eretz Yisrael in the revitalization of the Jewish people. In his denunciation of the Jewish Army resolution, Morris Lazaron was very careful to preface his critique with the assurance that "while it is written by one whose opposition to Jewish political nationalism is well-known, it is pro-Palestine." Lazaron hoped that it would be understood in precisely that context, as "the affirmative and constructive position of one who loves Palestine and, rejoicing in what has been accomplished there, would like to see Jewish settlement there not only maintained but extended."[135]

The Zionist majority rarely acknowledged this distinction in their attacks upon the Council minority. Lazaron's motivations were attributed to "the result of fear" and he was accused of urging American Jews "to appease a few Arab hotheads and politicos who have been flirting with Hitler . . . by making a total sacrifice of the Jewish national home and the hopes of millions of Jews in Europe regardless of any consideration of justice . . . ."[136] The non-Zionist supporters deeply resented the epithets hurled at them by Zionists, including such terms as "quislings" and "traitors." They resented almost as deeply the failure of Heller as President of the CCAR to object publicly to such a "campaign of vituperation."[137]

The name-calling was not limited to one side only. In the heat of anger and exasperation, the Council supporters often complained that the Zionists "dominated" American Jewish life, exercised authority in "tyrannical" fashion and were rapidly becoming "power mad."[138]

In spite of the fact that this war of words was fought in two directions, the advocates of Zionism still delivered far more abuse than they received. It often reached such a pitch of intensity that observers were prompted to report how they were "horribly shocked to read intemperate denunciations by their (American Council for Judaism's) rabbinical brethren in some of the Jewish press," and to remind these spiritual leaders that "if rabbis exist for the purpose of leading the brotherhood of man to the mountaintop, they should make a start by loving each other or, at least, by tolerating one another."[139]

Even more deplorable than this verbal assult was the evidence of devious manipulations and pressure tactics adopted by Zionists to impose their will upon the Conference and its membership, especially since the methods were often morally questionable. In 1939 at its convention in Washington, D.C., the CCAR seemed certain to nominate Jonah Wise as vice-president, an office which is almost always a preliminary step to the Presidency. At the last moment James Heller reportedly worked behind the scenes to prevent Wise's nomination and to arrange instead the election of Felix Levy as Vice-President.[140] In 1943 the New York Board of Ministers passed over Hyman Judah Schachtel who was automatically scheduled to become its next President. Schachtel made no secret about his opposition to Jewish nationalism, and it was evident that his convictions had cost him this recognition by his colleagues.

The grim irony surrounding all the abuse and disabilities which the Council supporters suffered stems from the probability that they represented the majority view of American Reform Jews. The UAHC itself had repudiated the Jewish Army resolution at a meeting of its Board of Directors and had avoided a public confrontation only for tactical considerations.[141] Most Reform laymen very likely would have subscribed to the view which pledged "to contribute toward the building of a Palestine that . . . will be a Shangri-la for Jews but not a political state."[142] One of the most prominent lay leaders of the American Council for Judaism claimed the overwhelming support of Reform Jews who opposed the creation of a Jewish state, because "it embraces the very racist theories and nationalistic philosophies that have become so prevalent in recent years, that have caused untold suffering to the world, and particularly to the Jews."[143] Even the most fervent Zionist could only presume that Reform laymen were "becoming better and more widely informed about Zionism" or that they were producing "greater support for the Zionist ideal" or that "many" laymen in Reform congregations were now members of Zionist districts.[144] They were cautious about any claims of capturing "most" or "the majority" of Reform Jews.

Many Reform Jews undoubtedly supported the American Council, because they were indeed afraid. They were constantly shaping their commitments in terms of "_mah yomru hagoyim_," opposing Zionism because it "tends to separate Jews from other Americans" and raises all sorts of questions about dual allegiance. Very likely, many of them gravitated to the American Council for Judaism for those considerations, but this obsession for acceptance among non-Jews and fears of alienation also led to the resignation of most of the rabbinic leadership from the Council. Most Reform rabbis who affiliated with it had envisioned the organization as a vehicle for restoring the priority of religion in American Jewish life. They were not prepared to support it solely for its denunciations of Jewish nationalism.

The non-Zionist rabbis resigned, because they had envisioned the Council as an instrument for expressing their convictions not their fears. What was most crucial to them, and what both their supporters and detractors ignored most of all, was their ideology. That ideology posited an emphasis upon religion as the dominant quality of Jewish life which they believed Jewish nationalism would obliterate. The Jewish community was for them a religious community, and they were primarily absorbed with "the growing secularism in American life, the absorption of large numbers in nationalistic endeavors and a tendency to reduce the religious basis of a life to a place of secondary importance."[145] Their conflict of conscience over the accelerating impact of Zionism had made them feel like "religious acrobats," and they had simply refused any longer to defend "the untenable position in society which nationalism as a creed imposes upon us."[146] They seriously questioned whether "a return to God means a return to nationalism, whether or not our salvation is in our religion or in a Jewish soil, whether the nationalistic movement is counter to every thought and emotion of Jewish history, whether retreat to a nationalistic ghetto is a surrender of the great universal messages of Jewish prophet and sage . . . whether we should consent to the destruction of our faith."[147]

These adversaries raised objections of practical consideration as well. They considered it "sheer arrogance" to petition for political control of Palestine after an absence of 2000 years. One critic suggested that "were I an Arab, I too would resist trespassers upon my political and moral rights, even though I would welcome them as immigrants come to join me in making the country good."[148] The major thrust of the objection at this level was the proposition that the establishment of a Jewish state would aggravate, not diminish, Jewish difficulties the world over. The status and condition of Jews in any country could suffer, "now that they will have the excuse that the Jews have a place to go and a place to which they belong anyway."[149] Not least important was the emergence of Arab nationalism which the anti-Zionists predicted would never accept the reality of Jewish sovereignty in Palestine. Certainly it should not be difficult for Jews who realize what nationalism means to them, to understand what it also means to Arabs.[150]

The Zionists complained that the opposition somehow found the courage to support every just cause of every other people except their own. They were among the first "liberals" to sign petitions for the complete independence of India, a second front to aid Russia and more ammunition for China. At the same time, they refused to embarrass the British government to suggest that "if in the civil strife, Jewish hopes will be devastated and opportunities for a large-scale immigration to Palestine destroyed -- who cares? The patient is unimportant; only the pet theory must be saved."[151]

Heller himself touched upon the most sensitive Zionist source of distress in declaring that what was supreme in this period of tragic turmoil is "not the insistence upon creedal or practical points of view, however ardently or sincerely held, but defense, unity, life . . ."[152]

That essentially points to the fairest judgment of all concerning the rise and development of the American Council for Judaism. Many of its supporters were sincere, but they turned out to be wrong. They may have been naive, but they certainly were not dishonest. They were misunderstood, misquoted, and mistreated, but they were also misguided. They seemed to realize the critical condition of world Jewry, but they failed to grasp the necessity for Jewish independence.[153] They were able spokesmen for the religious quality of Jewish life, but they could not detect the ties between torat-Yisrael (religion of Israel) and eretz-Yisrael (land of Israel). Attachment to the soil of Palestine was intimately associated with matters of Jewish faith. The Bible proclaimed the country as the eternal land of the Jewish people. The Jew prayed repeatedly in his worship every day for a return to that land. The Jewish calendar was predicated on the cycle of seasons in Palestine and even Jewish holy days and festivals recounted significant events in that place. The anti-Zionists largely ignored these associations out of revulsion for the evils of political nationalism.[154]

It is not known how many Reform Jews the American Council for Judaism may have actually attracted or repelled by awakening them dramatically to the dimensions of a conflict they never knew existed. It is clear, however, that after the conflict over the Jewish Army resolution and the fierce struggle that resulted in the creation of the Council, the die had been cast in Reform Judaism. It was evident at least that the Zionist momentum was accelerating with increasing support for its cause in Reform circles and would be extremely difficult to reverse.

In contrast to the plank on Palestine in the Columbus Platform of 1937, the Jewish Army issue of the early 1940s had produced a change in deeds as well as words. A growing segment of the Reform movement was acting with increasing militancy, and the non-Zionists of their own volition had dissociated themselves formally and officially from any endorsement of Zionist positions. The CCAR had at last committed itself to the political sanction of a Jewish homeland in Palestine after the war, and even the UAHC was edging toward that stand.[155] The American Council for Judaism remained a determined antagonist of any such development. Rabbinic and lay leaders might speak eloquently about respect for all points of view, but it was clear that non-Zionists were no longer comfortable or numerous in the highest councils of Reform Judaism.

CHAPTER 3
THE HOUSTON CONTROVERSY

In 1954 Congregation Beth Israel of Houston, Texas celebrated its centennial anniversary. The available evidence indicates that the Jews of Houston acquired a cemetery in 1844 and formed Congregation Beth Israel ten years later.[156] The official minutes of the congregation do not appear until 1861 but refer to the incorporation of the synagogue by an act of the Texas legislature on December 23, 1859. The early beginnings of the congregation and its development are somewhat difficult to establish, but it is fairly clear that Beth Israel is the oldest existing synagogue in Houston, Texas.

Originally, Beth Israel was an Orthodox congregation, but as early as 1867 the Minute Book discloses the first reference to the use of Isaac Mayer Wise's prayerbook, Minhag America.[157] In 1868, the congregation installed its first organ,[158] and by 1860 it engaged its first rabbi, the Rev. Zacharias Emmich.[159] He was followed in the pulpit by several distinguished Reform rabbis including the anti-Zionist Jacob Voorsaenger and the devoted Zionist Maximilian Heller.

The first serious conflict within the congregation occurred in 1879 over the issue of head-coverings. At the annual meeting on May 11 of that year, a motion carried to instruct the Shamus (ritual director) to require all non-members visiting the Temple for services to remove their hats before entering the Temple.[160] Apparently a portion of the membership already worshipped with uncovered heads, but two years later another motion directed that no male child would be permitted to enter the sanctuary with a head-covering.[161]

In 1883, however, the congregation defeated a motion which would have made head-coverings mandatory for all members and visitors. A year later, it also defeated a resolution instructing the rabbi to wear a gown, tallit (prayer shawl) and head-covering. In her review of congregational records, Anne Nathan Cohen concludes from this constant vacillation over the problem that by May, 1884 it was obvious that "a conflict is stirring within the congregation which will result in the first cleavage in Beth Israel's history."[162]

Evidence of that rupture follows with the resignation of a gentleman who left to become the first president of the Orthodox congregation in Houston.

According to the synagogue's recorded history there was only one other major "cleavage" in Congregation Beth Israel, which far exceeded the first in its impact and ramifications. That conflict erupted over the question of Zionism and became known throughout the Reform movement as "The Houston Controversy." It spawned a number of similar actions in several other Reform synagogues, stimulated spirited debate in the highest national councils of Reform Judaism, and elicited sharp rebuttals from the Presidents of the Hebrew Union College, the Central Conference of American Rabbis and the Union of American Hebrew Congregations. It was in many respects the last determined stand of "classical" Reform against the inroads of Zionist sentiment.

The Houston controversy sprouted out of the political infighting over the choice of a successor to Rabbi Henry Barnston (who planned to retire on September 1, 1943). The Assistant Rabbi at the time was Robert L. Kahn who was temporarily on a leave of absence with the armed forces as a United States Naval Chaplain. In the search for a successor to Rabbi Barnston, the Rabbinic Selection Committee reported that it had considered but rejected the candidacy of Rabbi Kahn as the next Senior Rabbi.

Some confusion exists regarding the reasons for this decision of the Rabbinic Selection Committee. The Committee acknowledged that Rabbi Kahn had served in the most satisfactory fashion as Assistant Rabbi and richly deserved the esteem and affection in which he was held by so many members. They even invited him in their report to return to Beth Israel as Assistant Rabbi after the completion of his military service; but they withheld from him the post of Senior Rabbi, out of several considerations. They explained, first, that Rabbi Kahn's availability, in light of his military obligations, could not be determined precisely. In addition, they claimed that the primary responsibility of the Board of Trustees should not rest upon personal preference or concern for any particular rabbi, but only upon "the best interests of the congregation." Finally, it was the committee's judgment that Rabbi Kahn was "too young to cope with the more mature leadership of the churches of other denominations in this community." The committee informed Rabbi Kahn of its decision regarding his candidacy in terms of the provisions cited above and invited Rabbi Hyman Judah Schachtel of West End Congregation in New York City to succeed Rabbi Henry Barnston as "Chief Rabbi."

Mr. I. Friedlander, who served as chairman of a special Policy Formulation Committee which eventually drafted the Basic Principles, indicated that other considerations affected the choice of successor. He reported that his committee was confronted with conditions within the congregation and the community which required "correction" and "action." One such condition was the rapid influx of Eastern European Jews into what was once a predominantly German Reform congregation. This influx of more traditional elements in turn triggered a fear among old, established families at Beth Israel that control of the congregation would eventually fall into the hands of these "neo-Reformers."

The major objective of these newcomers, in Friedlander's view, was not American Reform Judaism but "nationalism." Their intent, he charged, was to direct Beth Israel "toward a rapprochement with traditional or conservative Judaism and, of course, in the interest of political Zionism, then and now an issue in American Jewish life."[163] To achieve that end, he continued, they attempted to capture the congregation by convincing it to reject the unanimous recommendation by the Trustees of a successor to Dr. Barnston. Their only motive, he claimed, was a victory for Zionism. "How better could this be accomplished than to replace Dr. Henry Barnston, an uncompromising advocate of Israel's universalistic mission and ever an opponent of political Zionism, with a 'reform' rabbi favoring a Jewish "Commonwealth?"[164]

The Board of Trustees recommended the election of Rabbi Schachtel, because they believed that "he would guide Beth Israel along accustomed ideological lines and in conformity with the teachings and philosophy of a liberal Judaism similar to that which Dr. Barnston had supported." In approving the Board's recommendation, President Leopold Meyer urged the membership "to approach the matter with composure and equanimity." He summoned them to discount their personal differences and to resist reactions of emotional outbursts. He maintained that the primary issue should not be personalities of any kind, but the grave issues affecting the future of their temple. Personal friendships and selfish objectives were totally inadequate criteria for decisions of this dimension. The President did concede, however, that it would have been most surprising if Rabbi Kahn, after having served over a few years, had not endeared himself to a segment of the congregation which would solicit actively for his promotion. For that reason, Mr. Meyer explained, they might not endorse the appointment of Rabbi Schachtel.[165]

On August 4, 1943 the congregation met to approve the recommendation of the Board of Trustees for the election of Hyman Judah Schachtel as Chief Rabbi of Beth Israel. That special meeting was recorded as "the most exciting and hectic one in the history of Beth Israel, and unhappily, may compare too favorably with the most turbulent meeting ever held by any Congregation anywhere."[166] It was evident from the outset that the recommendation of the Board was not without opposition from several quarters. A sizeable segment of the membership rejected the Board's appraisal of Rabbi Kahn's qualifications and tried to overturn its decision. An attempt was made to dissociate Rabbi Kahn and Rabbi Schachtel from the bitter debate over Zionism, but to little avail. Each side identified one of the two men as the champion of their position. The President himself acknowledged that the election of Schachtel would mean a decisive defeat for Jewish nationalism at Beth Israel and settle the conflict once and for all within the congregation. It quickly became apparent that the congregation was caught between two hopelessly irreconcilable factions, and that the advocates of Zionism, despite their zeal and determination, were clearly a minority. When the ballots were counted, Rabbi Schachtel had been elected by a margin of 346 to 91. It was then moved and carried that his election be made unanimous.

The battle however did not leave the congregation unscarred. The meeting had not been confined exclusively to issues. It had also included brutal accusations and personal attacks which the victims did not easily or quickly forget. The victors assumed that the election results had earned them a final and decisive truimph. The President, Leopold Meyer, announced that the entire Jewish community had been aroused by the nature of the "claptrap" presented at the August 4 meeting. "Despite the fact that the Zionist contingent had been soundly thrashed . . . the lengths to which the obstructionists proceeded in their efforts to defeat the constructive purposes of the Board of Trustees was a revelation to many members of the congregation . . . After what transpired at the meeting no further argument or evidence was necessary, to the strictly Reform element of the membership, that the Zionist ideology was hopelessly incongruous with the temper of Beth Israel as well as incompatible with the doctrines and percepts of Reform Judaism . . ."[167]

However convincing they may have considered their victory to be, the leadership of Beth Israel was not convinced they could prevent a recurrence of such conflict without further remedial action. The time had arrived, in their mind, to state precisely the principles and philosophy which they believed had guided and should continue to guide Beth Israel in the future. It did not take long to reach that decision. Six days later at the regular meeting of the Trustees a special ad hoc body was appointed known as the Policy Formulation Committee. This committee was charged with a mandate to prepare a set of principles, policies, rules, regulations and procedures which would govern the future management of the congregation's affairs.

President Meyer emphasized that this committee was not appointed solely as a result of the special meeting on August 4. In fact, that meeting, he suggested, was only the consequence of prolonged turmoil that had been brewing within the membership for a considerable length of time. He maintained there was never any serious question whatever but that Beth Israel was clearly and unalterably Reform in its manner of worship, and definitely non-Zionist ideologically. It was simply a matter of when Beth Israel would take its stand in connection with the Zionist controversy, and August 4 was simply the occasion for the showdown.

I. Friedlander, who chaired the Policy Formulation Committee, was an eloquent spokesman for the anti-Zionists forces and not without a gift of dramatic metaphor. In his report to the President, he included as a preamble to the committee's proposals a reference to Abraham Lincoln's proposition that "a nation cannot endure half-slave and half-free" and claimed it was "equally axiomatic that a congregation cannot endure and attain for its membership the highest spiritual aspirations, 'half-traditional and half-Reform'."[168] He further added that if the existing membership policy remained unchanged, the temple would surely risk further disunity and a complete transformation of the Reform character of the institution.

Friedlander informed the Board at its regular meeting on September 7, 1943, that his committee, after long and lengthy deliberations, was now prepared to submit for approval a Restatement of Principles which would henceforth be known as "The Basic Principles of Hebrew Congregation Beth Israel." After some discussion and reflection, the Board adopted the Principles, instructing and authorizing the committee to incorporate the changes and modifications approved by the Board. The Board further instructed the Executive Secretary to print a sufficient number of copies of the Basic Principles for distribution to the membership. The final, approved draft of the Basic Principles read as follows:

PRINCIPLE NO. 1

We believe in the mission of Israel which is to witness to the Unity of God throughout the world and to pray and work for the establishment of the kingdom of truth, justice and peace among all men. Our watchword is "Hear, O Israel, The Lord our God, the Lord is One." We accept it as our sacred duty to worship and to serve Him through prayer, righteous conduct and the study of our Holy Scriptures and glorious history.

PRINCIPLE NO. 2

We are Jews by virtue of our acceptance of Judaism. We consider ourselves no longer a nation. We are a religious community, and neither pray for nor anticipate a return to Palestine nor a restoration of any of the laws concerning the Jewish state. We stand unequivocally for the separation of Church and State. Our religion is Judaism. Our nation is the United States of America. Our nationality is American. Our flag is the "Stars and Stripes." Our race is Caucasian. With regard to the Jewish settlement in Palestine we consider it our sacred privilege to promote the spiritual, cultural and social welfare of our co-religionists there.

PRINCIPLE NO. 3

We believe in the coming of a Messianic Age and not in a personal Messiah. We recognize that it is our hallowed duty to speed the coming of the Brotherhood of Man under the Fatherhood of God, which is the Messianic ideal for which the righteous of all people work and pray.

PRINCIPLE NO. 4

We accept as binding only the moral laws of Mosaic legislation and Prophetic teaching. While respecting the convictions of our Orthodox and Conservative brethren concerning the rabbinical and Mosaic laws which regulate diet, priestly purity, dress, and similar laws, we, however, as an American Reform Congregation, reject the religious obligatory nature of the same, as having originated in ages and under influences of ideas and conditions which today are entirely unsuited, unnecessary and foreign to the beliefs and observances of progressive Judaism in modern America. We shall maintain and use in connection with our religious services only such ritual and ceremonies as may be approved by the Congregation from time to time and which may symbolize, in effective and beautiful form, the principles of our faith, and, which are adapted to the progressive and liberal spirit of our times.

PRINCIPLE NO. 5

We recognize the complete religious equality of woman with man.

PRINCIPLE NO. 6

> The treasures of Divine revelation were given in the Hebrew language and in such language are preserved the immortal remains of a literature that influences all civilized nations. As the fulfillment of a sacred duty therefore, the cultivation of the Hebrew language has become unintelligible to the vast majority of our co-religionists; therefore, while a measurable content of Hebrew is essential and desirable in our rituals and services, it must be used wisely as is advisable under existing circumstances.

PRINCIPLE NO. 7

> The basis of brotherhood among the Jews throughout the world is Religion. Hence, it is our duty to help our co-religionists whenever and wherever the need may arise, even as we must help all mankind that may be in need, in accordance with the principles of our faith.

With only minor modifications, this declaration was essentially a restatement of the 1885 Pittsburgh Platform and a repudiation of the Columbus Platform adopted little more than six years earlier by the Central Conference of American Rabbis. It was likewise a rejection of the increasingly more flexible posture toward Zionist efforts by Rabbi Eisendrath and members of the UAHC Board of Trustees. Beth Israel's leadership was acting vigorously to dissociate itself from any trace of traditionalist influence.

The Basic Principles provided also for the printing of formal applications for membership in the congregation. These applications would include two categories of membership. Associate membership would include individuals who desired to affiliate but who would not subscribe to the Basic Principles. They would be entitled to all benefits, privileges and obligations of Beth Israel, but they would not enjoy the right to vote or to hold office. Regular members who subscribed to the Basic Principles would not suffer any disabilities.

This provision for dual categories of membership precipitated lengthy and heated discussion within the Board but, after extensive deliberation, it approved the proposal which resulted in two applications for membership. Both were virtually identical, with the exception that the Basic Principles were incorporated into the regular form, implying the willingness of the applicant to affirm those regulations. The associate membership form did not include the Basic Principles. The reasoning invoked to explain the distinction was based on the premise that "no person who was unwilling to subscribe to the fundamental principles upon which any organization was conceived should have the power, through the ballot, to incite active opposition thereto, and perhaps plant the seed for the destruction thereof."[169]

Mr. Friedlander also explained that at any annual meeting, without prior notice, a minority number of members attending such a meeting could change the ritual, the form of worship or even dispose of the physical properties of the congregation. There was nothing in the by-laws to safeguard or prevent such a possibility. He went on to observe that the largest influx of new members occurs just prior to Rosh Hashanah, and that there was not sufficient time therefore to propose changes in the by-laws to meet the requirements constitutionally. He regarded the Basic Principles as an instrument in an "educational" task, the task of orienting present and future members to the fundamentals of American Reform Judaism. He underscored the necessity for this procedure "because of the confusion even among the Rabbis themselves, arising from the accent lately upon the political rather than upon the religious nature of the Jewish people."[170] He felt it was imperative to correct this state of affairs before the prevailing majority position slowly eroded.

Finally, he defended the passage of the Basic Principles by vigorously insisting that there was nothing new in the Principles, that its formulators did not invent any new concepts, but had merely restated what had been the accepted, cardinal and underlying basic principles of American Reform Judaism. He explained that "we simply reworded and re-grouped the classic statements of the Philadelphia (1869) and the Pittsburgh Statement of Principles (1885)."[171] Friedlander conspicuously omitted reference to the Columbus Platform of 1937 which by then was already widely recognized as the successor to the Pittsburgh Platform.[172]

The formal adoption of the Basic Principles and the accompanying dual categories of membership by the Board of Trustees infuriated the traditional, Zionist minority within the congregation, as well as others who protested that such action violated every precept of freedom of conscience. In sharp rebuttal to the Board decision, forty-four members of Beth Israel filed a petition to the President, dated October 25, 1943 requesting a special meeting of the congregation at the earliest possible date.

They stipulated that the purpose of such a meeting should be a willingness to determine whether or not the majority of the Beth Israel membership agreed with the sentiments expressed in the Basic Principles attached to the application for membership. They objected to the retention of this application form on the basis of three major considerations.

First, they claimed it was not compatible with the fundamental philosophy of modern, liberal, Jewish thought as expressed by the two parent bodies of American Reform Judaism, the Union of American Hebrew Congregations and the Central Conference of American Rabbis. Congregation Beth Israel, they emphasized, was affiliated with these two bodies and should act in accordance with the principles of its organizational spokesmen.

Secondly, they insisted that the majority of the Beth Israel membership actually objected to the introduction of dual membership forms, because it set up a "second-class" membership, it flagrantly ignored all the rules of democratic procedure, its "test" for membership was un-American, it endorsed a policy that was irreligious and tended to undermine and destroy the prestige and influence of Congregation Beth Israel in its own membership and in the community at large. Finally, these petitioners demanded as a fulfillment of the purposes of this specially called meeting, that the vote on the dual membership proposition be carried through with democratic procedure and a closed ballot.

Two days later, the President announced receipt of another petition from those supporting the action of the Board requesting a special meeting to be called not earlier than December 1. The purpose of such a meeting in their view would be three-fold. It would permit, first, the entire membership to adopt the _Basic Principles_ as approved and adopted by the Board of Trustees at its meeting on September 7, 1943 and as set forth in the printed copies that had been mailed to all members.

The meeting would also provide the opportunity to formulate and send several resolutions, clarifying their position on Zionism, to the UAHC, the Hebrew Union College and the Central Conference of American Rabbis.

In addition, the entire congregation could officially approve, ratify and adopt the revised forms of Application for Membership which were actually already in use anyway, but endorsement of which would now discredit any further organized opposition. This petitioning group, in contrast to their Zionist opposition, demanded that any decisions be considered by voice vote only.

The battle lines were now clearly drawn for the final showdown. Petitioners on both sides began a campaign of propaganda to win over whatever constituency still remained undecided. A circular in opposition of the Principles was distributed unsigned by reportedly the effort of congregational members in opposition. A reply to that circular was signed and delivered by a "Committee Representing Petitioners Favoring the _Basic Principles_." This discredited the earlier leaflet of the dissenters by associating it "substantially with the language and thought contained in a recent letter written by a Brooklyn, N.Y. Rabbi of an Orthodox Synagogue to a recently admitted member of our Congregation."[173]

Whatever substance if any there may have been to such a charge, the intent of these supporters was clear. They suggested to the congregation that the opposition to the Basic Principles presumed to know more about Reform Judaism and Congregation Beth Israel than did the Board of Trustees. They accused the opposition of attempting to rewrite the principles "from the standpoint of traditional (Orthodox) Judaism with its legalistic, nationalistic interpretation."[174] They charged that such presumption by the protesters was completely unwarranted, because more often than not, members from non-Reform backgrounds are not equipped to judge the merits of Reform Judaism.

The supporters did not cite any evidence or statistics for their claim, but they alleged that Orthodox and Conservative synagogues "frequently lose members to Reform congregations, where such members have no clear idea of the principles of Reform and do not in fact accept such principles." They then proclaimed that the interests of harmony and unity within the Jewish community would be better served where "those who worship together understand and adhere to the same religious ideology than where an attempt is made to effect compromise on fundamental principles which ends usually with dissatisfaction upon the part of all."[175]

A special meeting of the congregation to ratify the Basic Principles and the dual categories of membership was called for November 23, 1943. The agenda also included the presentation of four resolutions, as requested by the anti-Zionist petitioners. The first three were directed at each of the major institutions of Reform Judaism--the UAHC, the CCAR and the Hebrew Union College.

One called for a thorough investigation of the Union and all its departments for the avowed purpose of "effecting a vigorous promotion of the historic principles of American Reform Judaism . . ." Another directed the Hebrew Union College to investigate thoroughly the curriculum, requirements and personnel of the College in order to ensure a greater number of students with Reform background and graduates with a more vital interest in Reform Judaism. It expressed the confidence that more Reform congregations would develop if a larger number of "strictly Reform rabbis" were graduated. The third resolution castigated the CCAR for what it termed a "departure of the Conference from the historic pattern and essential principles of American Reform Judaism." The final resolution appealed to all Reform congregations to join with Beth Israel in this protest.

The historic gathering of Beth Israel Congregation on November 23 attracted more than eight hundred members to debate the proposals of the Board of Trustees. Both factions were allotted equal time within which to present their arguments and were permitted to discuss every facet of the issues so long as it did not involve reference to personalities.

The meeting lasted several hours. The Chair called for a motion, which subsequently passed, to record the ballot by a standing vote. With representatives of both sides serving as vote tellers, the Congregation approved all issues on the agenda by a margin of 632 to 168. The Basic Principles and the resolutions now became an official policy statement of Beth Israel Congregation and copies were mailed to all rabbis, officers and members of the boards of trustees of all temples affiliated with the UAHC.

An immediate though not wholly unexpected repercussion of that official endorsement was the resignation of Rabbi Robert Kahn as Assistant Rabbi. Rabbi Kahn confessed that his decision was neither easy nor hasty. In fact, it was not even the content of the Basic Principles which disturbed him so much as the double standard of membership. He regarded the Principles as a "poorly written hodgepodge of theology, anti-defamation, anti-Zionism and anti-Orthodoxy," but what "shocked" him completely was the decision to cite the Principles as the basis for voting membership in the congregation. He submitted that never before in Jewish history had any congregation legislated a creedal formulation as a requirement for full membership in the community, and that Beth Israel's action was therefore completely unfounded and unprecedented. "If such a step had been taken by any other congregation, I would have spoken out against it. Such a step having been taken by the congregation of which I am Associate Rabbi, I, because I am a Reform Rabbi and an American, must protest by resignation."[176]

Rabbi Kahn also charged in his letter of resignation that the Basic Principles actually placed one segment of the congregation in the position of a permanent minority. Those who could not vote could never exercise control, and this restriction would apply forever to those who disagreed with the official policy of Beth Israel. Rabbi Kahn considered such procedure wholly inconsistent with democratic principle and Jewish tradition.

The President's reply to Rabbi Kahn on March 28, 1944 accepted his resignation with regrets and with the hope that he would find a suitable position elsewhere. He responded in no way whatever to the substance of Kahn's letter involving the injustice and immorality of the Board's action. The Board was undoubtedly aware of Rabbi Kahn's position on such matters, which in turn may have influenced their decision to by-pass him in favor of Judah Schachtel as successor to Henry Barnston. They evidently feared that with Kahn as Senior Rabbi, Zionism would sweep up Beth Israel in its momentum as indeed it was gathering momentum throughout the Reform movement. To avoid that eventuality this Houston congregation persisted in its denunciation of Jewish nationalism and rejected any growing criticism to the contrary. The feeble reply to Kahn was evidence of their determined resistance to any modification of their position.

In addition to the copies of Beth Israel's policies, mailed to Reform congregations throughout the country, an article by Rabbi Schachtel was distributed to the Anglo-Jewish press as an attempt to explain the rationale for the new regulations. According to Schachtel, his congregational leaders had culminated a three year period of study, thinking and planning which had produced these documents. He openly acknowledged that they were motivated by "an increasing concern over the growing power of political Zionism in shaping the future of Reform Judaism," but he still maintained that this was "clearly and inspiringly a layman's movement to revitalize and reaffirm the principles of American Reform Judaism as these laymen, after careful research, understand them."[177] At the same time, he disavowed any personal responsibility for their decision, and even though he was actively involved in the emergence of the American Council for Judaism, Schachtel conspicuously omitted from this press release any personal endorsement of their action.

Schachtel's effort did not succeed very well, because it bore many traces of a contrived exercise in apologetics on behalf of anti-Zionism. At this juncture, such a strategy was clearly incompatible with the dominant mood and attitude of American Jewry. Even as a defense for the action taken by his Board, no less as a legitimate step derived from Jewish tradition, Schachtel's statement was inadequate. In fact, some of his explanations produced more objections than they eliminated. He explained that even though the _Principles_ declared that "our race is Caucasian," his laymen knew that there were also other races among whom Jews could be found, "but they were writing principles for their congregation in Houston, Texas, and in their congregation the membership and the potential members in the city belonged to the Caucasian race."[178] The _Principles_ did not include, nor did Schachtel mention, provision for Jews who might arrive in Houston from non-white communities. In Houston, apparently, Reform Jews would always be white Jews.

He also dismissed the whole issue of "second-class membership" by comparing creedal categories with financial categories. He suggested that other congregations make it difficult for many to affiliate because of burdensome financial requirements. Very often elsewhere, full privileges of membership depend upon ability to pay, but here at Beth Israel, they depended only upon "a readiness to believe." That belief, of course was subject to definition and approval by the leaders of Beth Israel, but at least no one could complain about financial barriers.

Despite its highly explosive quality, the response to the Basic Principles and to Schachtel's explanations was not exclusively adverse. Rabbi Morris Lazaron telegraphed his approval to I. Friedlander, Chairman of the Policy Formulation Committee.[179] Louis Goldberg, President of Mt. Sinai Congregation, Sioux City, Iowa, later registered his support with a blistering rebuttal to Solomon B. Freehof's repudiation of the Principles.[180] Congregations in Baton Rouge, Louisiana and Pontiac, Michigan, which became early advocates of the American Council for Judaism, also endorsed the objectives of Beth Israel in Houston.

But the response to Beth Israel's decision and Schachtel's defense of it touched off an overwhelming avalanche of devastating criticism. As might be expected, the non-Reform community was virtually unanimous in its denunciation. The sharpest and angriest rebuke was delivered by David de Sola Pool, the distinguished rabbi of the Sephardic synagogue, Shearith Israel in New York, who wondered why the entire statement did not begin with a notice that "No Jews Need Apply." He strongly urged that "this truly shocking statement should not be allowed to pass unchallenged."[181]

Even in Reform circles, the reaction was almost totally negative. In a formal, public rebuttal, Louis I. Newman charged that "the Houston folly . . . is only Council (American Council for Judaism) anti-Zionism in masquerade."[182] He attacked every argument in support of the Principles and conceded to Beth Israel the dubious distinction of achieving for itself a status "by the side of the 'Protest Rabbiner' in the days of Herzl, whose synagogues today have been ravaged by the Nazis, and many of whose congregants have found asylum in Zion."[183] Newman spared no fury in attributing Beth Israel's action to Council influence. "Behind the Houston mischief-making," he announced, "stands the American Council for Judaism supported by Lessing Rosenwald . . . . They will stop at nothing to vent their spleen upon Zionism, despite the ever-enlarging tragedy of Jewry . . .[184]

Abba Hillel Silver refused to dignify the Houston episode with any expression of outrage. Instead, he declared he was not "very disturbed" over the whole matter and considered it as simply one of those adumbrations that appear on the surface whenever there is considerable tension.[185]

Beth Israel's conduct prompted even a well-known Reform Jewish news columnist to deplore a decision which "excommunicated" a segment of its membership from "the blessings of Reform Judaism" and to assure his readers that such procedure was extremely irregular in Reform congregations. He apologized to the avid Zionist who "will be denied the streamlined ministrations of the Union Prayerbook at his grave and will have to be content with a much longer Orthodox ritual."[186]

James Heller found the whole affair much less amusing. He conceded that there had been separatist movements and schisms before in Jewish life but never before over the question of a creedal test to determine sufficient credentials for membership in the Jewish community. He also conceded the right of any particular group to adopt and advance their own religious principles but not "with a fanaticism like that of the Houston congregations." Heller rejected any suggestion that the Beth Israel decision was motivated by sincerity or genuine concern for basic precepts of Reform Judaism. On the contrary, he insisted that "high-sounding phrases, protestations of fealty to the principles of our faith, do not suffice to cloak the cowardly and utterly impertinent treason to them which the cold fact of these actions involves."[187]

Heller was not alone in his furor. The denunciations were often so bitter and fierce that more moderate observers were prompted to plead for a discussion of Zionism "on the basis of the issues involved--without epithets, without animadversions, without reflections upon the characters or reputations of the principals." It seemed that the most fervent adversaries on both sides failed to realize that "the dignity of a people surpasses in importance the right to licentious speech that currently characterizes much of the controversy."[188] Unfortunately, the voices of moderation did not achieve any measure of reconciliation between the parties to the conflict.

Shortly after the controversy erupted, Schachtel visited the Hebrew Union College and ran headlong into the opposition of the student body. Some reminded him of his Orthodox lineage which seemed to them incompatible with his new posture toward Jews who observe Kashruth and support Zionism. They subjected him to endless recriminations and arguments on the subject, and, in the dining room, chanted the grace after meals with the words "boneh b'rachamav y'rushalayim" (May God in his mercy rebuild Jerusalem) especially for his benefit.[189]

A student editorial in the Hebrew Union College Monthly castigated Beth Israel for "doing its best to prohibit any change in the status quo."[190] It further informed the Houston leadership that the present rabbinical student body embraced a wide range of attitudes toward the principles of historic Reform Judaism. Very likely, it continued, not many future rabbis would be eligible for membership there, because "uniformity has not become our highest ideal."[191]

The first official reaction from the UAHC appeared in the December, 1943 issue of its monthly publication, Liberal Judaism. Editorially, the Union acknowledged the right of every congregation to its own opinions about Zionism, but added that "by no stretch of the imagination is there warrant for this action." The editorial reviewed the past record of Reform Judaism and Zionism, observing that even in the most vigorously anti-Zionist period, no resolutions ever excluded Zionist rabbis from the ranks of Reform Judaism or relegated them to second-class memberships. The Union declared that "the action of the Houston congregation runs counter to the tradition and practice of Liberal Judaism, which must rest upon a decent regard for divergent opinions, allowing for valid differences of opinion within its own fold."[192]

The stage was now set for a furious debate. On the one hand, a major Reform congregation had deliberately repudiated a growing sympathy in Reform circles for Jewish nationalism which had now become the central issue in the movement. On the other hand, the established institutions of Reform Judaism all now advocated at least a conciliatory policy toward Zionism, especially in a period of increasing urgency for the survival of Jews in Europe.

In a larger context, however, the controversy was evolving into a struggle for authority within the Reform movement. Could a congregation defy its parent bodies on a matter of primary concern and remain exempt from any penalties or disciplinary action? To what extent could the national bodies control the policies and procedures of its constituent members?

The opposition within Beth Israel itself warned against infringing "upon the rights of the rabbis of our Conference and of our faith by setting up principles which more than 90% of them would not accept."[193] Aside from the inflammatory character of their resolutions, the Beth Israel majority was chided for its arrogance in refusing even to consult with eminent authorities in Jewish life before reaching their decision.

The Union first offered to send a conciliation committee consisting of the Presidents of the UAHC, the CCAR and the Hebrew

Union College, but Beth Israel would not agree to receive them.[194] Rabbis Jonah B. Wise and James Heller, now immediate Past-President of the CCAR, offered to mediate personally, but received no invitation. Even Dr. Louis Finkelstein, President of the Jewish Theological Seminary, was willing to intervene, but he too was rejected.[195] Rabbi Maurice Eisendrath, who had just recently been appointed executive director of the Union, personally requested a meeting with the Board of Trustees but received a negative reply.[196]

Eisendrath undoubtedly had Houston in mind when he declared that "only the blinded partisan could fail to give serious attention to its (Reform Judaism) program which seeks the fullest implementation of the Balfour Declaration, while refraining from reducing all Israel to a mere political entity which would make our proud and historic people 'like unto all the nations.'"[197]

In the absence of Beth Israel's willingness to negotiate their differences with the movement, the Union Board formally repudiated the action undertaken by the Houston congregation on the grounds that a Reform synagogue "should not exclude from the full privileges of membership anyone who seeks in sincerity and in truth to join in the fellowship of our religion."[198] The Board also deplored any "creedal test for full membership" and "urged" Beth Israel to "reconsider" its recent action "in the hope" that it would abolish the Basic Principles.[199]

In a lengthy and detailed formal reply to Beth Israel, Solomon B. Freehof, the newly-elected President of the CCAR, denied the congregation any right to deprive the Conference of its privilege to change previous policies or even to exclude from their own Temple membership those who disagreed with the majority. He did not deny that the collective opinion of the Reform rabbinate on this question might be incorrect, but, he concluded, "if the judgment of the majority of the Reform rabbis on this question is not acceptable to you, whose judgment will you accept?"[200]

Freehof was further concerned about the decision of Beth Israel to distribute their resolutions against the Conference to all member congregations of the UAHC without any prior consultation with the CCAR. He therefore announced that he was regretfully compelled to issue a public refutation, even though he would have preferred "to avoid further disturbance of the peace in American Reform Judaism by public disruptations."[201]

Beth Israel firmly refused to retract its decision or even to soften it through any channels of conciliation. It rejected any overtures to achieve that end, and despite the public embarrassment it caused the movement, it remained adamant in its decision.[202]

National Reform leadership was helpless in the face of this determined resistance. Whether it could not or would not execute reprisals against Beth Israel, the national bodies absorbed more humiliation in this episode than they could inflict. The Union virtually admitted as much when Eisendrath proclaimed that "the accused" (national Reform institutions) would receive a "hearing . . . before the bar of American Jewish opinion."[203]

The major emphasis of Eisendrath's appeal was a plea for reconciliation. He urged Beth Israel to realize that the "Union was only as strong as the sum total of its constituent congregations acting together for the common cause" and reminded them that "the Union has no authority other than that which its constituent congregations, meeting in its Biennial Councils, confer upon it."[204]

The principle of autonomy and freedom of inquiry which Reform Judaism had invoked as a movement to achieve its independence could not be denied to individual congregations within the fold. The national leadership might protest the activity of a congregation like Beth Israel and denounce its decision, but it could not censure such a group without betraying its own principles. Eisendrath therefore could only remind the Houston temple that sufficient opportunity existed to lodge complaints through "regular channels" and to voice its opinion on matters affecting the movement "through written communication directed to the Executive Board."[205] The national office could not "forbid" a constituent congregation to issue public resolutions in opposition to the parent body, but could only contend that such procedures were "inappropriate" and "unnecessary." Since Houston had not communicated to the widest possible audience, the extensive publicity it received would hopefully persuade them to close the entire episode which, in Eisendrath's words, "has proved embarrassing to those leaders of Reform who still believe that Reform is not of yesterday, but of today . . ."[206]

The Union was clearly concerned, however, for a more pragmatic reason than the ideal of religious freedom. Eisendrath repeatedly stressed his fear that this issue was so explosive it could conceivably split the Reform movement into two irreconcilable factions and destroy such hopes for unity as might have still existed. He rested almost all of his efforts at comprise with Houston on the gnawing intuition that "if we do not succeed . . . in arriving at a formula, Reform Judaism will be split into two opposing camps. They will be fighting each other instead of fighting together for Reform Judaism."[207] Eisendrath's struggle to retain the Union's participation in the American Jewish Conference derived from similar concerns, as will be discussed in further detail below.

In rabbinic circles, not every response to the Basic Principles was adverse. Several Reform rabbis praised it for its "idealism" and commended the Houston congregation if not for its procedures, at least for its motivations. A few Reform leaders considered the Houston action a long-over-due reaffirmation of the principles which had distinguished Reform Judaism from its inception. In their view, the rapid growth of Conservative Judaism and the added impact of Reconstructionism had begun to tarnish the "spiritual supremacy" of Reform Judaism. For them the Basic Principles embraced a restatement of faith for the American Jew. "If you agree that the future of Judaism depends upon Reform Judaism, then why denounce a congregation, even if it is mistaken?" asked Louis Witt. "They (the Basic Principles) tell us that Reform Judaism is at stake. Those opposing points of view, like the Reconstructionists, have become aggressive and are trying to invade every city in America . . . There is no excuse for the meagerness of our numbers today except that we have been indifferent. The Conservative group has become aggressive and is increasing in power."[208]

The fear of diminishing vitality in Reform Judaism was not the only rationale among those who applauded the Houston action. A few blamed the national bodies for denying to Beth Israel the same freedom of expression which they charged Beth Israel had denied to its own members. They argued that in a liberal movement any group is entitled to govern its own internal affairs without fear or intimidation by its parent body. "We talk a whole lot about 'Freedom of Speech'," said Solomon Foster, "we say that every congregation and every rabbi have a right to think or speak as they please, and then we denounce those who do not happen to agree with us."[209]

Despite the occasional statements of support for Beth Israel, the overwhelming response was decidedly unfavorable. It embarrassed Reform leadership, both lay and rabbinic, virtually repudiated the Zionist plank of the recently-formulated Columbus Platform (1937), and invited widespread disenchantment with Reform Judaism in most sectors of the American Jewish community increasingly sympathetic to the growing demand for a Jewish state.

The Houston affair also troubled traditional elements in Reform, because it provided a cause célèbre for the newly-formed American Council for Judaism. The Council had organized only a year before the announcement of the Basic Principles, but had not yet uncovered a specific episode as suitable to its purposes as the Beth Israel controversy would prove to be. Rabbi Schachtel at the time was a member of the American Council, and undoubtedly the Council embraced his "victory" as their own as well. For them the bitter recriminations which the principles evoked only demonstrated how imperative was the need for an organization such as theirs to defend the position of "authentic" Reform Judaism.

The daring initiative of Beth Israel in fact spawned a sporadic but shortlived outburst of similar incidents in other communities in support of the American Council for Judaism. B'nai Israel in Baton Rouge, Louisiana issued a set of resolutions protesting recent policy decisions of the Union and the CCAR similar in nature to the Houston series. One of its resolutions even envisioned the prospect of "a new league of American Reform Jewish congregations that shall be loyal to the ideals of Isaac M. Wise and the Pittsburgh Platform."[210] Reform congregations in Iowa, Michigan and other states also derived support and encouragement from the declaration of opposition which emanated from Houston.[211]

The Basic Principles remained on the record at Beth Israel, at least formally, until they were rescinded on December 8, 1968.[212] In retrospect, the Houston Controversy did not alter the increasingly favorable attitude in Reform circles toward Zionism and the establishment of a Jewish state in Palestine. At the time of their release, and for a while thereafter, the Basic Principles produced considerable agitation at the highest levels of leadership and perhaps may even have compelled that leadership to re-examine and reformulate its ideological assessment of Zionist aims.

Ironically enough, the Houston Controversy and the aggressiveness of the American Council may even have accelerated the growth of support for Zionism among Reform laymen. The magnitude of opposition to these two phenomena dramatized as nothing else could how outmoded and irrelevant the position of earlier Reform Judaism had become on the issue of Jewish nationalism, which was extremely difficult to defend any longer. It was an increasingly lonely task; and with polarization intensifying between the two sides, Reform laymen may now have found it far more comfortable to support the majority of their rabbis and lay spokesmen; and that meant an endorsement of Zionist objectives.[213]

The conflict over the Basic Principles also provided an excellent illustration of the ideological clash between Jews of German extraction and their East-European peers. At the Hebrew Union College and in the CCAR, a similar clash had prevailed, but in both those bodies the influence of German Jews was waning and with it their opposition to Zionism. In Houston, Jews of German lineage still controlled the leadership ranks at Beth Israel and therefore could successfully repudiate Jewish nationalism. Even that victory, however, was of short duration. The Beth Israel majority won their battle, but lost the war. Their efforts did not effect any substantial change in the direction of Reform Judaism on this issue.

It was clear from the widespread denunciations which the Houston affair evoked that the movement was decisively committed at the national level, if not to direct an active support of Jewish sovereignty in Palestine, at least to a position of non-interference.

Indeed, there was more than a modicum of merit to the anti-Zionist charge that at least two events had committed Reform Judaism to more than a position of neutrality. Support for a Jewish Army in Palestine was a major issue in Zionist circles, and the CCAR resolution in favor of it could be viewed as little less than an endorsement of Zionism. In addition, although the American Jewish Conference was summoned primarily to unify American Jewry on all post-war issues affecting Jewish life, little doubt existed but that the single, most important item on the American Jewish Conference agenda was the creation of a Jewish state. The Union and the CCAR did not fully support the Zionist resolutions on this subject; but their participation in the proceedings of the Conference and their proposals for substitute resolutions clearly implied more than simple neutrality on the issue. Freehof acknowledged as much in his reply to the Houston congregation when he conceded "There has been a definite change of mood in our Central Conference of American Rabbis." Alluding to the revised neutrality resolution passed by the CCAR in 1943, Freehof admitted: "We recognize the fact, plainly observable in the life of hundreds of our Reform rabbis, that Reform and Zionism are quite compatible."[214]

The Basic Principles of Beth Israel established the fact, however, that this "new mood" was by no means unanimous, and that large numbers of Reform laymen, as well as rabbis, could still be mobilized to resist the intrusion of nationalist sentiment upon their religious idealism. They reminded the new majority that while they shared the same abiding concern for the remnants of Hitler's death camps, they could not and would not assume that Zionism afforded the only, or even the best, solution to Jewish homelessness. Even more than its ultimate objectives did they resent its tactics and a strategy which implied for many that rejection of Zionism was equivalent to rejection of the Jewish people.

Although the tide had thus turned, the turbulence by no means abated. A helpful vehicle for understanding the agitation which still engulfed Reform on this question is a glimpse into the lives of those who grappled with the crisis and their consciences as it developed. The analysis which follows focuses on three major leaders of Reform Judaism during the period under study, each of whom responded differently to the swift and convulsive developments of this transitional phase.

CHAPTER 4
ADVOCATES AND ADVERSARIES: THE INNER CONFLICT OVER ZIONISM

Understanding the transition in Reform Judaism on the issue of Zionism requires more than an understanding of the dynamic developments within the movement. In addition, it is imperative to explore the minds and hearts of those who wrestled painfully with an ideological legacy from the past and the requirements of both present and future. Zionism was a highly-charged emotional issue, even in traditional Jewish circles. For Reform Jews with doubts and questions about "dual loyalty," with a commitment to Judaism solely in religious terms, with an ambivalence about Jewish "peoplehood" and the merit of ethic differences, a campaign for separate Jewish sovereignty served only to compound their inner conflict. An appreciation for the magnitude of that conflict clarifies considerably the events which produced the transition.

This is the major purpose for examining the Zionist odyssey of the following three Reform leaders: Morris Lazaron, Julian Morgenstern, and Maurice Eisendrath. The controversy over Zionism in Reform Judaism produced eloquent and impassioned spokesmen on both sides of the issue. Advocates and adversaries could all claim a depth of conviction and idealism which few other questions in American life evoked. The inner turmoil experienced and endured reveals, far more effectively than any recitation of chronological events, the enormous volatility in the movement and the shattering clash of ideologies at the moment of critical impact.

All three men whose positions are analyzed here were colleagues and contemporaries in the Reform rabbinate. Both Julian Morgenstern and Maurice Eisendrath are cited as spokesmen for the majority who began their journey as anti-Zionists but shifted to support of Zionist objectives, although Morgenstern did so with seemingly less enthusiasm and commitment than Eisendrath. Morris Lazaron deserves careful recognition as a classic representative of the anti-Zionist ideology, even though he originally supported the restoration of Jewish life in Palestine. Each of them, however, labored diligently and courageously for their own deepest, heartfelt convictions.

Morris Lazaron received his rabbinic ordination at the Hebrew Union College in 1914. He served as spiritual leader of Congregation Leshem Shomayim in Wheeling, West Virginia from 1914 to 1915. He was then elected to the pulpit of Baltimore Hebrew Congregation where he remained for almost thirty-five years until 1949. In 1922 he officiated as the Jewish chaplain at the burial of the Unknown Soldier in Arlington National Cemetery. Following his retirement from the pulpit, he was appointed as visiting professor of religion and sociology at Rollins College. He was also executive chairman of the Maryland Association for the United Nations from 1940-47.

His foremost distinction, however, stemmed from his personal crusade, first in behalf of Jewish nationalism and, later, in vehement opposition to it. Early in his career he not only affiliated with the Zionist movement, but, in 1931, was elected a member of its National Committee. A little more than ten years later, he resigned from all his Zionist associations and accepted the office of vice-president of the American Council for Judaism.

In recollections about his views on Zionism, Lazaron recalls that his daughter once asked her aunt, the wife of a distinguished Zionist leader (perhaps Abba Hillel Silver?), "Why do the Zionists hate my father so?"

"Because," her aunt replied, "he was once a Zionist. But he left the Zionist camp. They consider him a traitor. That is why they hate him."[215]

The Zionists did not always "hate" Lazaron. Indeed, at one time, they counted him among their brightest young prospects.[216] When he finally affiliated formally with the Zionist movement in 1931, he recalls that Dr. Henry Friedenwald, first president of the Zionist Organization of America and a distinguished Baltimore physician, called on him personally to congratulate him. A short time later at a large Zionist gathering in Baltimore, he remembers that the principal speaker, Justice Louis D. Brandeis, welcomed him officially and publicly into the movement.

Lazaron's first introduction to Jewish nationalism dates back to his earliest boyhood in Savannah. There he remembered hearing Jacob De Haas lecture on the re-nationalization of the Jew. De Haas appeared not long after the entire Jewish world had been thoroughly shaken by the notoriety of the Dreyfus trial. The young Lazaron was deeply touched and felt a warm glow not only from what De Haas said but from the man himself. "In a boyish way," he explains, "I recall sensing some strange organism far-scattered, numbering millions, that reacted like an individual who had been wounded. The entire organism felt the pain and shock."[217]

Savannah, however, at that time was a rather atypical Jewish community in terms of its low incidence of anti-Semitism and limited exposure to the larger Jewish world. De Haas and the Dreyfus affair therefore did not leave more than a passing impression.

Lazaron attended the Hebrew Union College under the administration of Kaufmann Kohler. Kohler's anti-Zionism, however, apparently did not affect him substantially. Lazaron admits that there had been some controversy at the College between Zionism and anti-Zionism during his student days, and even some discussion about the compatibility of Reform Judaism and Zionism, but it simply was not a major item yet on the agenda of American Jewish affairs. Reform Jews especially did not take it very seriously. As Lazaron points out, the popular statement, "We are Jews by religion and America is our home, our Zion was "not a slogan; it was a conviction."

The young rabbi, however, was not wholly untouched by the climate which then prevailed at the Hebrew Union College. He arrived in Baltimore as a moderate non-Zionist. He was not overly concerned about the issue at all until a chain of events began unfolding which offended his sense of fairness and justice. One of the events he cited was the refusal of a Reform congregation to elect Dr. Max Heller as spiritual leader, because he was a Zionist.[218] Shortly thereafter, he heard an address by Stephen Wise on Zionism and responded with a feeling of "something welling up from the depths of my being."[219]

By far the most decisive influence was the impact of World War I. Lazaron realized that the incredible distress of European Jewry and the urgent necessity for relief required major assistance from American Jews. With the announcement of the Balfour Declaration, he began to view Zionism as a powerful instrument for the rehabilitation of devastated Jewish communities. He envisioned the return to Palestine at that time as a movement in which politics was minimized for the sake of emphasis on philanthropy and resettlement.[220] He was deeply concerned about channeling the enthusiasm for Jewish nationalism into specific projects for the strengthening of Jewish life and Jewish unity. Lazaron insisted that the well-being of the Jewish people always remained his major priority.[221]

Devotion to the Jewish people was, in fact, the foremost consideration which eventually led Lazaron into the ranks of the Zionist organization. In 1921 he undertook his first trip to Palestine. He went with an open mind and with an inclination to regard the ancient homeland as a modern cultural center. The reality of Herzl's _Judenstaat_ seemed extremely remote, whereas the vision of

Ahad Ha'am seemed far more functional and inviting. Upon his return to America, Lazaron wrote to Henrietta Szold to express his immense satisfaction with the fruit of Jewish efforts in Palestine, especially the wonderful accomplishments of Hadassah. He hoped she would suggest to him "the best way in which we can do something on this end so that the work of splendid service to which you are giving so much, may not be limited," and he assured Miss Szold of his "earnest desire to do anything I can to further and maintain what I consider to be one of the finest pieces of constructive service our people are conducting in Palestine."[222]

As pleased as he was with the progress in Palestine and its possibilities, Rabbi Lazaron did not always endorse the tactics which produced it. He was very disturbed from his earliest associations with Chaim Weizmann with the political maneuvering and manipulation for Jewish statehood. He claimed that Weizmann acknowledged in his autobiography that his major strategy included a deliberate effort to "soft-pedal politics in order to get money from American Jews."[223]

In the fall of 1922 Rabbi Lazaron testified before the Congressional committee on the Joint Senate-House Resolution supporting the Balfour Declaration. He affirmed the merit of the Resolution but qualified his endorsement with emphasis on the "spiritual" and not the "political" virtues of a Jewish "homeland."[224]

Less than a decade later, he joined the Zionist Organization of America. He did so largely out of sympathy for the very tenuous condition of European Jewry and out of commitment to the concept of Jewish peoplehood--"k'lal Yisrael." In his own city of Baltimore, he became an active member of the Public Information Committee of the Baltimore Zionist District during 1934-35. He served also as a member of the board of directors of the Baltimore District.[225]

In subsequent years he participated actively in building a constituency among American Jews for the relief, rescue and rehabilitation of Jews everywhere. He lectured constantly throughout the country for the joint Distribution Committee and the ZOA. He repeatedly emphasized Palestine as a cultural homeland and appealed for funds to develop the country solely on that basis.[226]

He crystallized the distinctive features of Jewish nationalism, as he envisioned them, in a book which he authored in 1930 entitled, <u>Seed of Abraham: Ten Jews of the Ages</u>. He argued there that "nationalism is here to stay. It is a force in our civilization which must be reckoned with. We must dominate it, or it will dominate us. We can and must spiritualize it. . . ."[227]

Lazaron's enthusiasm for the potential of Palestine in Jewish life bridged a significant period of development. In 1931, he wrote a pamphlet, "Reform Judaism and Jewish Nationalism," which was an examination and refutation of the "misinformation, misstatements and misinterpretations" in an article by a Reform colleague, Rabbi Morris Feuerlicht of Indianapolis, on "Hatikavah and Reform."[228] Feuerlicht had objected to the action of the CCAR which voted to include Hatikvah in the new Union Hymnal. He objected on the basis that Jews are nationals of the land in which they live and appeals to Jewish nationalism endanger the status of Jews everywhere. He repeated the well-rehearsed theme that the mission of Judaism is world-wide and spiritual, not Palestinian and political.

Lazaron acknowledged that the emphasis of early Reformers upon the universal message of Judaism was still sound and their success in salvaging a vacillating generation of Jews, no small achievement. In their zeal to revitalize Judaism, however, they had neglected a basic component of Jewish consciousness -- the concept of Jewish peoplehood. The preservation of the people Israel was no less important than the preservation of Judaism, the religion. Lazaron insisted the two were inseparable.[229]

Such Zionist sympathies predictably elicted a wave of opposition, especially among Reform spokesmen. Hyman Enelow, who then served as rabbi of Temple Emanu-El in New York City, was numbered among the most severe and cynical critics of Zionism. He registered his strong repudiation of Lazaron's assessment of the early Reformers, informing him that "I don't remember being taught by any of them to disbelieve in the reality or the ideal of the Jewish people. They did teach me that there was a difference between a political nation and a people."[230]

In the revision of the Union Prayerbook, the prayer for the rebuilding of Palestine was regarded as a concession to the Zionist element of the CCAR. The prayerbook revision in its entirety represented the labor of a special committee, but the author of the prayer for Palestine was Morris Lazaron.

Ironically, Lazaron's enthusiasm for Zionism began to wane at a time when its appeal was never more promising. His disaffection was complete by the outbreak of World War II, but the disillusionment had set in slowly. He was troubled by doubts very shortly after he had formally affiliated with the movement. Zionist leaders, he claimed, seemed to be less than completely candid in their conversations with those from whom they sought financial contributions. Lazaron claimed that the level of discourse in this context was radically different from what he was reading in the

Zionist press. Publicly they advocated a democratization of Jewish life; but, in reality, the party line and discipline were in the hands of a select few who exercised an autocratic authority which no one could effectively challenge.[231]

He finally convinced himself that the Zionists were exploiting the crisis of world Jewry to serve their own political goals. He painfully concluded that to promote the Zionist cause, the leadership manipulated every sacred feeling of the Jew, every instinct of humanity, every deep-rooted anxiety for family and every cherished memory.

In 1939 Lazaron wrote an article for The Christian Century which published appropriately enough as part of a series on the subject, "How My Mind Has Changed During This Decade." In that article, he noted that his sympathy for Zionism had originated long before the present danger to Jewish survival in Europe. His sympathy then embraced Zionism as a "spiritual nationalism" which, when achieved, would not diminish but enhance the prospects for world peace.

The rise of Hilter and a more ferocious anti-Semitism, however, had blunted the edge of this promising possibility. Instead, "the bewildered, driven Jew, caught in the matrix of mighty tides of undisciplined feelings, his sense of community identity, his group consciousness sharpened, sought to sustain his self-respect by Jewish secular nationalism."[232] Although such reaction out of fear and despair was understandable, it was, nevertheless, for Lazaron self-defeating. It was a distortion and misreading of the original purpose of Zionism, and in fact was wholly unrealistic in light of world opinion and Arab opposition.

He warned that Judaism cannot accept as the instrument of its salvation the very philosophy of nationalism which was leading the world to destruction. Indeed, the approaching disaster could be attributed to a world that was going mad on nationalism; and, in Lazaron's analysis, this was no small cause for anti-Semitism. Nationalism was an enemy of the Jew, because fundamentally and primarily the Jewish genius flourished in a climate of universalism.[233]

The experience which perhaps most influenced Lazaron to change his course was his trip to Germany and his personal encounter with the full magnitude of the approaching slaughter. He recalled that on one occasion he would dine with a Jewish family making futile attempts to be cheerful in the midst of impending disaster. The next time he visited them, the head of the family had disappeared. When he returned again, he found a small tin can of ashes left at the door.[234]

When he returned to America, Lazaron could hear Zionists pounding away at only one theme -- no place but Palestine. He objected to what he considered to be the impact of Zionist pressures on the allocation of funds for the United Jewish Appeal. As the expenditures for Palestine became larger, those for the emergency relief work of the Joint Distribution Committee organized to provide relief and rescue for Jews in all countries became smaller and smaller.

He insisted that the issue was not anti-Zionism and pro-Zionism, as most of his critics claimed. The issue was only a question of priorities. For the Zionists, rescue was apparently impossible without Palestine. In Lazaron's view, Palestine was incidental to the urgency of saving Jewish lives. He chided the Zionist leadership for misleading Jews into believing that the world would always and inevitably reject them, because they were Jews. He blamed the Zionists for breaking down the self-confidence of American Jews and forcing them to surrender the promise of emancipation, because it had failed in Germany.[235]

With such a discouraging assessment of the Zionists' ideology, it is not difficult to understand why Lazaron, in spite of his abiding concern for constructive work in Palestine, now felt the time had come to part company. He had decided in effect that Zionist leaders had established the premise that if you were a Zionist, you were a loyal Jew; if you were not a Zionist, you were a traitor. When he concluded that this premise had finally become an operating principle in the arsenal of Zionist strategy, he terminated his support of the movement. Exasperated, frustrated and bitterly disappointed, Lazaron officially withdrew from the Zionist Organization of America -- ten years after joining the ZOA.

He was not however a silent dissenter. He became in fact a formidable adversary. He outlined the basis for his reversal in an address before the Union of American Hebrew Congregations at its biennial convention in New Orleans in January, 1937. In that speech he denied what he called two major premises in the present emergency -- that the plight of German Jewry proved the failure of the Emancipation and that the only hope then for the Jew was the development everywhere of an intense Jewish nationalism that centered in Palestine. He reaffirmed his unequivocal, disinterested loyalty to economic projects on behalf of Palestine, but rejected once again the uncompromising campaign to establish an independent, political state. The obstacles of Arab nationalism and British imperial policy would be impossible to hurdle.[236]

Ironically, in spite of his animosity for the Zionist program, Lazaron joined with his prominent Zionist colleagues, James Heller and Samuel Gup at the same UAHC convention, to sponsor the Resolution on Palestine, which called upon all Jews, "irrespective of ideological differences, to unite in the activities leading to the establishment of a Jewish homeland in Palestine. . . ."[237] It is impossible to resolve this apparent inconsistency without recognizing the distinction to which Lazaron clung between the spiritual and political fulfillment of Zionism.

In the years that followed, Lazaron and his constituency were still receptive to a possible compromise with the Zionists, but events and circumstances constantly eroded whatever common ground existed between them. One of the incidents which precipitated a final separation through the formation of the American Council for Judaism was the Jewish Army controversy. Lazaron denounced it as only a facade for the ultimate demand of complete sovereignty and statehood for Palestine. The political future of Palestine, was, in his view, a matter for Palestinians to decide. "Let us keep hands off," he warned, "Don't let our hearts lead us where our heads won't follow."[238]

The Jewish Army debate in the CCAR and the obvious implications of the American Jewish Conference for Zionist success persuaded Lazaron in the fall of 1943 to become a founding member and vice-president of the American Council for Judaism. He was convinced that Zionism had stifled the voice of dissent.[239]

Lazaron himself paid a heavy price in prestige and recognition for his persistent opposition. Shortly after his association with the American Council, he was invited to address a combined meeting of all Reform temple sisterhoods of Boston, but the invitation was suddenly withdrawn when Zionist members of the program committee threatened to resign if he was the principal speaker. A speaking tour, requested by a lecture bureau, never materalized, because whenever the booking agent sought to place him, some Zionist member of a program committee would invariably object and cancel the arrangements.[240]

After the war, he was invited by the National Conference of Christians and Jews to visit Europe to meet with leaders of France, Germany, Holland, Italy and Belgium to help develop a working organization for the World Brotherhood movement. Again, the invitation was withdrawn because of Zionist pressures. They reported, Lazaron claims, that he had rejected the highest traditions of his faith and that such a conference could expect no support from the Zionists if Lazaron represented the Jews. He had disqualified himself for any important assignment because of his anti-nationalist stand.[241]

He even suffered repudiation from his own family circle as well. Lazaron was a brother-in-law to Abba Hillel Silver, and the latter hardly applauded the decision of his relative and colleague to abandon the Zionist movement.

Lazaron's quarrel with Silver however was the result of his Zionist opposition, not the cause of it. Lazaron repudiated Jewish nationalism for all the reasons already discussed and he recited them to Silver personally.[242] He registered his strenuous objections to the visit of Chaim Weizmann in 1939 personally and privately to Silver, emphasizing that "this is no time for pressure for a political nation by American Jews vis-a-vis British policy in the Near East."[243]

The most crushing blow followed Lazaron's address on the "Message of Israel Hour" in which he objected to the contemplated visit by Chaim Weizmann.[244] Lazaron invited Silver to be the principal speaker on the occasion of his twenty-fifth anniversary in the pulpit of Baltimore Hebrew Congregation and Silver refused. He told him that his "sinister act" had made it impossible for him to attend and that any participation "would greatly embarrass me and I am afraid, also you--for I would have to take occasion to publicly dissociate myself from the position you took and to repudiate it."[245] Such a blanket denunciation could not but have hurt Lazaron deeply and left an indelible scar. What probably distressed him more than all else was the total disregard for his principles and convictions.

Aside from any value judgments about Lazaron's encounter with Zionism his recollections and reflections disclose helpful insights into the intensity of feeling which this issue evoked in Reform Judaism. It was not a question of logical deduction or disinterested reasoning. It touched off a bitter feud of unprecedented proportions and it aroused the deepest emotions in all corners at all levels.

Lazaron's encounter also helps to establish that the matter was not settled at all by the time of the Columbus Platform. The Columbus Platform disclosed for the first time officially a more sympathetic response to Zionist aims which previously could only be implied, but until 1937 Lazaron was still a Zionist. The Jewish Army controversy, the emergence of the American Council for Judaism, the debate over participation in the American Jewish Conference, all of which explained his reversal on the issue, were still waiting to unfold.

Finally, Lazaron's review of events teaches a valuable lesson about the folly of judging motives and intentions. At the height of the unfolding crisis in Nazi Europe and the consequences for Jews and Jewish life there, loyalty to Judaism became almost synonomous with loyalty to Zionism. The relief and rescue of Jewish refugees became the paramount priority on the agenda of Jewish leadership, for sound and urgent reasons; and the only practical hope they envisioned for such a rescue operation was the establishment of a Jewish state in Palestine. Rejection of such a plan was almost equivalent to rejection of the Jewish people.

Lazaron and others like him suffered the stigma of that equation. They were classified as anti-Semites, self-haters, traitors to the cause of Jewish survival. Undoubtedly many marginal Jews did hide behind the cloak of anti-Zionism as a disguise or excuse for their own rejection of Jewish identity. That misfortune, however, was by no means a universal truth. Some, like Morris Lazaron, opposed Zionism not because they despised Jews, but because they loved them. Many did believe that Palestine could or would develop into a Jewish state in the face of British opposition and Arab belligerence. Many were apprehensive about the status of Jews elsewhere in the world if attention were focused exclusively on the Middle East. Many were convinced that at least equivalent emphasis should be devoted to finding havens of refuge in other countries besides Palestine, that Jews should be entitled, as any other human beings, to live wherever in the world they chose to pledge their loyalty. Many feared that the emergence of a secular Jewish state would completely obliterate the religious quality of Jewish life in Diaspora by absorbing the major share of Jewish money, time and effort.[246]

Morris Lazaron was among that group. The resistance he mobilized, the convictions he articulated so eloquently and the abuse he endured so courageously should be sufficient testimony to his abiding attachment to his faith and his people. In retrospect, his critics might question the wisdom of his judgments on Zionism but certainly not their sincerity.

Equally sincere but eventually more moderate in his opposition and ultimately an advocate of Jewish sovereignty was the fourth president of the Hebrew Union College, Julian Morgenstern. Morgenstern traveled the same path as Lazaron but in the opposite direction. He began as a staunch adversary of Zionism but eventually yielded and endorsed the principle of Jewish settlement and reconstruction in Palestine.

Morgenstern himself explains that his long-standing opposition was largely the result of early conditioning.[247] He was only seven years old when his family moved to Cincinnati where he lived until he was ordained as rabbi from the Hebrew Union College in 1902. His parents had affiliated with the Mound St. Temple (the forerunner of the Rockdale Ave. Temple) where he attended and later taught religious school under the supervision and influence of Dr. David Philipson. Philipson was a leading anti-Zionist and convinced the young Morgenstern that the endorsement of the concept of a Jewish nation in Palestine implied political loyalty to that state and rejection of American citizenship. Morgenstern claims that he "cherished this sentiment" during his student days at HUC and through the early years of his career until 1907 when he returned to the College as a professor of Bible. Even there he remained an anti-Zionist, he recalls, until 1921 when he was elevated to the presidency of HUC.

At that juncture signs of a transformation began to develop. The intensity of his opposition diminished and it was evident that his whole approach to the issue was conditioned by a measure of ambivalence. Rabbi Henry Berkowitz circulated petitions to several leading rabbis and laymen from 1919 to 1921 in opposition to the Balfour Declaration urging their signatures on several anti-Zionist resolutions. Morgenstern withheld his signature, explaining that the resolutions "go far beyond my own point of view," especially in their opposition to the principle of minority group rights. In addition, Morgenstern could not attach major significance to the Zionist campaign and probably chose not to dignify it even by his rejection of it.[248]

Only a few years later, however, he participated in the deliberations of the annual ZOA convention. He emphasized that for him Judaism was still primarily a religion, but added that even Jewish religion was difficult to understand without an appreciation for "the consciousness of Israel as a unique people in the world." He hoped that this endorsement of Jewish peoplehood would establish the truth that Reform Judaism "has advanced from its established position of our great honored pioneers and reformers of the nineteenth century."[249]

Following the Arab riots in 1929 in Palestine, the Zionist district of Cincinnati gathered at Plum Street Temple in protest as part of a worldwide demonstration of outrage over the tragic unprovoked violence. Morgenstern not only attended that rally but affixed his signature to the petition that was delivered to Secretary of State Henry Stimson. The resolution included demands upon the British to increase their protection of Jewish settlements and not deter the Jews of Palestine from equipping themselves for self defense until such protection was assured; and it rested those demands on grounds of "historic justice to a people reft of its land, Jewish sacrifice during the World War, Jewish initiative and investment in Palestine and . . . Jewish martyrdom . . . upon its ancient soil."[250]

At least one explanation for this shift in Morgenstern's posture, slight as it was, involved his awareness as president of HUC that the student body at the College and even members of the faculty were becoming increasingly sympathetic to Zionist aspirations. It was a gradual process, of course, the implications of which Morgenstern himself might not have realized at the time. There was no single incident or sudden crisis (including the events in Palestine in 1929) which accelerated the developments at HUC; but, as Morgenstern acknowledges in retrospect, "it was growth, education, expanding knowledge and adjustment to a changing world."[251]

Whatever concessions Morgenstern was prepared to yield to the Zionists, however, were not yet a consequence of any inner personal reassessments. He was attempting as best he could to reflect changing conditions at the College, but he still had not modified his own individual stance on the issue. As late as 1935 he flatly rejected the proposal for a World Jewish Congress, which would represent Jews of all lands and all groups, because it rested on an appeal to "Jewish separation and racial nationalism." He warned the Jewish community that it had arrived at a critical juncture in its spiritual development in America. Every American Jew must decide for himself, he declared, whether to support the cause of Jewish nationalism "with all the inevitable consequences of jingoism, suspicion, antagonism and warfare of one kind or other" or whether to advance the idea, as he would urge, of Israel as "a united people dwelling in countless lands, yet bound together by the eternal imperishable bond of a common religion . . . ."[252] Morgenstern may have recognized that the Zionist climate was changing at the College, but he had not yet by any means changed his own mind on the subject.

Morgenstern's opposition to Zionist objectives rested upon a challenging set of conceptual propositions. In fact, his rebuttal to Zionist affirmations ranks among the most eloquent, articulate and analytical of all refutations. Morgenstern was primarily a scholar and not an activist or antagonist for either side. He based his argument almost entirely upon those principles in Jewish history and religious thought which, in his considered judgment, embodied the essence of Judaism. He, of course, could not divorce himself entirely from some emotional appeal for his position; but he pleaded his case largely on the basis of its rational merits.

The way in which Morgenstern stated his case is significant in still another context as well. As impressive as it was, it was not convincing enough even to persuade Morgenstern that it was true regardless of changing times or conditions. The arguments he formulated so skillfully and precisely only demonstrated the ultimate futility of even the staunchest, most formidable resistance. The failure of the anti-Zionist cause was not only a result of poor tactics; it suffered from a faulty ideology as well.[253]

Essentially, Morgenstern rejected Zionist claims out of consideration for the nature of Reform Judaism as he conceived it, the fallacy of "cultural pluralism" as a functional concept in American society and, finally, a general repudiation of the merits of political nationalism. Fundamental to Morgensterns' understanding of Reform Judaism was the concept of a constant, ceaseless fusion of two primary forces, tradition and environment. Reform Judaism thrived on an harmonious synthesis of its past (tradition) with its present (environment) to create and sustain a program of life and action for the future. Orthodoxy, in his view, continued to stagnate, because it stressed only the past and minimized the present. The assimilationist, on the other hand, exaggerated the present and forgot the past.[254]

Morgenstern's appreciation for "temporal conditions and considerations" may have been a crucial factor which enabled him eventually to accept the "reality" of Zionist claims, but what undoubtedly delayed that recognition was a pronounced "messianic" chord in his vision of the possible future in American Jewish life. He envisaged a time when the emergence of a universal ethic might eliminate the need for Judaism and hence, the Jewish people. Without religion, in his view, there was no _raison d'etre_ for Jewish identity. This prospect, in fact, was not merely an idle dream, since Jews had never experienced in all their history an environment such as America "whose spirit is so closely akin to the eternal spirit of Judaism and of the Jewish people."[255]

The major difficulty with this excessive optimism, however, was the absence of any clear, programmatic method to achieve the spiritual ideals he projected. Morgenstern was a bit vague and ambiguous in outlining particular tactics, as when he described the "specific" task of Jews as one which required them "to build a true, creative American Progressive Judaism which, . . . safeguarding its basic historic, spiritual and traditional relations with the whole of Israel . . . still seeks . . . to express itself as American Progressive Judaism in sympathetic, eager and constructive response to the influence and demands of our American environment."[256]

This "messianic" theme is his appraisal of the Jewish future also contributed to his renunciation of the concept of cultural pluralism. Morgenstern believed emphatically that isolation was as dangerous for Jews as was assimilation. He argued that Jewish history confirmed the thesis that creative Jewish survival always followed a pattern of first accepting an alien culture, then resisting it, and, finally, adapting it to the features of the Jewish community. The secret, then, of Jewish existence was a recognition that "the only program of salvation is to assimilate without being assimilated."

Morgenstern charged that cultural pluralism in this context was equivalent to isolation. It was not an effective vehicle for Jewish survival in America. In his view it was a vestige of the Old World mentality which always resulted in rigid social stratifications that constantly excluded Jews from the society they lived in. A society of "cultural pluralism" would be only an "infection of our American national existence with the festering sore of racial rivalries and antagonisms and the cancer of persistent minority groups and minority group rights." Those who advocated such a course failed to realize that such a "foreign virus would be suicidal."[257]

The rejection of "cultural pluralism" explained Morgenstern's distinction between "Judaism in America," which he deprecated and "American Judaism," which he advocated. By "Judaism in America," he meant the establishment of a Jewish civilization apart and independent of American culture, such as he charged the Reconstructionists were attempting to achieve.[258] Such an attempt was doomed to failure, because it would only establish a dichotomy for Jews between their religious commitments and national loyalties. Like "cultural pluralism," this dichotomy was "dangerous" for American Jews, because it would lead to a stale and stagnate religious practice which totally ignored existing realities in American life.

The only viable alternative for American Jews, in Morgenstern's analysis, was "American Judaism." This approach to Jewish life would be as compatible as possible with the major features of American culture, and its advocates would exercise every attempt to achieve an harmonious and congenial association between the two. Morgenstern stressed, however, that this arrangement would flow from already-existing groups in Jewish life, not from any new constellation or any single organization. It would require, of course, a readiness and willingness among all groups to cooperate with each other to achieve the best possible accommodation with American culture, but it would not be a unity based on uniformity. Even though he welcomed support from all sources, Morgenstern contended that the Reform movement would become the principal catalyst toward the evolution of this "American Judaism."

Morgenstern not only believed in this ultimate development. He was almost dogmatic about it. He insisted that not only could there be, but that there must be, and would be, a consensus among Jews in America. He summoned all Jewish leaders to realize that "to this integration every Jew and every Jewish group in America must conform," because "its course is imperative, its force irresistible."[259]

As dogmatic as he was on this subject, Morgenstern still left open the possibility of some reapprochement with the Zionists as participants in this grand alliance of "American Judaism," Obviously, a summons to enlist all sectors of the Jewish community in a search for unity and cooperation could not ignore so central a segment as the Zionist movement. Morgenstern may not have endorsed their objectives completely; but he acknowledged that his "American Judaism" would never materialize unless it became "the unity of a large family, with many members, all sprung from a common ancestry, but each in his day and in his land having his own character, his own individuality, his own strength, his own obligations to his brothers and to all his fellowmen."[260]

Such occasional concessions to other points of view in the Jewish community probably enabled Morgenstern eventually to accept the merits of Zionism for the sake of Jewish unity. It would be a reluctant concession, however, not only because of his convictions about the nature of Reform Judaism or his misgivings about "cultural pluralism." In addition, he resisted Zionism, because he vigorously repudiated political nationalism of any kind. He attributed the pain and suffering to two world wars to the evils of rampant nationalism and was most disturbed with what he considered to be a tendency among new immigrants to cling to their old-world cultures. He was convinced that such "militant cultural loyalties" would severely retard the growth of a "distinct, integrated American people."[261] Morgenstern never denied that political nationalism was once a feature of Jewish existence, but it was wholly incidental even then and in the twentieth century dangerous and regressive, especially if it did not attach a higher priority to the religious dimension of Jewish tradition.[262]

None of Morgenstern's pronouncements on the subject of Zionism ever received a warm response from the Zionists in Reform circles, but one in particular infuriated them far beyond their ordinary displeasure. Their anger and wrath may have prompted Morgenstern to reconsider his own adamant opposition in light of changing conditions in Nazi Europe and in the Reform community. For that reason alone it deserves more than casual notice.

It was customary at the Hebrew Union College for the President to deliver the major address each fall at the Opening Day Exercises, a ceremony which marked the official beginning of the academic year. Morgenstern chose as his subject in October, 1943 the question of authentic Jewish identity and proceeded to discredit the claims of Zionism to any major role in Jewish affairs. He charged that, in truth, Jewish nationalism did not rest upon any urgent necessity other than that of "sheer desperation and despair."

He declared that the history of ancient Israel as a sovereign nation was in no way any different from that of numerous other small and equally powerless nations. Israel, he repeated, was distinguished only for its religious insights and that the peoplehood of Israel and its covenant were meaningful only in religious terms. The Jewish people, he emphasized, enjoyed special distinction only for religious considerations and did not require a reconstituted nation to fulfill its "God-appointed destiny." He concluded with regret and disappointment that it would be "foolish, sad and tragic for the Jewish people, which has dreamed the dream and proclaimed the message of world unity, to itself reject its message, faith and destiny and to seek for itself a salvation impossible of realization, an exploded theory of restored, racial statehood."[263]

The response to Morgenstern's address from his Zionist colleagues was swift and furious. So indignant was Rabbi Samuel Wohl at the Isaac M. Wise Temple that he published a formal rebuttal in which he submitted that ancient Israel far exceeded its sister-nations in its level of morality and intellectual achievement. He further denied that Zionism represented any kind of "regression" in the universal thrust of Judaism but that, to the contrary, "the Zionists cherish and put into practice in Palestine the universal teachings of prophetic Judaism."[264]

Abba Hillel Silver denounced Morgenstern's statement at an Executive Committee meeting of the CCAR.[265] A Conservative colleague called the statement "an act of treachery" and appealed at least for a retraction.[266] Several alumni of HUC signed a telegram, circulated by Joshua Liebman, Barnett R. Brickner, James G. Heller and Felix A. Levy, in which they "deeply deplored the remarks on Zionism of Doctor Julian Morgenstern" and especially his reference to Jewish nationalism as being "practically identical with Nazi and

Fascist theory."[267] It seems that only a bond of personal esteem and affection for Dr. Morgenstern prevented several Reform rabbis from seeking a more severe censure than the statement had in fact produced.[268]

Morgenstern was probably stunned by the extent of the distress his remarks had already created. They certainly had not involved any departure from his previously stated position on the issue, and he surely must have wondered why his most recent exposition on the subject had loosed such a flood of invective. One explanation would suggest that he caught his opposition completely by surprise. Only a few months earlier, Morgenstern had voted in favor of the CCAR neutrality resolution, reaffirming that Zionism and Reform Judaism are not incompatible, and had also supported the Conference resolution urging the dissolution of the American Council for Judaism. Dr. Morgenstern's students and colleagues evidently interpreted these gestures as a sign of at least some moderation in his opposition so that they hardly expected the harsh denunciation of their objectives which he delivered. They were puzzled, perplexed and hence, outraged.[269]

In addition, the occasion which Morgenstern chose for this attack on Zionist aims could not have been more poorly timed. The American Council for Judaism had only recently emerged, much to the dismay and embarrassment of the CCAR; and only a few weeks earlier, the American Jewish Conference, in which the UAHC participated, had adopted a resolution calling for the establishment of Palestine as a Jewish commonwealth. Added to those developments were the reports already beginning to leak out of Houston, Texas, concerning the adoption of the Basic Principles which would establish separate categories of membership at Beth Israel for Zionists and non-Zionists. The President of HUC had repudiated Jewish nationalism just at the moment when the possibility of the establishment of a Jewish state was reaching its most critical juncture in Reform circles. A censure of the concept by such a distinguished leader of Reform Judaism, so unexpectedly and so untimely, produced a storm of indignation.

Following this outburst of widespread disapproval for his position, Morgenstern carefully avoided any further harsh refutations of the Zionist position. He was undoubtedly deeply disturbed over the furor he had caused, and it is not unlikely that this experience persuaded him to reconsider the basis for his opposition. Those who knew him best report that Morgenstern maintained his convictions regardless of their popularity but was always willing to change them when he became inwardly convinced that a new course of action was more correct.[270]

That "new course of action" with respect to Zionism began to emerge most visibly in his Opening Day address at the College in the fall of 1946. Essentially, his reassessment of Jewish nationalism developed out of a reconsideration for the role of Jewish peoplehood. He still did not surrender his belief that the character of American Judaism was primarily religious, but he now acknowledged that an unexplainable kinship among Jews everywhere superseded even the religious quality of Jewish life. He was still convinced that American Jews could survive only as a religious community but different conditions elsewhere might well merit different adjustments. He still could not subscribe to a classic Zionist ideology which summoned all Jews to recognize the re-establishment of a Jewish state as the primary goal of their existence. He still stressed the priority of spiritual concerns. Nonetheless, he now agreed that "even though the fulfillment of historic Jewish destiny . . . lies in a direction which leads away from nationalism toward universalism, in its broadest and loftiest concepts there is nothing specifically unJewish in nationalism; it is quite within the bounds of reason and propriety that a section of the Jewish people, dwelling anew in the land of its fathers, should under favorable and warrantable conditions, become once again a Jewish nation, independent and self-governing, wholly or conditionally, as the case may be."[271]

It is also likely that, by 1946, Morgenstern realized that the establishment of Jewish sovereignty in Palestine was not only inevitable but imminent. He alluded to such a prospect as a "blessed day" soon to arrive which "at last should mark the end of our Jewish bickerings and party strife and disunity at least upon the issue of Jewish nationalism." That development would transform the issue into a matter that was "only academic at the very most, and the issues will have passed from our control or influence completely."[272]

Morgenstern's conversion might have been a reluctant one, but it was also swift. He probably never abandoned his perenial hope in the ultimate triumph of the spiritual values of Judaism, but he rather quickly adapted to the new realities of the post-War era. In a Conference lecture to the CCAR in 1947, he established the aspiration for Jewish sovereignty as a legitimate, historical component of the Jewish spirit.[273] Morgenstern outlined what he considered to be the four major areas in Jewish history as the conquest of Palestine to the Babylonian Exile, the Exile to 90 A.D. (or even 135 A.D.), the complete termination of national existence from 135 to the dawn of the Enlightenment, and from the Enlightenment to the present time. That this leading opponent of Zionism should have shifted his position at all would have been remarkable in itself, but that he now reconstructed his conceptual framework of Jewish history in terms of Jewish nationalism was a significant transformation.

Again, Morgenstern stressed the concept of peoplehood as the common denominator of Jewish experience. Only peoplehood was a constant and absolute fundamental of Jewish life. Everything else was secondary and incidental. The modern Zionist movement then was a response to one of the basic, historic principles for self-realization and fulfillment. In fact, Morgenstern added, "From Bar Kochba to Herzl there was no movement of political nationhood in the life of the Jewish people comparable to the present Zionist movement in magnitude and in realistic and positive character."[274]

He acknowledged that the vast majority of Jews now supported the Zionist cause in thought, belief and program beyond any conceivable question. He attributed that phenomenon to a growing realization everywhere that, in light of the recent disasters in Europe during the previous two decades and the precarious stability of the Middle East, it had become absolutely essential for Jews in Palestine to organize along political lines. That is why, he concluded with the statement so widely quoted and distributed, " . . . At heart, we are all Zionists of a kind to a degree. This we realize clearly today as never before. We have learned anew and through pain and sorrow, our difficult and inescapable task is to devise a proper workable, saving harmonization of universalism and particularism and of particularism necessarily expressing itself today as nationalism."[275]

Morgenstern's transition was not only a tribute to his scholarship. It was also a testimony to his own inner struggle with the implications of a changing world order. His own metamorphosis on Zionism reflects better than any other model could the enormous impact of new realities and new developments upon partisans of the "classic" Reform position. His public repudiation of that position was a tribute to his courage, his honesty and his integrity.

Morgenstern's stance also disclosed another major feature of the accord which Reform Judaism reached with Zionism. Support for a Jewish state in Reform ranks was not simply the result of a "*coup d'etat*" by aggressive Zionists and their desire to repress all Zionists dissent. In the absence of any practical alternatives, most anti-Zionists began to recognize the merits of Zionism and the inevitable necessity of a Jewish state. It was not so much a matter of events prevailing over obsolete assumptions. Zionist supporters, of course, eventually captured key leadership posts in the Reform movement, but they soon found their opposition joining them rather than resisting them in their efforts.

* * * * * * * * * * * * * *

A leading spokesman of Reform Judaism who endorsed Jewish nationalism much earlier than Morgenstern and campaigned much more vigorously as a Zionist supporter was the president of the UAHC, Maurice N. Eisendrath. Whereas Morgenstern, by virtue of his position as president of HUC, was preoccupied with the theoretical justifications of Zionism, Eisendrath, as the chief executive officer of the national lay body of Reform Judaism, concentrated on matters of tactics and strategy.

Eisendrath began his career as an unqualified adversary of the Zionist movement. Like Morgenstern, he was raised in a home and synagogue that were strongly anti-Zionist. The ideology which pioneers of Reform Judaism formulated in Europe and which later inspired the Pittsburgh Platform only reinforced his early conditioning.[276] During his student days at the College he recalled that the movement was still predominantly anti-Zionist and that there were still very few Reform rabbis who supported Zionism. One of the most heated controversies among the student body erupted over the invitation extended to Rabbi Maximilian Heller to address the College audience.[277] Eisendrath also attributed much of his early attitude to the teaching of his esteemed professor of Bible, Moses Buttenweiser. He remembered Buttenweiser as a vigorous proponent of prophetic universalism who emphasized the needs of humanity much more than those of his own people.[278] Eisendrath also wrote his rabbinic thesis under the direction of Julian Morgenstern.

That was the orientation which Eisendrath brought with him to his first pulpit in Charleston, W. Virginia and subsequently to Holy Blossom Temple in Toronto, Canada. There, however, the similarity with Morgenstern ended. Eisendrath shifted his position much more quickly, completely and enthusiastically. He dated his "conversion" from 1935 following his first trip to Palestine. As late as 1934, however, he furiously denounced all Zionists as "madmen in Israel" who promoted their cause by using "almost the very words of the Nazis themselves" and reducing Judaism to a "jingoistic connotation of that term." He declared then that he would battle and protest this movement regardless of its popularity, because it was "quite as dangerous to the essential spirit of the Jew as Fascism, Communism and Hitlerism are to the essence of Christianity."[279]

Within one week after his arrival in Toronto, his anti-Zionism nearly succeeded in ostracizing him from the Jewish community. Eisendrath was a pacifist and he began his service at Holy Blossom Temple in September, 1929 just a few weeks after the series of widespread Arab assaults on Jewish settlements in Palestine. Several Jewish leaders were demanding the creation of a Jewish Brigade to retaliate against any future incursions. It seemed wholly incongruous to Eisendrath to relate such militarist activities to traditional pronouncements that hunting, fishing, war and all such "sadistic practices" were not for Jews. He objected strenuously to such a Brigade and stated so vociferously as a contributing editor of the Canadian Jewish Review, immediately upon his arrival in Toronto. In addition, he openly supported the recommendations of Judah Magnes which advocated reconciliation with the Arabs through the establishment of a bi-national state in Palestine.[280]

His dissenting opinion met with a blistering denunciation. He was indicted as a mamzer (bastard) and a meshummed (traitor) and even summoned to a meeting with leaders of the Canadian Zionist movement and the officers of his own congregation who ultimately resisted the pressure to discharge him immediately. The opposition even went so far as to establish a rival publication designed to drive the Canadian Jewish Review out of business in reprisal for its refusal to condemn Eisendrath and force his resignation. The effort failed, but it obviously did not endear Zionism to Eisendrath.

What softened his opposition more than all else was his developing friendships with several members of the Labor Zionists in Canada who did not share the "fanaticism" which he had found among the General Zionists. To the contrary, their social idealism began to intrigue him and prompted him to consider the possibility of Palestinian Jewish settlers' establishing a commonwealth of equity and righteousness. He mixed frequently and closely with members of Histadrut who, in turn, introduced him to such leading spokesmen of Poale Zion as Golda Myerson, Moshe Shertok, David Ben-Gurion and Zalman Shazar.

His Histadrut friends soon persuaded him to visit Palestine in order then to judge afterwards for himself the merit of their efforts. He readily agreed to the proposal and accepted an invitation to spend two weeks in Palestine as a special guest of Golda Myerson.

Upon his return from Palestine, Eisendrath was as firm in his support for Zionism as he had been previously in his opposition. Much of this transformation was undoubtedly the consequence of his abiding dedication to the ideals of social justice. From the very outset of his career, he had assigned highest priority to the moral mandates of Judaism, including its imperatives regarding justice, human equality, personal dignity and social welfare. In Palestine he found the most promising possibilities for their fulfillment.

The "spark of conversion" was kindled when he surveyed the devastation and destruction which Arab marauders had inflicted on Jewish settlements without provocation. He realized for the first time what it meant to be a victim of insensate violence; and what a difference there was between the comfort of the pulpit and the virtues of pacifism, on the one hand, and the grim, painful realities of the struggle for sheer survival, on the other.

More importantly, Eisendrath discovered in the Kibbutzim (collective agricultural settlements) a dramatic application of prophetic idealism. He was enraptured with the vision of young men and women building an entire society on the principles of Jewish law and spiritual precepts. Here in the land of the prophets the rights of the individual and the community finally seemed to achieve a common purpose.[281] Eisendrath was astounded to discover a functioning community free of graft, corruption and abuse of power and he was determined to support such experiments with every resource at his command. He recalled all of the earlier idealism which had convinced him that a cooperative human existence, such as the "kibbutz," was possible so long as its supporters mobilized sufficient will and determination. He confessed how he "searched here, there and everywhere for concrete substantiation. And, finally, I found it, appropriately enough, in Zion."[282]

So enthused was Eisendrath with his discovery and reassessment of Zionist goals that when he returned to Toronto, he advocated the example of the pioneers in Palestine as a model for all "miserably exploited toilers" who would be better advised to emulate their brothers in Palestine than to trust in conventional "revolutionary propaganda." The substantive achievements of young Jews there could inspire so many "disillusioned, anchorless, despondent" youth far better than the usually "raucous and splenetic oratory" they often hear.[283]

Whereas Morgenstern regarded Jewish settlement in Palestine as an impediment to the ethics of universalism, Eisendrath now viewed such settlement as a major step toward its fulfillment. With such a vision as a theoretical consideration and the increasingly ominous developments in Nazi Germany as a pragmatic consideration, Eisendrath soon realized that, by word and by deed, he was now committed to the Zionist cause.

Still, he was not so rhapsodic as to believe that everyone else would now accept the wisdom of his judgment. By 1937, he was pleased with the passage of the Zionist plank in the Columbus Platform; but he conceded that it was a "very, very bitter fight" and in light of the small attendance at the CCAR sessions and the narrow margin of victory, "it probably did not represent the majority of the rabbis at that time." In fact, he continued, it may well not have passed at the beginning of the meetings when the attendance was much larger.[284]

The Zionist statement, he acknowledged, certainly did not represent the position of most Reform laymen. There was very little Zionist programming or Zionist activity of any kind in most Reform congregations. Those few laymen who did support Jewish nationalism such as Julian Mack (New York), Mortimer May (Nashville), Henry Monsky (Omaha), and Robert Goldman (Cincinnati), did not find their congregations a suitable vehicle for their involvement. Financial support for Palestine projects from Reform temples was also insignificant. By all standards of measurement, Eisendrath's reappraisal of Zionism and subsequent support were still a decidedly minority position.

If he entertained any illusions about that question after his return from Palestine, they were very quickly dispelled when he accepted the appointment by the UAHC Board of Directors in 1943 to succeed Dr. Nelson Glueck as President of the Union of American Hebrew Congregations. Eisendrath assumed direction of Union affairs immediately following the creation of the American Council for Judaism and the furor surrounding the publication of the _Basic Principles_ of Beth Israel Congregation in Houston. It was also the same period which required the UAHC to decide whether or not to participate in the newly formed American Jewish Conference. The debate over Zionism had reached crisis proportions precisely at the moment when Maurice Eisendrath donned the mantle of leadership of the UAHC.[285]

The Zionist debate occupied the highest priority on his agenda. Shortly after assuming his position, he assembled a mixed body of rabbis and laymen, representing both sides of the controversy, to explore all possible avenues of compromise or accommodation.[286] The most conspicuous absence was that of Abba Hillel Silver who refused to meet with any spokesmen for the American Council and whose rigid resistance sorely hampered Eisendrath's attempts to bridge the distance between the two sides.[287]

The meeting accomplished very little. The combined body of rabbis and laymen had been authorized by the Thirty-eighth Biennial

Council of the UAHC, but it was invested only with consultative powers. The major subject under discussion was a search for compromise on the matter of the Union's participation in the American Jewish Conference, or at least its endorsement of that body's Palestine resolution. Zionist supporters claimed that the anti-Zionist extremists were creating a schism in Reform Judaism and that participation in the American Jewish Conference was little more than an act of solidarity with Jews everywhere. The anti-Zionists emphasized that dissolution of the American Council for Judaism was out of the question and continued association of the UAHC with the American Jewish Conference was equivalent to an endorsement of Zionist goals.

Judge Joseph Proskauer, President of the American Jewish Committee attempted to soothe tempers on both sides by suggesting that each party had committed serious mistakes. As a step toward reconciliation, he urged all parties to accept the existence of the American Council, to request, however, that the Council "seek a (new) name descriptive of its real purpose," that the Council moderate the tone of its publicity and that all parties urge a recognition for the voice of non-Zionists in the election of delegates to the American Jewish Conference.[288] All the participants agreed to report such recommendations to their respective constituencies; but the whole proposal never advanced beyond the stage of discussion, and Eisendrath still had not persuaded the opposing camps to resolve their differences.

Eisendrath finally achieved a tentative compromise between both factions at an informal meeting of rabbis which he called in Cincinnati on November 30.[289] All the men agreed that it would be impossible for the UAHC either to withdraw completely from the American Jewish Conference or to endorse completely its resolution on Palestine. Therefore, the assembled representatives approved the resolution of a sub-committee which included a key paragraph that declared "the Union, as an organization, is unable to associate itself with those parts of the Palestine Resolution of the American Jewish Conference which call for exclusive Jewish control of immigration into Palestine and the establishment of a Jewish Commonwealth."[290] This compromise among the rabbinic spokesmen for both sides produced at least a temporary truce in the conflict which eventually resulted in a victory for the Zionist supporters at the next UAHC Biennial in 1946.

Eisendrath did not accomplish his task, however, without severe criticism. Abba Hillel Silver was furious. He threatened to resign from the Board of the UAHC if it adopted any such resolution of the rabbis' meeting and accused Eisendrath of having been "intimidated by the determined opposition within the Executive Board."[291] He charged that the situation had deteriorated because of Eisendrath's "own blundering and inconsistencies" because he had been "scared stiff by the opposition" and had thus "seriously messed up the situation by convoking the rump rabbinical meeting in Cincinnati."[292]

In addition to the verbal assaults from militant Zionists like Silver, Eisendrath also endured bitter recriminations from other colleagues and laymen who resented the activities of all "extremists" and urged Eisendrath to state clearly and unequivocally the neutrality of the Union on this whole issue."[293] He was criticized both for acting too aggressively and not aggressively enough. He was caught on both horns of a dilemma -- moderation infuriated the extremists in both camps, while extremism infuriated the moderates. What pained him even more than all the recriminations, however, was a haunting premonition that the very survival of the Union and the Reform movement would turn on this issue. He feared the imminent development of a schism within Reform ranks that would immobilize Reform Judaism permanently.[294] He was convinced that unless there had been strong and vigorous leadership pulling the Union in the direction of Zionism and subsequently to the State of Israel, Reform Judaism might have abandoned any concern for Jewish nationalism and might well have become "some kind of obscure sect in American Jewry with very little influence or appeal."[295] In order to prevent Reform Judaism from drifting out of the mainstream of American Jewish life, Eisendrath decided to promote as persuasively, but as firmly, as he could the argument for the Union's support of Zionist objectives.

At the Hebrew Union College he politely but earnestly responded to the historical and theological opposition which colleagues like Julian Morgenstern had raised. He stated categorically that those who minimized or assigned a lesser role to the concept of Jewish peoplehood than to the concept of Jewish "faith" were quite simply in error. He cited the prophetic theme that even in the "end of days," the _acharit hayamin_, the people of Israel would not only continue to exist but would be restored to their beloved land of Zion.

He pleaded, in addition, for a rejection of ideological dichotomies. Nothing which revitalized the Jewish spirit was ever alien to Jewish tradition, he declared. To the contrary, "body and soul, Judaism and Jew, Zion and the Diaspora, the preservation of our people and the mission of Israel--none is antithetical to the other."[296]

Finally, he proclaimed his abiding conviction that Reform Judaism, and the UAHC as its collective voice, was especially suited to restore this balanced perspective to American Jewry. He urged his present and future colleagues to accept that responsibility, because, as he explained, "I conceive it to be the task of the Union to bend its every effort to achieve such a synthesis today."[297]

The UAHC Biennial Assembly of 1946 was the first in which Eisendrath participated as its President. Almost the entire proceedings of this convention were devoted to the question of a Jewish Commonwealth or issues related to it and Eisendrath took the opportunity to rally the Reform movement in support of a Jewish homeland in Palestine.

In his initial State of the Union Address, Eisendrath assured the delegates, were he living, Isaac Mayer Wise himself would have applauded the position adopted by the UAHC Executive Board which declared in effect that Zionism or anti-Zionism is not a matter for the Union to determine for everyone, but a matter for each individual to resolve for himself within the sanctity of his own conscience.

He then proceeded to establish the principle of liberalism in Jewish thought with elaborate citations from Ibn Daud, Maimonides, Leo Baeck and David Philipson. Having established the principle of free inquiry in Reform Judaism, he then established the corollary that neither Zionism nor anti-Zionism could be considered an "eternal" or "inviolable" precept of Judaism in general or Reform in particular. It was simply indefensible to presume that the tenets of Reform Judaism were fixed forever.

Since only Reform Judaism could embrace this reverence for individual conscience, the UAHC President pleaded for unity and continued membership in the American Jewish Conference by appealing to Reform Jewry to "let it be henceforth understood that although this Union, as an organization, takes no official position on this much debated question, it offers unstinted hospitality to the proponents of both viewpoints within its fold. This means that henceforth there shall be no witches' hunt, which totally un-American and un-Jewish action has been called for in some quarters, to purge from our staff the followers of one or the other 'partyline'."[298]

Eisendrath was actually rephrasing much of Freehof's earlier appraisal of the controversy as being a question not of which doctrine on Jewish nationalism was correct, but of where each doctrine was correct.[299] Reform Judaism, he (Eisendrath) explained, was not by definition committed to either Zionism or anti-Zionism.

The merits of Zionism and the urgency of a Jewish state depended upon the place and circumstances in which Jews lived throughout the world and did not involve any cardinal percepts of Reform ideology. The theories of neither side embraced the total reality of Jewish life and therefore Reform Jews should not demand allegiance to either position as a pre-condition of participation in the movement.

Eisendrath's statement before the Biennial, however, required an added measure of courage, inasmuch as it repudiated once again the action of Beth Israel Congregation of Houston two years earlier which had established two categories of membership. Beth Israel had not been alone in its revolt and other, smaller congregations had derived comfort and encouragement from Beth Israel's defiance. Eisendrath may well have decided to settle the matter once and for all through a public appeal to the Union membership. Never having tested his influence at a plenary session of the Biennial and realizing that a defeat could well have destroyed his tenure as President of the UAHC, Eisendrath understandably cherished the overwhelming approval of the delegates to remain in the American Jewish Conference and to endorse its program.

The complaint which ardent Zionists lodged against Eisendrath because of his caution and compromise was largely unfounded. Whatever moderation he exhibited stemmed not from any lack of enthusiasm for Zionist objectives but from genuine consideration for the convictions of the opposition and the overriding quest for unity. He demonstrated that concern on several occasions but never more convincingly perhaps than in his personal reply to Morris Lazaron who registered a vigorous protest against any decision to support the American Jewish Conference. Eisendrath assured him that he was fully committed to a "constant and conscientious effort" to avoid embarrassment to the non-Zionist component of the movement.[300]

He attached to his letter to Lazaron a copy of the telegram sent by the American Jewish Conference to the State Department including a statement that the UAHC had not concurred in the Commonwealth resolution and was therefore listed as a "non-Zionist" organization.[301] Such evidence, declared Eisendrath, should have been sufficient to assuage any fears Lazaron may have had about the integrity and fairness of the Union leadership.

He reminded Lazaron that the Union had never indicated at any time that it regarded Jewry as a "nation." More than any other organization, the UAHC had demonstrated as tangibly as possible in concrete deeds and definite action its insistence upon the religious priorities of Jewish life in America. Eisendrath made unmistakably clear that he considered Lazarons's protest completely unwarranted.

It might be said that Eisendrath ended his odyssey where Lazaron began and that Lazaron ended his where Eisendrath began. Both men, however, were vigorous protagonists of their respective positions, and neither ever apologized for his change of mind and heart. Both were eloquent and devoted ambassadors for a cause they each considered crucial for the future of liberal Judaism in America. Morgenstern, too, was no less sincere or eloquent; but his ardor was not equivalent, at least not at that critical juncture when his active support would have added so enormously to the merit of Zionist claims. Morgenstern shifted, to be sure, and eventually abandoned his opposition; but his words and deeds suggest that he did so more out of necessity than out of conviction. He realized eventually that rejection of Jewish nationalism had become indefensible. He yielded to the demands for a Jewish state, but not without, it seems, a twinge of regret for the old emphasis on spiritual ideals which somehow had suddenly vanished. Lazaron still clung to them; Eisendrath transcended them; Morgenstern reluctantly set them aside.

CHAPTER 5
DEBATE OVER THE AMERICAN JEWISH CONFERENCE

If Zionism was a major issue among Reform laymen as it was among their rabbis before 1937, the evidence is very scanty. Temple bulletins, periodicals, newsletters and other publications indicate very little serious concern with Jewish nationalism. For all the controversy it created in the ranks of the CCAR, Zionism received only occasional passing interest among the members of Reform temples.

Periodically, temple auxiliaries would sponsor musical programs or discussion groups focusing on some features of Jewish culture in Palestine. The Emanu-El League of Temple Emanu-El of New York City, an organization of young Jewish couples, gathered for a debate on the subject, "Resolved, That The Jewish Heritage in America Should Be Preserved As A Separate Entity."[302] The Women's Auxiliary reported that at one of its meetings "a most interesting program was presented and enjoyed by members of the Women's Auxiliary. Moshe Rudinov and Ruth Leviash rendered beautiful selections of traditional Hebrew melodies and closed the program with Palestinian songs."[303]

Temple Rodeph Shalom of Philadelphia invited Dr. Ben Zion Mussinsohn of Tel Aviv to speak from the pulpit on "Education In Palestine."[304] Dr. Mussinsohn was described as the principal of a Jewish school in Tel Aviv. Although he was "no stranger to America," he was "an ardent Zionist who, consistent with his views, has dedicated his life to the Zionist cause in Palestine." He was also considered "a man of broad culture and of very engaging personality." Another report from Rodeph Shalom announced that the charity collections of the Religious School included allocations of $25.00 to the United Jewish Appeal, $5.00 to German refugees and $5.00 to the Young Israel Farm Fund."[305]

Occasionally a Temple men's club scheduled a discussion program on Palestine,[306] or a Zionist organization utilized the facilities of a Reform synagogue for a meeting on some issue concerning Jewish nationalism;[307] but such events were conspicuous by their rarity. Rabbi Maurice Eisendrath could not muster any sizeable audience in Toronto for his series of lectures on Palestine after his visit there in 1933.[308] Although Rabbi Abba Hillel Silver often reproduced in his bulletin items of Zionist interest from other sources, such as praise for the Hebrew University or arguments for Jewish sovereignty by Chaim Weizmann, rarely if ever did his Temple publication include a statement of commitment to Zionist goals by any lay leader or congregant.[309] Surely he would have welcomed and published such responses if he had received them.

Except for a few scattered exceptions, Zionism was not a matter of concern to Reform laymen, at least not in their congregational lives, and certainly in no way comparable to its priority in Jewish affairs among their rabbis. One survey in 1930 found that despite the "traditional opposition" of Reform Judaism to Zionism in the past, one member out of every five families affiliated with a Reform congregation belonged to Hadassah or the Zionist Orangization of America; but whatever increasing support for Zionism such associations might imply, that support did not visibly affect Temple affairs.[310] Even the Zionists among Reform Jews simply did not relate their cause to the agenda of their congregational activity.

The tranquility began to crumble shortly after the passage of the Neutrality Resolution by the CCAR in 1935. In that same year, the UAHC re-examined the role of Palestine in Jewish life as a potential haven of refuge from the rising Nazi terror, and passed a resolution in support of Jewish settlement in Palestine.[311] In 1937 the Union endorsed the Columbus Platform, including the plank on Palestine; but it still had not confronted the Zionist demand for an independent Jewish state. For most Reform Jews, Zion was at best only one of several homes for the Jewish people. They argued that Jews should feel "at home" in whatever countries they chose to live.

Only a few years later the quarrel erupted in all its fury in the aftermath of the Jewish Army controversy, the emergence of the American Council for Judaism and the spectacular defiance of Congregation Beth Israel of Houston concerning the policies of its parent bodies. These decisive episodes prompted laymen to question whether a religious commitment to Jewish peoplehood required or even permitted support for the establishment of a Jewish state. For Reform Judaism, the forum which generated that debate was the American Jewish Conference of 1943 and thereafter.

The American Jewish Conference consisting of representatives from national Jewish organizations came into being as a result of a preliminary meeting that was held in Pittsburgh. The initiative in calling the preliminary meeting was taken by Henry Monsky, then President of B'nai B'rith, at whose invitation delegates from thirty-two national organizations convened at the Hotel William Penn on January 23-24, 1943.[312] Its avowed purpose was to organize a representative body of American Jewry to unite upon a common program of action to deal with the unprecedented problems of rescue, relief and rehabilitation of those Jews who would survive the Nazi Holocaust.

Beginning in January, 1942 a series of reports began emanating from Europe confirming the truth of Hitler's "Final Solution."[313] In February, the Danubian steamer Struma sank outside Istanbul harbor with a loss of 767 lives. Another ship, the Patria, met a similar fate, because it, too, was denied passage to Palestine, even though the passengers were all refugees from the Nazi inferno.[314] By early 1943 it became readily apparent that the ordinary channels of protest and petition would be wholly insufficient to cope with the magnitude of this unprecedented disaster. The American Jewish Conference was an attempt to meet that emergency.

A principal decision of the opening meeting was the establishment of a temporary Emergency Committee for European Jewish Affairs. It was agreed that such a body would function only until a central organization or steering committee could be established by national elections. Unfortunately, that plan never materialized. Instead, even the nominal unity embodied in the Emergency Committee did not survive the year.

After the call for elections, issued in May, 1943,[315] approximately 500 delegates representing 171,000 voting members of 65 national Jewish organizations met at the Hotel Commodore in New York on August 29 - September 3.[316] The overwhelming majority of representatives supported the Zionist program, but it was impossible to accommodate the small but vigorous non-Zionist minority. The Zionists were not prepared to compromise their ideology, and the anti-Zionists as well as the non-Zionists were not willing to disappear.

Louis Wolsey, a prominent anti-Zionist delegate to the Conference, complained that "no dissenting opinion was permitted" and that the leaders of the sessions were careful to exclude any speakers who opposed the Zionist program.[317]

Most of the sessions were marked by flaming rhetoric and impassioned oratory but less impressive results. Many critical issues were subordinated to a ventilation of personal animosities. One American observer warned that "it is not necessary to wait for a situation like the one in which the Jews of Warsaw found themselves before you learn to cooperate, to compromise, to form a united front for the common good."[318]

The Conference actually involved more than a matter of personalities. The Zionists knew at this date that they could depend for support upon a clear majority of American Jews. They were convinced that any hint at abandoning the leadership to which that support entitled them would be equivalent to betrayal. They considered themselves the guardians of a mandate which did not distinguish between rescue efforts and a Jewish commonwealth. Each was dependent upon the other. They argued that had there been a national Jewish homeland, rescue efforts would have been unnecessary. This was the central lesson of the Holocaust for Zionists, and they repeated that theme continuously at the Conference sessions. For most American Jews, the Zionist argument was extremely convincing, and they did not respond with any fervor to what they regarded as fine distinctions between the concepts of "a national home" and "an independent commonwealth" as presented by the non- and anti-Zionist organizations.

That distinction, however, was not such a minor consideration for large numbers of Reform Jews. Indeed, their demand for such distinctions explained in large measure their opposition to participation by the UAHC in the proceedings of the Conference.

The critics of participation rested their dissent on four primary considerations.[319] First, they argued, the majority of organizations invited to form the American Jewish Conference stood for a "maximal political nationalist program." These organizations evidently presumed that Jews are a nation and must have Palestine as a national homeland. It was not at all likely that they would retreat from this posture, and hence any attempt to reach a compromise with them would be an exercise in futility and frustration.

Secondly, the Union would suffer irreparable damage if it decided to join the proceedings and then withdraw at a later date if the program proved to be unsatisfactory. The onus of responsibility would rest upon the Union to explain its dissent and not upon the Conference to justify its actions.

In addition, these non-Zionists claimed that Jews could better serve their own interests at the Peace Conference as a religious group fighting for religious freedom for all peoples everywhere, rather than as a special minority seeking special status and privilege. Finally, they insisted that the emphasis upon Jewish nationalism in the program of the Conference could not but react unfavorably upon the position of Jews in America and other free countries. The non-Zionists were still worried about the repercussions of too much "visibility" by American Jews.

The advocates of participation, however, were equally adamant in their own convictions. They maintained, first, that the Jewish position in the world was catastrophic. American Jewry would despise the Union if it failed now to join in a united endeavor to deliver Jews from certain death and to safeguard the future rights of Jews everywhere.

Next, they noted that the Union would very likely lose the confidence of its own membership if it failed to explore every possible avenue of cooperation with fellow-American Jews. They repeatedly stressed the impact which only a united Jewry could wield on behalf of its brethren in desperate circumstances. Five million Jews acting in unison could exert enormous pressure for just and equitable compensation, but a divided Jewry would destroy any possibility of effective action.

Therefore, to achieve the desired result, they concluded, ideological considerations must yield to the urgent, existing needs of whatever Jews could still be delivered. Indeed, the presence of the Union in these activities, as a force in Jewish religious life, might help to achieve a moderate and religiously based program of action. Judge Joseph Proskauer, president of the American Jewish Committee, declared in his address to the Conference that no delegate should require any other to sacrifice his principles but that the purpose of their gathering was an attempt to "emphasize not our differences but our agreements."[320]

The advocates of participation eventually prevailed and firmly established in Reform Judaism a favorable response toward Zionist aspirations for a Jewish state. They achieved their victory, however, not without a long and bitter struggle. The American Jewish Conference fell far short of its expectations, in terms of its goals; but for the Reform movement, it proved to be a major turning-point in the Zionist controversy. It served that function not because it did so much, but because so many Reform leaders feared it might.

The Executive Committee of the UAHC voted to participate in the Conference at its regular session on April 1, 1943, immediately preceding the opening of the Biennial Assembly the next day. One of the most persuasive arguments in favor of that decision appealed to considerations beyond ideology. The President of the National Federation of Temple Sisterhoods, Mrs. Hugo Hartman, simply reminded the Committee bluntly and pragmatically that "we must send people there who know what it is that we as Reformed (sic) Jews believe in, we must get our proposals written into the proposals which will be presented, and I submit to you gentlemen that the only way that can be done is if we are there. From the outside, we cannot dictate what a body shall do."[321]

At this April 1st meeting the Executive Board of the UAHC approved a motion to participate in the American Jewish Conference, but only on condition that the Union would not be bound by any actions of the Conference without the approval of the Executive Board. In addition, a sub-committee of rabbis and laymen met in Philadelphia on May 31, to draft a statement of principles, subsequently adopted by the Executive Board and designed to guide the Union's participants in the deliberations of the American Jewish Conference, scheduled for late August.

Those principles expressed the hope that the Conference "will attain unity on the following objectives":

> 1. No peace to follow this war can be judged enduring unless, as for all other men, it provides for Jews complete civic equality, guarantee of the right to worship, and full parity of economic opportunity.
>
> 2. In view of the especially tragic condition of the Jews in Europe, exceptional measures need to be taken . . . to rehabilitate and to restore the Jews in Europe to a full share in European life.
>
> 3. Even with this, great masses of Jews in Europe will be in such a deplorable condition after the war that their plight can be alleviated only by resettlement. A world in which persecution and slaughter of large masses of Jews have been possible, owes those remaining alive the right to find a place where they can live in peace . . .[322]

The principles then reaffirmed the resolution of the UAHC in 1937 affirming support for "the establishment of a Jewish homeland in Palestine." The statement concluded with a set of preliminary recommendations, suggesting that (1) provisions be made for <u>large-scale</u>[323] immigration into Palestine, (2) Palestine remain under international supervision until it was possible to establish self-government "without jeopardizing the rights or status of any group in Palestine, and (3) such eventual self-government be democratic and non-sectarian "with complete separation of Church and State."[324]

These statements which the Union formulated to guide its own delegates in the deliberations of the Conference were positive but cautious. They were responsive to the grim realities of the unfolding catastrophe, but they were certainly no endorsement of Zionist objectives. First, the statements refrained from focusing any exclusive concern upon Palestine as the sole haven of Jewish refuge, but instead summoned the post-War community to restore Jews and all minorities to full equality. Where such developments were unlikely to occur, then the world must recognize the necessity for resettlement. It is interesting to note that the Union statement on this subject did not specify Palestine as the only area for resettlement.

Secondly, the statement of principles hedged on the subject of immigration. It was not prepared to endorse the concept of unlimited entry into Palestine, but hoped that an influx on "a large scale" would be sufficient to meet post-War needs without incurring the wrath of resident Arab populations.

Finally, and perhaps most important, the Executive Board did not include in its principles any immediate concern for the establishment of a Jewish state. Contrary to the Zionist aim, the formation of a Jewish commonwealth was still for Reform laymen entirely an incidental issue. The aversion to Jewish nationalism still ran deep, despite the grave conditions in Europe. Rescue was one matter, but political independence was entirely another.

It is not difficult therefore to understand why Reform lay leaders were profoundly concerned by the Resolution on Palestine which the American Jewish Conference passed at its meeting in New York in August, 1943. It called for "the fulfillment of the Balfour Declaration and of the Mandate for Palestine whose intent and underlying purpose . . . was to reconstitute Palestine as the Jewish Commonwealth." It further demanded unlimited immigration to Palestine as a requirement for "the attainment of a Jewish majority and for the re-creation of the Jewish Commonwealth."[325] In contrast to the Union's directive, the American Jewish Conference Resolution concentrated almost exclusively on Palestine without even passing reference to equal rights for minorities, rehabilitation in lands of origin or resettlement in other areas other than Palestine.[326]

As might be expected, the Palestine Resolution touched off a furious debate at the next meeting of the UAHC Executive Board on October 3, 1943. In the course of a long and heated discussion, it became clearly evident that the Board was almost evenly divided on the question. Unable to arrive at a decision themselves, members of the Board voted to refer action on the Resolution to the next Biennial Assembly of the UAHC which would meet in 1946.

That decision, however, met with immediate protests. Several congregations reportedly complained to the Union that time was of the greatest urgency and that the date of the next Biennial Assembly was far too remote for reaching a decision on such a vital question. Others contended that the deadlock within the Executive Board was itself evidence of disaffection for the Resolution, and therefore sufficient reason for the Union to withdraw completely and immediately from the American Jewish Conference.[327]

In an attempt to resolve the impasse, President Adolph Rosenberg invited thirty Reform rabbis, representing every shade of opinion on the subject of Zionism, to a special meeting in Cincinnati on November 30. The purpose of this special conference was to formulate a position with which all factions could live peacefully, if not enthusiastically. The rabbis drafted at their meeting a resolution which exactly duplicated the one which the Executive Board had endorsed in May with the exception of two additional paragraphs which stated candidly the considerations which prevented the Union from approving the Palestine Resolution of the American Jewish Conference. Those two key passages explained that:

> Because in the congregations of the Union there are divergent opinions on the question of Zionism the Union recognizes the right of each individual to determine his own attitude on this controversial question.
>
> Therefore, the Union, as an organization, is unable to associate itself with those parts of the Palestine Resolution of the American Jewish Conference which call for exclusive Jewish control of immigration into Palestine and the establishment of a Jewish Commonwealth.[328]

During the period between this November meeting, however, and the next session of the Executive Board on January 18, 1944, another storm of criticism had erupted over these embarrassing additions and it was sufficient to force the deletion of both paragraphs. Rabbi Abba Hillel Silver vigorously objected to the nature of the November meeting itself and questioned the soruce of its authority as well as the basis for influence on the Union Administrative Committee.[329] Rabbi Maurice Eisendrath explained that the anti-Zionist faction had petitioned the Union for a clear statement of opposition to the Resolution of the American Jewish Conference and for outright withdrawal from that body. The insertion of the additional two paragraphs was an act of compromise to salvage at least the Union's association with the Conference.[330] Silver's influence, however, prevailed, and the added paragraphs were subsequently eliminated.

The Union had thus returned full circle to its position of nearly a year earlier. It should be noted that this immobility coincided with a period of the most startling revelations concerning the plight of Jews in Europe, beginning in early 1942 with the disclosure of the Nazi plans for the Final Solution.[331] Apparently, not even the evidence of mass extermination was yet adequate to bridge the distance between Zionist and Reform strategies.

One of the most articulate spokesmen for Reform Judaism, Rabbi Solomon B. Freehof, substantiated the existing difference and acknowledged that "the theories of both movements, when boldly stated, are apparently as incompatible as they ever were."[332]

Nevertheless, if differences still existed, the basis for disagreement was gradually changing. The adversaries of Zionist activity were shifting their opposition from a position of ideological hostility to one of practical objections. Again, Freehof observed that large numbers of rabbis in both camps "have grown weary of the entire controversy and feel that somehow it has lost its vitality." Freehof concluded by questioning whether "the facts of actual experience have not sapped the strength of older doctrinal statements and whether or not the older theories now need a general reconstruction."[333]

The old arguments were not necessarily disregarded completely. The controversy still continued over whether Jews were a nation or a community of faith, whether universalism and the Messianic vision precluded Zionism, and whether or not the longing for a return to Palestine amounted to a repudiation of emancipation. These debates, however, were ceasing to dominate the forums of discussion and were beginning to yield to challenges of a far more pragmatic quality. Non-Zionists began to voice serious misgivings about the wisdom of creating a Jewish state to survive in the face of uncompromising Arab opposition. The Arab world, they emphasized, was bitterly opposed to the establishment of such a state; and it was useless, they claimed, to attempt to reach any accord with the Arab states on this issue. The Zionist program therefore was misconceived in this regard, because, they concluded, it was totally unrealistic.

Secondly, the non-Zionists rejected Jewish nationalism, because of the entrenched opposition from the British Foreign office. Winston Churchill himself had earlier denounced the British White Paper, restricting Jewish immigration to Palestine; but the urgencies of war and other emergencies had compelled him to yield to the policy of the Foreign Office. Non-Zionists were fond of citing the fact that even Zionists had despaired of changing the British attitude. It was, therefore, sheer folly to create a state in Palestine which would fan the hostility of both the Arabs and the British.

Finally, the Zionist opposition pointed to the pragmatic consideration that not even the United States was prepared to support Jewish independence in Palestine. Despite a long list of

Congressional signatures on public petitions, newspaper advertisements and mass meetings,[334] the State Department had not agreed to interfere in the Palestine Affair and would very likely resist Zionist pressures to reformulate United States policy. Any coercive tactics in this direction might even be construed as subversive and incompatible with American interests.

The non-Zionists were equally as pragmatic in their proposals as in their objections. Any effort on behalf of Jewish survivors, they insisted, must appeal first to the provisions of the Atlantic Charter and President Roosevelt's Four Freedoms which proclaimed equality of political and economic rights for all people wherever they may be situated. Secondly, immigration to Palestine must depend upon the practical capacity of the country to absorb them. That decision would be the proper function of a commission appointed by the United Nations. Finally, the non-Zionists appealed for a concentrated search for other places of refuge beside Palestine. They were confident that the limited economic and industrial potential of that area could only sustain a limited number of Jewish inhabitants. In addition, since Arab fear of Jewish control of Palestine was the major obstacle to any peaceful settlement, it would be more productive to declare Palestine a unique Holy Land of the World, ruled neither by Arab nor Jew, but by a special United Nations commissioner.[335]

This new emphasis on "practical" considerations also helped to shape the Executive Board's decision at its January 18th meeting. Dr. Freehof urged the Board to endorse the activity of the American Jewish Conference and its work of rescue, relief and rehabilitation and to leave the controversial question of Palestine out of consideration altogether. Such a position of strict neutrality, he argued, would be one which "we will be able to support next year and any year when opposing forces might attempt to capture our Union. We don't want anyone to capture our Union on the question of Zionism. The Union does not commit itself on this question, and the time to say it is now."[336] The rationale for such a decision was simply that "this is the only sure thing, the only just thing, the only lasting step to take."[337]

In an attempt to placate the many conflicting factions, the Executive Board followed Dr. Freehof's counsel and approved for consideration by the next Biennial Assembly of the UAHC the following resolution:

> The Union declares that its function is to interpret, maintain and promote Reform Judaism and reaffirms its loyalty to its spiritual purposes.

> The Union, continuing as a member of the American Jewish Conference, declares its sense of fellowship with all Israel and will associate itself with all worthy and practical efforts designed to ameliorate the tragic plight of world Jewry and to assist in reconstructing those communities that have suffered from the ravages of Nazi tyranny.
>
> Because in the congregations of the Union there are divergent opinions on the question of Zionism, the Union recognizes the right of each individual to determine his own attitude on this controversial question and therefore the Union refrains from taking any action on the Palestine Resolution adopted by the American Jewish Conference.
>
> We call upon our congregations and their members to rally loyally to the support of the Union so that its great and noble work may continue to enrich the spiritual life of American Israel.[338]

The significance of the passage of this resolution consisted not so much in any resounding support for an independent Jewish commonwealth, about which it actually said very little, but rather in the fact that it enabled the UAHC to remain a member of the American Jewish Conference. It was clear to any intelligent observer that a primary goal of the Conference was to establish an independent Jewish state and that membership in the Conference, regardless of any verbal qualifications, implied at least tacit support for such an objective. The objections of anti-Zionists to continued participation on these grounds was thus well justified, and no Zionist claims to the contrary could alter that fact.

That is why the next Biennial Assembly which met on March 3-6, 1946 generated a blistering debate on the question of endorsing the resolution of the Executive Board and remaining a member of the American Jewish Conference. The delegates were well aware that approval of such a resolution would lend the support to the Union to the creation of a Jewish state in Palestine. Each side summoned its most articulate spokesman in an eleventh hour attempt to win the patronage of undecided delegates. It was apparent to all that the decision of this Biennial Assembly on this subject would shape the future direction of the UAHC in the post-war world.

It was by no means certain at the outset that Reform laymen would approve the action of their leadership. Shortly after the Executive Board meeting which affirmed the resolution, the President of the Union received word that the local Reform rabbis of Baltimore had met with their temple presidents to consider withdrawal from the Union. Although that drastic action was averted, one temple president still served notice to the UAHC that "The

Conference has become a political Zionist issue, and it is foolish for the Union to remain in the Conference on any basis. So foolish that it is exasperating."[339]

In addition, Congregation Beth Ahabah of Richmond, Virginia announced that it would accept neither the Palestine Resolution of the American Jewish Conference nor the Union's tacit endorsement of it by its failure to withdraw completely. It also stipulated that it would make no further financial commitments to the Union "until we could reach a conclusion as to the adequacy of the standing of the Union in respect to Jewish nationalism."[340]

Several distinguished laymen had registered their own vigorous opposition. Judge Horace Stern declared that "the very essence of Reform Judaism depends on the opposition to nationalism and to a secular commonwealth in Palestine. Deprived of that philosophy, the Reform movement becomes merely a matter of more modern rituals and ceremonies . . . not a sufficient basis on which to sustain a schism in Jewish ranks."[341]

Lewis Strauss labeled the Conference as "a vehicle for the Palestine Resolution, all the rest being window dressing" and stated further his belief that "a religious organization should not subject itself to conditions in which it is either forced to participate in political decisions or compelled to periodically proclaim that it is abstaining from such decisions."[342]

The strongest objections of all were received from I. Edward Tonkon who charged that Eisendrath and Rosenberg were "the fair-haired boys of the Zionists" who had "unwittingly succumbed to their devious, imperceptible but definite pressures."[343] For this reason, he continued, both Reform leaders had become "personae non gratae" among many in the Union, and he summoned them both to "suggest forthwith formal withdrawal from the Conference."[344]

Eisendrath himself conceded that "American Jewry has never been more bitterly divided than it is today." He hoped that the next session of the American Jewish Conference would realize that "it cannot function efficiently and effectively with the present contradictory arrangement which seeks to commit organizations to programs that are contrary to the will of at least a goodly portion of their respective constituencies."[345]

The next session of the American Jewish Conference met before the Biennial Assembly of the Union, but it produced little satisfaction for the non-Zionist opposition.[346] The principal debate at this session concerned the question of whether or not to extend the activity of the Conference into the domain of local American Jewish affairs as well as the international scene. That proposal was quickly and thoroughly defeated, but the Conference did not retreat at all from its position on Palestine.

In a final attempt to accommodate the dissidents, while at the same time retaining the Union's membership in the Conference, Eisendrath and President Adolph Rosenberg registered their displeasure with the Conference leadership for its failure to take official cognizance of the necessary reservations among several constitutent organizations toward Conference positions.[347] They objected that in public statements on the subject, Conference spokesmen had insisted that the Palestine Resolution had received "only four negative votes" without any indication that these dissenting organizations were unable to concur because of serious divergence of opinion in their own ranks.

They directed particular irritation to the testimony of Louis Lipsky before the House Committee on Foreign Affairs of the 78th Congress. Lipsky had announced that "today an overwhelming majority of the members of the Central Conference of American Rabbis is on record in favor of this (Palestine) Resolution, in favor of our position (the position of the American Jewish Conference). At that time, the UAHC was wholly against us . . . Today the Union of American Hebrew Congregations is a member of the American Jewish Conference." Eisendrath and Rosenberg rejected the implication that membership was equivalent to endorsement. They explained very candidly that such misrepresentations had made the Union's position within the Conference extremely difficult to maintain. The Union had been constantly embarrassed by the absence of any statements from the Conference leadership that divergence of opinion existed on the highly controversial issue of the Jewish Commonwealth.

"For this reason," they stated "the Union of American Hebrew Congregations finds it imperative to insist that at the forthcoming meeting of the United Nations Conference in San Francisco, as well as in all pronouncements bearing on the Palestine Resolution preliminary thereto, as well as in all future official representation or publicity on the part of the American Jewish Conference, it be clearly indicated that the Union of American Hebrew Congregations -- although a member of the American Jewish Conference -- has taken no positive action on the Palestine Resolution."[348]

Eisendrath and Rosenberg apparently hoped that some evidence of cooperation from the Conference in this regard would provide sufficient compensation to reduce the intensity of Zionist opposition at the forthcoming Union Biennial. One sign of such cooperation appeared in a subsequent telegram from the American Jewish Conference to the State Department. Claiming the support of all sectors of American Jewry, the telegram added that "the non-Zionist viewpoint is represented in the Conference by organizations which have remained in the Conference out of respect for the majority decision, although they did not, as organizations, support the Palestine Resolution in its entirety. These include . . . the Union of American Hebrew Congregations. . . ."[349]

This dominant mood of expectancy produced the kind of atmosphere which attended the opening of the Biennial Assembly in Cincinnati on March 3-6, 1946. Although the entire proceedings of this convention were devoted to the question of a Jewish Commonwealth or issues related to it, the plenary sessions were devoted almost exclusively to a debate over continued membership in the Conference. All the addresses and arguments hinted at a recognition that the moment of reckoning on the subject of Jewish nationalism was at hand.

A highlight of this Thirty-Ninth Council of the UAHC was a town meeting forum on the issue of creating a Jewish Commonwealth. The principal participants included Rabbis Joshua Liebman and Irving Reichert as well as two laymen, Isaac Heller of New Orleans and M. M. Dannenbaum of Houston. Much of the rhetoric was only a repetition of ideological platitudes for and against Zionism, but several observations touched upon certain obvious dilemmas. Rabbi Liebman reminded the audience that Reform Judaism "cannot have it both ways, to deny the supernatural revelation at Mt. Sinai and at the same time endow a kind of supernaturalism at Pittsburgh, Pa."[350] Isaac Heller, who was a committed Zionist but who [as a delegate to the American Jewish Conference] advocated a moderate Palestine Resolution appealed for a pragmatic treatment of the dilemma with a summons that "we must not adopt, if it can possibly be avoided, any program for this Union that will unreasonably divide our people at a time when our greatest need is for unity of action."[351]

Rabbi Irving Reichert of San Francisco was one of the most vigorous anti-Zionist spokesmen in Reform circles. It was he who rebuked his Zionist Reform colleagues most severely for their passage of the Jewish Army resolution and whose public renunciation of Zionist aims prompted Rabbi James Heller, as president of the CCAR, to visit San Francisco and deliver there a formal rebuttal. Reichert demanded to know at this "town meeting" who in the audience has "yet to hear a responsible Jewish religious organization in this country stand up and say to America, 'We Jews in the United States consider ourselves no longer a religious community, but a nation'."[352] It should be unmistakably clear to all, Reichert argued, that the basis of Jewish life in America was religious and that support of Jewish nationalism was a violation of those conditions upon which Jews accepted equality of citizenship in this country.

He dismissed as "an infamous libel" the charge that non-Zionists were indifferent to Jewish suffering, because they opposed the establishment of a Jewish state as the solution to the Jewish catastrophe in Europe. The record will disclose, he declared, that "Zionists conveniently forget to mention that non-Zionist generosity is responsible in no small measure for the miracle of modern Palestine."[353] He included on that distinguished list of non-Zionist benefactors such philanthropists as Baron de Hirsch, Sir Moses Montefiore, Louis Marshall and Felix Warburg. He indicted the Zionists with responsibility for distorting the goals of post-war reconstruction. He charged that "neither religion nor rescue nor relief nor the abrogation of the White Paper are the objectives of this secular nationalism--not 100,000 visas for persecuted Jewry, but one certificate for admittance as a Jewish state into the United Nations is their goal."[354]

Although he would have preferred that the Union completely withdraw from any associations with Zionist activity and repudiate Jewish political nationalism, Reichert admitted that such a course would only cripple the Reform movement and lead to disaster. He agreed with his opposition on at least one principle--the necessity for compromise, if only because "we dare not destroy this organization to satisfy our personal preferences."

Despite the sharp lines of difference, both sides were moving increasingly closer toward some attempt at compromise with common overriding concern for the well-being of all Jews. Much of the discussion at the plenary sessions focused precisely on this priority of Jewish peoplehood. One Southern layman from Sheffield, Alabama, Nathan Gilbert, confessed that he was not a member of the Zionist party, nor did he ever consider himself in any way a Zionist, but he suggested that in the absence of any better solution, the Zionist proposal deserved serious consideration. "I believe," he said, "that if we were to forget that we are one with our brethren in Europe, if we were to say that in the moment of their critical need, we are neutral, it is the same as saying that you are neutral about whether you bleed or not. Can you be neutral about that?"[355]

Henry Monsky explained that as president of B'nai B'rith, most of whose members were probably Zionists, he nevertheless did not commit B'nai B'rith to the Palestine Resolution out of deference to the minority who were not Zionists. At the same time, however, he would not withdraw B'nai B'rith from the American Jewish Conference. He claimed that the same analogy applied to the Union as well.

Even Rabbi Morris Lazaron, who had reversed his earlier espousal of Zionism,[356] conditioned his opposition with a readiness to "recognize the fact that there are brother Jews who are just as sincere and devoted in their belief and that they can be Reform Jews and be Zionists, as I am in my own belief rejecting the national philosophy of the Zionist movement. That is fact. We start with that."[357]

The decision of the Union to remain in the Conference according to several participants was debated with equal fervor and sincerity from every perspective. It produced a lengthy and arduous round of arguments; but, in the words of one veteran observer, these sessions "were the most spontaneous, the least rigged, the most unrehearsed expression of deep-felt views by men and women consecrated to the cause of peace and progress in the household of Israel. It was a model convention, worthy of emulation by all other groups in America."[358]

When the question was finally submitted to the Council delegates for acceptance or rejection, the assembly registered an overwhelming vote in favor of the resolution orginally adopted by the Executive Board of the UAHC on January 18, 1944.[359] Even more surprising than the sizeable margin of victory was the motion to register the unanimous vote of the Council offered by Rabbi Hyman Judah Schachtel and seconded by Rabbi William H. Fineshriber, both of whom had been spearheads of the opposition. Schachtel acknowledged that "this question had been freely, democratically, gravely and beautifully debated . . . The decision has been arrived at in a spirit of real unity . . ." Fineshriber admitted that he regretted the decision, "but the fight was a fair one. . . . I pray that the Conference . . . with the impact of the Union behind it . . . will become a forceful, dynamic factor in Jewish life in all the world."[360]

It was left to Rabbi Freehof, who had labored many years to bridge the distance between both sides, to specify the role of the synagogue as "a moderating and mediating influence" in the struggle between Zionists and anti-Zionists. The final disposition of the Palestine question by the international community, he cautioned, might be less than Zionists seek and more than anti-Zionists would wish, but the religious priority in American Jewish life should dictate an endorsement of that decision by all parties.

In retrospect, the resolution to remain within the American Jewish Conference marked a decisive moment in the Union's changing posture on Jewish nationalism. Never again would the merit of a Jewish state ever be subject to parliamentary debate in the councils of the UAHC. Not every Reform Jew, of course, became a convert to Zionism, but the tide of sentiment had shifted dramatically, and the movement's support for the goals of Jewish nationalism was no longer in serious doubt.

When the Jewish Telegraphic Agency reported the results of the Union's vote on the Conference issue, it headlined the item, "U.A.H.C. Votes to Remain Within American Jewish Conference; Neutral on Zionism."[361] A discriminating observer realized, however, that endorsement of the Conference by the Union implied reconciliation. More perceptive was the editorial observation of the Hebrew Union College Monthly that "ever since the formation of the American Jewish Conference, the Union has been plagued sporadically by certain congregations which have even threatened to withdraw from the Union should it fail to secede. Now that the issue has come to a showdown, it is doubtful whether this type of coercion will ever be attempted again. It may even be that Rabbi Schachtel's resolution that the vote be recorded unanimous stemmed from his realization of the tenor of the delegates and the strength of the Zionists."[362]

Much credit for this shift in attitude belongs to Maurice E. Eisendrath. He assumed the presidency of the UAHC at a critical juncture in terms of the Zionist question. Depending upon his response to the Houston Controversy, the vacillation of his executive board, the barrage of protests from influential and prosperous laymen, Eisendrath might have tilted the balance of Zionist sympathy either way, or at least postponed interminably any positive support from the Union. That he chose to encourage and urge the Union to support Jewish nationalism and the creation of a Jewish nationalism and the creation of a Jewish state, even at the risk of losing his appointment, is a tribute to both his foresight and his courage. What made it even more notable was the realization that Eisendrath had begun his own career as a formidable anti-Zionist and had only changed his own mind less than a decade earlier.[363]

No single individual or group of individuals, however, was solely responsible for the Zionist transformation in Reform Judaism. That change was also due in large measure to an increasing bankruptcy of the anti-Zionist position. The ideology of the Pittsburgh Platform had grown stale, and in light of twentieth century realities, inconsistent with world events. In the aftermath of the Holocaust it was no longer so evident that human progress was inevitable, that universal justice and brotherhood was imminent, or even that human nature was essentially pure and good, and that the proper morality would produce a world of order and harmony, as the "mission" concept of earlier Reform Judaism had implied. Human behavior, it was discovered, was simply too complicated and unpredictable for any easy, conventional judgements. Self-interest was still the dominating incentive in human relations, and, hence, in international relations too.

On a pragmatic level, anti-Zionism could not provide a tangible promise of relief to Jewish suffering which the goals of Zionism offered. The old appeals to the "conscience of mankind" or to trust in "democratic principles" had been completely discredited by the Nazi slaughter in Europe and the callous neglect and indifference of the allied nations. Few if any havens of refuge other than Palestine existed at that time and even after the war was over and the full scope of the disaster was well-documented and widely-known. Petitions for new guarantees of "minority rights" and "equal citizenship" in lands of origin understandably met with less than eager enthusiasm in a Reform community now descended in greater measure from persecuted Russian and Polish immigrants.

For all these reasons, the readiness of the UAHC to participate in the American Jewish Conference, regardless of that body's accomplishments, signalled much more than an experiment in organizational cooperation. It marked the onset of an entirely new attitude in Reform Judaism toward Zionism. It not only saved the Union much embarrassment over the establishment of a Jewish state by the United Nations, which followed soon after, but enabled the Reform movement to welcome Israel from its very inception as a major ally in strengthening the quality of American Jewish life.

* * * * * * * * * * * * *

Armed with the UAHC decision to remain within the American Jewish Conference, most Reform leadership began to translate the increasing sympathy for a Jewish state into an explicit endorsement. Zionism now commanded the loyalty of an overwhelming majority of American Jews, at least in terms of its membership statistics; and it was difficult even in Reform circles to resist the rapidly growing momentum of the movement. As the reality of a Jewish state loomed larger, the opposition grew weaker; and greater effort was directed to formulating a definition of the most meaningful relationship which could obtain between the Yishuv (the Jewish settlement in Palestine) and American Jews, especially Reform Jews.

The manner in which this final phase evolved included at least three contributing components. The first was a slashing attack on the American Council for Judaism. The CCAR especially may have been encouraged in this strategy, inasmuch as most of the rabbinic leadership had resigned from the Council or at least withdrawn from its leadership. Many decided that the Council had undermined its original purpose of responsible dissent and had become a harmful influence in relieving the distress of world Jewry.[364]

Abba Hillel Silver, then President of the Conference, delivered a crushing broadside against the Council in his President's Message to the CCAR convention in Chicago in 1946.[365] Silver applauded the action of the Union Biennial in March and argued that the American Council, for all of its good intentions, had now evolved into a "purely political agency which has nothing to do with the advancement of Reform Judaism or, for that matter, any other kind of Judaism."

The American Jewish community at this juncture, in company with many non-Jews and numerous community organizations was struggling, with the support of President Truman, to persuade Great Britain to release 100,000 immigration certificates for Palestine to those Jews still detained in displaced persons camps in post-War Europe. Rabbi Silver castigated the American Council for actively seeking to enlist American support in denying those certificates. He declared that such interference was nothing less than "crude, conscienceless bigotry," instigated by "dark and bitter malice."

At that same convention Rabbi Morton Berman delivered the Conference lecture and echoed Silver's denunciation of the Council. He emphasized that the Columbus Platform could have included an even stronger plan on Palestine, if there had not been so much eagerness by the Zionist membership to show consideration and respect for the opposition.[366]

The Union, too, acknowledged that the past few years had been extremely trying and difficult in terms of preserving unity within the movement. Time and circumstances had unfortunately substituted raw emotions for calm and considered judgment and had polarized a significant segment of Reform leadership.[367] In fact, the prospect of a permanent split had been a distinct possibility; but recent events, most noticeably the Biennial Council of 1946, clearly demonstrated that the movement did not want "to cleave itself upon the rock of Zionism."

All these pronouncements constituted an unequivocal repudiation of the American Council for Judaism. The leadership of the Reform movement firmly rejected any equation which linked the Council to Reform Judaism. As Silver proposed in his President's Message, the Conference resolution in 1943 calling upon the Council to "terminate this organization" should now be phrased to "dissociate themselves from this organization."[368]

A second factor in this final stage of transformation on the issue of Zionism was the appeal to the desperate plight of the Jewish survivors of the Nazi terror and the shameful injustice of British policy in maladministration of the Mandate for Palestine. One of the simplest but most convincing arguments in this respect was the response of a non-Jew, Edgar Ansel Mowrer, author, foreign affairs columnist and Deputy Director of the Office of War Information until 1943. Even anti-Zionists had repeatedly claimed a paramount concern for the predicament of Jewish refugees, but that advocacy of a Jewish state would not necessarily contribute to their relief. Assuming such a premise, Morris Lazaron had asked Mowrer whether he believed that the most important issue was to save and rescue Jewish lives or to establish a Jewish state. Mowrer explained that he had become a partisan of Zionism only when he became convinced that "the establishment of a Jewish state in Palestine gives the only hope of the permanent salvation of the Jewish people."[369] He emphasized that nothing less than total independence would enable Jews in Palestine to find complete safety and security.

Morton Berman raised the same consideration in his Conference lecture in the context of "_k'lal Yisrael_" (the unity of the Jewish people). The reality of Jewish peoplehood involved all American Jews in the suffering of their afflicted brothers throughout the world. Whenever one Jew grieved, he submitted, the total community grieved. That was the most convincing rationale for urging the Conference to strengthen the faith and rebuild the morale of American Jewry by affirming the right of the Jewish people to establish in Palestine a free, democratic Commonwealth.[370]

The most shocking and convincing evidence of all, however, which disclosed the magnitude of the crises in Palestine and the episode which aroused the indignation of even the most dispassionate Conference members, was the wholesale arrest and incarceration of scores of Jewish Agency officials by British authorities on June 29, 1946. The incident occurred while the CCAR convention was in session and elicited immediate and almost unanimous condemnation by Reform rabbis as an act of brutal repression designed to break the resistance of the _Yishuv_ and compel its acceptance of the terms of the 1939 White Paper.

An initial resolution of protest met with opposition from two avowed opponents of political Zionism, not because it was too harsh, but because it was too weak. Dr. Julian Morgenstern, President of the Hebrew Union College, compared the British action to "the barbaric practices of ancient Syria and Rome."[371] His language was incorporated into the revised draft of the resolution.

Dr. David Philipson, who had remained a bitter adversary of Zionism for a lifetime, declared that the incident had made that day a "black Sabbath." He confessed that he had always harbored the highest esteem for Great Britain, "but by this act of hers today . . . she has forfeited all the respect and love which I and many others have had . . ."[372] Philipson even requested that he be appointed a member of the committee authorized to present to President Truman in person the resolution which vowed to "resist this act of flagrant injustice with all the moral powers at our command."[373]

Following the close of the convention, every member received a notice enclosed with a copy of the final resolution, urging him to bring it to the attention of his congregation and community for endorsement or similar action. An additional copy was sent to the president of every Reform congregation.[374]

The steadily deteriorating conditions in Palestine, compounded by the still-smouldering memory of the Holocaust, increased sharply the anxiety and sense of urgency among those who had previously remained aloof. Now, however, the magnitude of suffering and the grim prospect of an endless road of defeat and humiliation awakened those previously uncommitted Jews to the need for an independent Jewish Palestine, hopefully by negotiation, but if necessary by force.

A final factor in this last stage of transition was the gradual emergence of a new ideology which embraced Jewish nationalism as almost a kind of Hegelian synthesis of universalism and particularism. David Seligson of Central Synagogue in New York explored this theme by divorcing political considerations from spiritual ones. He submitted that a Jewish state in Palestine would be especially beneficial, because it was "the birthplace of our faith, the sacred spot from which emanated the great spiritual truths of Israel for all mankind."[375] He stressed the distinction between political and spiritual ties to a Jewish state and observed that no one ever questioned the American loyalties of those millions of Irish-Americans who celebrate St. Patrick's Day every year and hail Irish Republic. American Jews deserved equivalent consideration. He added that there are Americans of virtually every conceivable ethnic descent who maintained a sympathy for the institutions and culture of their fatherland and who support those institutions, but whose patriotism is never questioned. American Jews were entitled to the same criteria of judgment.[376]

On this threshold of the United Nations decision to partition Palestine, it could be expected that Reformers like Wise, Heller, Silver, Barnett Brickner, Phillip Bernstein, Louis Newman and Morton Berman would heartily welcome the arrival of Jewish nationhood. Far less likely, however, was the enthusiasm of relatively moderate supporters like Seligson, or the reversal of Morgenstern, the repudiation of British policy by Philipson, the decision by Schachtel and Fineshriber to join in a unanimous approval of the Union's association with the American Jewish Conference and the increasing defections of Reform rabbis from the American Council for Judaism. Such developments indicated clearly that resentment had yielded to accommodation and even cooperation.

This mood of harmony and mutual assistance was also aided by an increasing degree of support from non-Jewish circles. Edgar Mowrer's sympathies were already mentioned above. In addition, Dean Alfange (a founder of the New York State Liberal Party and National Chairman of the Emergency Committee to save the Jewish People of Europe) announced his endorsement in an address before the Bronx Zionist Region in 1945. He argued that Jews were at least as much a nation as religion. Indeed, they were persecuted in World War II not because they were a religious sect, but because they were stateless and homeless and lacking in those symbols of sovereignty which all other people possess. "Every Jew," he concluded, "should strive for the establishment of a free Jewish state in Palestine, because the establishment of such a state is the <u>one and only way</u> by which anti-Semitism can be rooted out at the source."[377]

Alfange also rejected the arguments about dual loyalties, patriotism and the acculturation of Jews to American society. "If I were a Jew," he concluded, "I would also view the fight for Jewish statehood as a struggle for self-perservation. I hope that some day all Jews will unite in support of this great ideal. It is the basic solution of their problem."[378]

Just after the long-awaited birth of Israel as a nation on May 14, 1948, Abraham Feldman, as President of the CCAR, announced that he had received a resolution from the Annual Meeting of the American Unitarian Association in support of this major event in Jewish history. The resolution recognized "the hopes of millions of Jewish people . . . in the creation of a Jewish state in Palestine" and urged Presidential action for "the prompt recognition of the Republic of Israel . . . together with the statement of our hopes that this recognition will be implemented in every way authorized by the Congress of the United States and by the Constitution of the United States."[379]

Actually, these statements of support from Christian groups and individuals contained little that had not already been voiced repeatedly by Jews themselves. If they served any purpose at all, it was a service of reassurance. It dispelled the fear among hesitant Jews that Zionism would evoke the suspicion and hostility of the Christian community. When these Jews heard their own spokesmen defend their right to self-determination, they listened very poorly. When, however, the Christian world also defended that principle, then the issue achieved merit and respectability. If the non-Jew recognized the moral and legal sanctions for Jewish nationalism, then certainly Jews need not fear the charges of "dual loyalties" or an "international conspiracy." It was once again a question of *mah yomru hagoyim*? ("What will the non-Jews say?"), and once they knew, they were able to relax. At least such expressions of encouragement did not impede the capacity of the Reform movement to achieve a notable degree of unity on this issue.

Once it approved the proposal for continued membership in the American Jewish Conference, the UAHC moved with increasingly greater confidence toward open endorsement of Zionist objectives, even though it still insisted it was maintaining strict neutrality. In response to a complaint that the Union was leaning too far in a Zionist direction, the official reply simply acknowledged that "practically all Jews, Zionist and non-Zionist, are agreed that Jews in Palestine, as elsewhere, are entitled in justice to a free, democratic home" and dismissed the complaints of "extreme anti-Zionists" as a symptom of "being obsessed by the very word 'Palestine'--somewhat like Mr. Dick was haunted by 'King Charles Head' in *David Copperfield* . . . "[380]

Even these vestiges of ideological debate were completely removed to the realm of the academic by the decision of the U. N. General Assembly on November 29, 1947 to sanction the establishment of independent Jewish and Arab states in Palestine. It ended for all practical purposes whatever festering resentment still remained; and Reform leadership, lay and rabbinic, generally agreed that "the time has come for joint counsel."[381]

As the heat of conflict in the Middle East intensified, the Union's position on Jewish nationalism gradually became firmer and surer. In response to the refusal of the Arab nations to allow Jewish self-government and the endless vacillation within the international community, it was unusual to hear the Union state categorically that "no matter which compromises are made by the nations, no matter how much they may hesitate to come to a forthright, implemented decision, the Jewish community in Palestine will never surrender. If it must rely upon its own strength, it will do so. . . ."[382] Reform leadership had clearly decided to end any ambiguity about their readiness to support the emerging Jewish state. Pockets of Zionist resistance remained and would remain even after the establishment of the state, but it would no longer receive encouragement from either lay or rabbinic spokesmen.

That is why Silver could declare with confidence at the UAHC Biennial Council in 1948 that "the long contention may not cease. The swords may be sheathed. The argument is over. Life had finally composed our quarrel. The State of Israel is here."[383] After having spent much of his career in opposition to the anti-Zionist position of Reform Judaism, Silver could now join in healing the "schism." He appealed to Reform Jews to realize that "the great debate having been ended by a fiat of history, all erstwhile antagonists may now join in amity in the common and interfused task to make Israel secure, to defend Jewish rights throughout the world and to make Judaism strong and vital in the world."[384]

As a fitting epilogue to Silver's appeal, Hyman Judah Schachtel, once a founding member of the American Council for Judaism, rose to announce that ". . . as one who up until November 29, 1947 stood out strongly for my point of view, which was contrary to that of Dr. Silver, I want to say tonight that I support what he has stated, and that I believe with all of my heart and soul that it is possible now and should be for every American Jew to help this State to become established in health and strength, in joy and in peace."[385]

The CCAR officially recognized and welcomed the State of Israel at its convention in June, 1948. President Abraham Feldman expressed the sentiment of his colleagues in observing that "the event (Israel independence) is one of those which is bound to have far-reaching influence upon the course of subsequent Jewish history, and Jewish life will never be as if this event had never happened."[386] He summoned his colleagues to extend to the new State their "warmest greetings and prayerful wishes" which they did in a report from the Committee on Palestine.[387]

The accommodation between Zionism and Reform Judaism was now almost complete. The Reform movement welcomed enthusiastically the rebirth of a Jewish state and offered its unconditional support in defending its integrity. The reality of the post-War world had delivered its own verdict about the necessity of Jewish self-determination, and Reform Jews sustained that verdict.

The Union itself stated the case most convincingly in voicing the hope that the "propaganda" phase of Zionism, both among its proponents and opponents, would tend to approach an end. It urged Reform Jews to realize that in light of the new realities, "no good end can be served by continued opposition" to the State of Israel, but that, "in generosity, Jews should put aside whatever differences still sunder them, and pray for its welfare."[388]

Whatever opposition to Israel thus resided in the movement dwindled steadily to a very insignificant force, while concern and interest for Israel gained rapid momentum. The debate over Jewish nationalism was now an academic issue. The establishment and existence of the State had superceded all the arguments about it.

SUMMARY AND CONCLUSIONS

The events and developments analyzed in the preceding pages should clearly establish the proposition that Reform Judaism did not reconcile its differences with the aims and objectives of the Zionist movement until the period following the Columbus Platform. It was evident in 1937 that large numbers of Reform rabbis were receptive to the Zionist program and that they could mobilize sufficient strength to reverse the stand of the CCAR on this issue by a slim majority. It was also evident that the rabbinic student body at the Hebrew Union College was decidedly sympathetic to the Zionist cause by 1937.

It was not nearly as easy to verify the thesis that most Reform rabbis and laymen now supported the claims of Zionism. Approval of the Zionist plank in the Columbus Platform represented only the majority sentiment of the modest number of rabbis still present at the convention at that time. Even the staunchest Reform advocates of Jewish nationalism conceded that adoption of the statement would never have survived a roll-call of all members of the Conference. As it was, the plank was adopted by only a majority of one vote.

Reform laymen were even less enthusiastic about the new Zionist position which the Columbus Platform articulated. The UAHC never endorsed support of Zionist efforts prior to that date, and at its meeting following the CCAR convention the Executive Board of the Union expressed serious misgivings over the action of the Conference at this matter. Some Union Board members even urged a public censure of the CCAR statement. Many Reform rabbis who supported Zionism still found themselves among a small minority within their own congregations. Nearly all the active participants in Zionist circles from the Reform movement were rabbis. Very few laymen joined them in that enterprise.

This large, dormant opposition explained the emergence of several serious threats to the unity and stability of the Reform movement. Passage of a resolution by the CCAR in 1942, affirming support for the formation of a Jewish Army in Palestine, was the precipitating factor which rallied the anti-Zionist forces into a unified constituency. Founded by rabbis in June, 1943, but monopolized by laymen, the American Council for Judaism became a disruptive if not destructive influence in the ranks of Reform prior to the establishment of the State of Israel. In fact, the American Council encouraged the development of staunch defiance among laymen, the most notable being the Basic Principles of Congregation Beth Israel of Houston, Texas in November, 1943.

Rabbi Maurice Eisendrath, as the newly-elected Executive Director of the UAHC in 1943 devoted much of his available time and energy toward reconciliation between the warring elements within the movement that threatened to shatter Reform Judaism into a hopeless multitude of splinter groups. He participated in several meetings with rabbinic colleagues on both sides in an attempt to achieve an acceptable compromise. He visited with the governing bodies of several dissenting congregations in an effort to alleviate their apprehension and preserve their loyalties.

Neither Eisendrath, however, nor any spokesman for Reform Judaism could predict the course which the movement would follow on the issue of Zionism until the debate over participation in the American Jewish Conference at the UAHC Biennial Convention in 1946. Overwhelming acclamation at that meeting for the aims of the American Jewish Conference demonstrated convincingly that substantial numbers of lay and rabbinic leaders had shifted dramatically to support of a program for an independent Jewish homeland in Palestine. When the State of Israel was finally re-established in 1948, the dominant sector of American Reform Jewry warmly welcomed the fulfillment of the Zionist dream.

The final reconciliation, however, in no way diminished the magnitude of the crisis that had existed earlier. The controversy over Zionism constituted one of the most bitter and divisive conflicts in the history of American Reform Judaism. No other single issue precipitated an equivalent outburst of words and actions, charges and countercharges, accusations and recriminations on both sides of the question.

These two movements had always tugged at each other from the very outset. It was only more conspicuous after the passage of the Columbus Platform. The Zionist conflict was the only major controversy which erupted in all three major bodies of the movement--its seminary, the Hebrew Union College, its lay organization, the Union of American Hebrew Congregations, and its rabbinic arm, the Central Conference of American Rabbis. It was the only quarrel which threatened to split the CCAR and undermine the unity of the UAHC. It was the only issue which threatened to separate Reform

Judaism from the remainder of the American Jewish community in its attempt to deal responsibly with the post-war problems of world Jewry through the American Jewish Conference.

Zionism was the antithesis of every principle that was sacred to the majority of early Reformers. Those who drafted the Pittsburgh Platform of 1885 had anticipated a new world of justice and freedom in which Jews would enjoy equal rights and privileges with all other citizens wherever they lived. Zionism, however, had declared that Jews would be strangers everywhere until they could reclaim their own homeland. Reform Judaism had regarded nationalism as the cause of Jewish suffering, but for Zionism it was a solution. For Zionists the essence of Jewish existence was the concept of peoplehood, and everything else depended on that premise, whereas for Reform Jews the essence of Jewish existence was faith, especially the conviction that creative survival depended upon recognition of a universal "mission" through which Jews would labor to achieve ideals of justice, brotherhood and peace among all men. Finally, Zionism emphasized the ethnic bonds that united all Jews and did not require any specific spiritual commitments; but in Reform Judaism the priorities were exactly the reverse: the spiritual ties transcended whatever other differences existed among Jews, and ethnic distinctions were among the least important or meaningful of all those differences. All Jews, in their view, were primarily "Americans of Mosaic persuasion."

Jewish nationalism, from its very inception, was always a thorn in the side of the Reform Jewish community; but it never reached any truly critical stage until the Nazi peril engulfed the Jews of Europe in the 1930's. The Nazi terror was not the only catalyst activating support for Zionism in Reform circles. Ideologically, the Reform movement had reached an impasse. Its entire prognosis of a new and better world for the future as a consequence of human striving had crumbled in the cataclysm of one world war and on the brink of another. The unprecedented optimism of the nineteenth century had been overtaken by the unprecedented suffering of the twentieth. All the exuberance and confidence in man's capacity for moral excellence sounded hollow and naive in light of past and imminent catastrophes. Zionism vigorously challenged Reform Judaism to re-examine its basic suppositions.

It involved even more than ideology. Conditions in Europe made it perfectly clear that physical survival was more urgent than heated debates about the merits of one or another ideology. Jewish life was collapsing everywhere on the Continent, and it was obvious that the order of priorities must begin with relief and rescue.

For stateless Jews who needed a refuge, none was available except Palestine. Anti-Zionists, as well as Zionists, encouraged large-scale emigration to Palestine and emphasized that they in fact had never discouraged support for Jewish settlement there for religious and cultural development. Their objections, they insisted, were aimed solely at political sovereignty; but realities in the Middle East made it increasingly clear that such fine distinctions would ultimately be impossible to maintain.

The composition of the Reform movement at this juncture had also changed. It occurred first and most visibly in the student body at Hebrew Union College. The sons of East European immigrants, saturated with the rich Jewish folk-culture of Russia and Poland and indoctrinated with the ideals of socialism or Zionism, now enrolled at the Reform seminary to become rabbis of Reform congregations whose memberships were still overwhelmingly of German extraction. A clash was inevitable. What exacerbated the conflict in ideology was the ordinary strains resulting from differences in age. Zionism found its strongest support in Reform Judaism among younger rabbis, its staunchest opposition among their older colleagues. "The recognition that on this question, as on all others, the position of youth would inevitably prevail did not facilitate the adjustment for the elder leaders of the movement."

As strange as it seems, the fierce controversy between Zionism and Reform Judaism also evolved out of a thread of similarity between the objectives of each. Zionism, like Reform Judaism, was deeply rooted in a vision of social justice. Both movements strove for the realization of the "justice society," a life of freedom, equality and personal dignity for all. Both were quick to cite deficiencies in the existing political, economic and social structures as a principal explanation for the exploitation of the Jew and other minority segments of the population. The redemption of society required a determined effort to rectify and reorganize the existing order. The early _Halutzim_ (pioneers in Palestine) incorporated that precept in their development of the _kibbutz_ (agricultural commune) as their model of collective social responsibility. It is interesting to note, too, that several Reform rabbis were among the most fervent members of the Labor Zionist movement long before the quarrel between Zionism and Reform Judaism was finally resolved. Obviously, these rabbis had discovered in Labor Zionism a significant social theme which did not conflict with their theology, but, on the contrary, only served to reinforce it. The clash between Zionist and anti-Zionists was thus not always a question of ends but of means. Zionists sought to achieve the "just society" through a unique brand of nationalism while Reform Jews pursued it as a matter of religious principle.

Theology affected the controversy, however, in yet another more subtle fashion. The battle over Zionism in Reform ranks involved more than just opposition to nationalism. It also disclosed a grave apprehension over the future dynamic character of Reform and its distinctive quality. Reform Judaism had always thrived on the supremacy of the religious dimension in American Jewish life until the rising prestige of the Zionist movement began to challenge those assumptions on which the foundations of Reform Judaism rested. The anti-Zionists were genuinely fearful that Jewish nationalism and the creation of a Jewish state in Palestine would seriously damage if not destroy the religious attachments of American Jews. The major focus in Jewish affairs would shift from America to Palestine and would diminish the stature of Jewish life in the Diaspora.

Such apprehension explained the ambivalence surrounding the Houston controversy. Although most Reform rabbis and lay leaders severely rebuked Beth Israel for its passage of the Basic Principles, several still praised the congregation for its motivations, if not its procedures. A few even considered the Houston decision a long-overdue reaffirmation of the principles which had distinguished Reform Judaism from the beginning. Such was the rationale which prompted Louis Witt to declare that "if you agree that the future of Judaism depends upon Reform Judaism, then why denounce a congregation, even if it is mistaken? They (the Basic Principles) tell us that Reform Judaism is at stake . . . There is no excuse for the meagerness of our numbers today except that we have been indifferent."

As increasingly large numbers of Reform Jews gravitated to the Zionist camp, the Reform movement attempted to stem further defections by shifting its emphasis from theology to peoplehood. The concept of Covenant and peoplehood was a major theme in the Columbus Platform and a radical departure from its predecessor in Pittsburgh. At Columbus, the CCAR reaffirmed the historic continuity of the Jewish people and the links of tradition which united Jews the world over and obligated them to a principle of mutual responsibility. They established a new rationale within the context of Reform Judaism that would enable Reform Jews to participate by reason of religious motivations in the relief and rescue of afflicted Jews and to support them in their efforts to achieve an independent Jewish state in Palestine.

The Columbus Platform, however, was clearly not the final statement on the question of Zionism and its compatibility with

Reform. It was a significant milestone, but hardly any more than that. Indeed, it actually led to more not less ambiguity. It applied only to the CCAR; and, even within that body, only the slimmest majority had chosen a Zionist direction. The most difficult and decisive journey was yet to develop.

Maurice Eisendrath has stated that the way in which the UAHC finally responded to the challenge of Zionism could well have determined the future existence of Reform Judaism in America. If it had repudiated completely the merit of Zionist goals, it might well have become dysfunctional and obsolete. It probably would have sailed right out of the mainstream of American Jewish life and drifted into a marginal, insignificant sect. That it did not is a tribute to the vision and courage of leaders like Eisendrath, James Heller, Abba Hillel Silver, Stephen S. Wise and countless others who battled persistently and successfully to reshape and redirect the ideology of Reform Judaism on this issue. The Reform movement could not have remained a major voice in American Jewish affairs if it had refused to budge from its anti-Zionist stance.

One of the most tragic misfortunes during the entire period of transition was the failure of both factions to understand each other. Perhaps the answer to this puzzling conflict was traceable to the emotional pitch of the moment, the uncompromising conviction on both sides, the mutual mistrust, personal jealousies and animosities or unfounded fears; but neither group ever fully appreciated the motivations of the other. The Zionists for their part, were severe, intolerant, abusive, even vitriolic, in their attacks upon the anti-Zionists. Had it not been for such verbal "overkill" by Zionist supporters, the American Council for Judaism might never have emerged. The Zionist opposition never repudiated the role of Eretz Yisrael (the land of Israel) in the revitalization of the Jewish people, but their objections to political sovereignty for Jews in Palestine were always met with scorn and contempt by Zionist supporters. They recalled the universal elements in Judaism and reminded their people, "Are ye not, O children of Israel, unto me as are the Ethiopians?".

At the same time, the anti-Zionists were rarely more considerate of their opposition. They attempted to discredit Zionist goals by proclaiming they were devoid of spiritual significance. It is difficult to believe that the anti-Zionists were convinced that all Zionists, including rabbis, were spiritually bankrupt; and yet they constantly spoke as if such were actually the case. Anti-Zionists insisted that the safety of the Jewish people was more important to them than a Jewish state and that their position rested on that premise. Had they listened to their opposition, they would have realized clearly there was no quarrel with the Zionists on the matter. The divisive factor that severed one camp from the other was not the priority of peoplehood over statehood but the cardinal Zionist principle that the safety of the Jewish people demanded the re-establishment of a Jewish state. With the re-emergence of that state in 1948, the debate became entirely academic; and the process of reconciliation between advocates and adversaries accelerated much more quickly.

In retrospect, anti-Zionism was not incompatible with Reform Judaism. It was a companion belief, an "ad-hoc" commitment as it were, not an essential doctrine. The essential doctrine of Reform Judaism was simply reform--the right to make radical changes in the rituals and forms of Judaism in order to preserve and perpetuate its basic precepts. That principle included the necessity to change the position on Zionism if conditions so required it. Consideration of such conditions was both the basis for the controversy and the process for its eventual resolution.

NOTES

1. For an introduction to the general philosophy and precepts of Reform Judaism, the reader may consult the following sources; Israel Knox, *Rabbi in America: The Story of Isaac M. Wise* (1957); J. J. Petuchowski, *Prayerbook Reform in Europe* (1968); D. Philipson, *Reform Movement in Judaism* (1967); W. G. Plaut, *Rise of Reform Judaism* (1963); *idem*, *Growth of Reform Judaism* (1965); *Reform Judaism*, essays by Hebrew Union College Alumni (1949); C. Seligmann, *Geschichte der juedischen Reform-bewegung* (1922); M. Wiener, *Juedische Religion im Zeitalter der Emanzipation* (1933); J. M. Wise, *Liberalizing Liberal Judaism* (1924); J. Wolf (ed.), *Rediscovering Judaism* (1965); S. B. Freehof, *Reform Responsa* (1960), 3-23, introd.; *idem*, *Reform Jewish Practice and its Rabbinic Background* (1963); *idem*, *Current Reform Responsa* (1969), introd.; *the Reports of the Committee on Responsa, Central Conference of American Rabbis Yearbook* (CCARY).

2. See Samuel Halperin, *The Political World of American Zionism*, Wayne State University Press, Detroit, 1961, pp. 78-79. Halperin notes that, however encouraging a statement the Platform may have been, the CCAR, no less the entire Reform movement, had not yet endorsed the Zionist position it had so long repudiated.

3. See Naomi Wiener Cohen, *Reform Judaism in America, and Zionism, 1897-1922*, Master's Thesis, Columbia University, New York, 1949; Milton Matz, *American Reform Judaism, 1890-1937*, Rabbinic Thesis, Hebrew Union College, Cincinnati, 1952; Melvin Weinman, *The Attitude of Isaac M. Wise Toward Palestine and Zionism*, Rabbinic Thesis, Hebrew Union College, Cincinnati, 1947.

4. Editorial, *American Israelite*, Vol. 45, No. 29, 19 January 1899, p. 4.

5. *American Israelite*, Vol. 37, No. 38, 19 March 1891, p. 4 Wise declared that the final redemption of Israel could be brought about only by "the final redemption of the Gentiles, their liberation from their fanaticism, their narrow-mindedness, their exclusiveness . . . we want the equality and solidarity of mankind."

6. *American Israelite*, Vol. 45, No. 29, 19 January 1899. Wise wrote that "the Herzl-Nordau scheme appears to us to be about as important to Judaism as was Pleasanton's blue grass theory to science or as is 'Christian Science' to medicine. Pleasanton's empiricism was at least harmless, but Herzl-Nordau's is so fraught with the possibility of mischief . . . it becomes the duty of every true Jew to take an active part in efforts to destroy it." As early as July 14, 1882, Wise had declared that "the colonization of Palestine appears to us a romantic idea inspired by religious visions without foundation in reality. . . . We take no stock in a dreamland; the idea of Jews returning to Palestine is no part of our creed. We rather believe it is well that the habitable

world become one holy land and the human family one chosen people." For additional observations by Wise in the American Israelite on the subject of Jewish nationalism, see Vol. 32, No. 4 (24 January 1879), Vol. 42, No. 30 (23 January 1896), Vol. 44, No. 14 (30 September 1897), Vol. 45, No.   (7 July 1898), Vol. 45, No. 11 (8 September 1898).

7. "Zionism," The H.U.C. Journal, Vol. 4, No. 3, December, 1899, pp. 45-47.

8. Wise also had some practical advice for aspiring philanthropists. He suggested that "if any of them want to carry out the original plan of assisting the poor of Israel in the lands of barbarism, turn them to agriculture and the practical arts; they must construct another organization, one which every charitable and intelligent citizen can support, without bringing upon himself the odium of being a traitor, a hypocrite, or a phantastic fool, whose thoughts, sentiments and actions are in constant contradiction." Ibid., p. 47.

9. Ibid., p. 47.

10. Ibid., p. 47.

11. Caspar Levias, "The Justification of Zionism," The H.U.C. Journal, Vol. 3, No. 3, April 1899, pp. 167-175. The Executive Committee of the CCAR later overruled the decision of the Conference, and Levias' statement was included in the Yearbook for the following year.

12. Essentially Levias attacked three major arguments of the anti-Zionists, namely that (1) Zionism eliminates the concept of "the mission of Israel," (2) Zionism is a distortion of Messianic prophecy and (3) nationalism is evil.

13. Occasionally, in those earlier years, Zionism would find pockets of support among the students such as the editorial in The H.U.C. Journal, December 1899 which declared, "Zionism is a fact in Jewish Politics of today." Far more frequent, however, were the bitter denunciations of men like Gotthard Deutsch who insisted that "history, sound reasoning, and the views of people guided by common sense declare the Zionist scheme, if it intends to be more than a charitable and an educational enterprise--a failure." (H.U.C. Journal, Vol. 4, No. 3., December 1899, p. 70). Louis Grossman, another faculty member, stressed that "a sober student of Jewish history and a genuine lover of his co-religionists sees that the Zionistic agitation contradicts everything that is typical of Jews and Judaism." (Ibid., p. 72)

14. See Adloph S. Oko, "Kaufmann Kohler," Menorah Journal, Vol. 12, No. 5, p. 517.

15. Minutes, Special Meeting, Hebrew Union College Board of Governors, May 3, 1905, American Jewish Archives, Cincinnati.

16. Ibid.

17. Samuel Cohon, "A History of the Hebrew Union College," American Jewish Historical Society Quarterly, Vol. 50, No. 1, p. 41. See Note 48.

18. David Philipson, "A History of the Hebrew Union College," H.U.C. Jubilee Volume, p. 44 ff.

19. Cohon, *op. cit.*, Cohon suggests that not even Zionism was an issue because the Board of Governors approved the appointment of David Neumark, an avowed cultural Zionist to replace Margolis. He neglects to add, however, that Neumark was not at all concerned with the political aspects of Zionism. Not even Wise had objected to the support of Jewish life in Palestine. The basic conflict centered on the question of an independent, political Jewish state in the Middle East or elsewhere.

20. Philip R. Alstat, "How Reform Judaism Is Reforming Itself," *Milwaukee Wochenblatt*, 1 August 1947.

21. In 1921, Kallen completed his own appraisal of the need for a sovereign Jewish state in his book, *Zionism and World Politics*, Doubleday, Page and Co., New York, 1921.

22. The author is indebted to Rabbis Abraham J. Feldman and James Heller who both shared with him their personal recollections of this incident during their student days at the Hebrew Union College. In addition, Rabbi Harvey E. Wessel, as a student, claimed that "Zionist themes were reported at the time to be taboo in relation to the College pulpit; a non-religious Zionist (Kallen?) was prevented by official action from addressing the student body, and prominent exponents of the anti-Zionist interpretation were being invited to address the students and combat their recalcitrant attitude. Anti-Zionism was then the principal theme of sermons delivered from local pulpits." Harvey E. Wessel, "How I became A Zionist at the Hebrew Union College," *Hebrew Union College Monthly*, Vol. 6, No. 6, May-June, 1920.

23. James G. Heller, "The Home of the Jewish Spirit," *Hebrew Union College Monthly*, Vol. 2, No. 6, March, 1916, p. 189.

24. "The Jewish spirit *must* work through a body--a strong, centralized body--must have a *normal*, healthy medium, a heart to send the blood coursing through the whole system, not merely for the more intensive realization of its past ideals, but even more for the opportunity to develop *new* ideals, to exercise its *creative* genius." *Ibid.*, p. 195.

25. Citing examples in Jewish history to verify his thesis about the necessity of sovereignty for creative survival, Heller concluded that "since the destruction of the Temple, it is only where there has been some semblance of a combination of body and spirit that the spirit has had a healthy growth. . . . You may take individual instances, such as the Golden Age in Spain, or the flowering of scholarship in Poland, but in every instance there is some semblance of a national life." *Ibid.*

26. Heller charged that the requirements of the present dictated the necessity of modern nationhood as the embodiment of the Jewish spirit. "It is not enough to say that it is the mission of Judaism to spread justice and righteousness . . . The really pregnant and paramount question as to *how* we can best work for the millenium is another matter . . . It is well possible that we may best work for an era of *universalism* . . by being a *nation*."

27. *Ibid.*

28. Kohler invoked the authority of no less a personage than the distinguished medieval philosopher Saadia Gaon, attributing to him the statement that "our nation is not a nation by virtue of race or of any political endeavor, but solely by reason of its Torah." See Kaufmann Kohler, "What The Hebrew Union College Stands For," *Hebrew Union College Monthly*, Vol. 3, No. 1, November 1916, p. 2.

29. _Ibid_.

30. For thorough and well-researched treatments of the issues and personalities responsible for the formulation of the Balfour Declaration, see Leonard J. Stein, _The Balfour Declaration_, Simon and Schuster, New York, 1961. Also, Ben Halpern, _The Idea of the Jewish State_, Harvard University Press, Cambridge, 1961.

31. See Harvey E. Wessel, _op. cit_.

32. _Hebrew Union College Monthly_, Vol. 17, No. 1, 15 October 1929, p. 4.

33. _Hebrew Union College Monthly_, Vol. 17, No. 2, 1 December 1929, p. 1.

34. _Ibid_.

35. _Hebrew Union College Monthly_, Vol. 15, No. 3, 15 January 1930, p. 2.

36. Joshua Trachtenberg, "Youth in the Temple," _Hebrew Union College Monthly_, Vol. 15, No. 4, 1 March 1930, pp. 16-18. Trachtenberg observed that "the interest in contemporary Jewish events is widespread; the desire to participate in them has created such bodies as the Avukah, the Junior Hadassah, the Young People's League of the United Synagogue, Young Israel, Young Judea, Mizrachi Hatzair, Young Poal Zion, Zeire Zion, Habonim, etc.", _Ibid_. p. 17.

37. _Hebrew Union College Monthly_, Vol. 17, No. 5, 15 April 1930, p. 2.

38. _Ibid_.

39. _Hebrew Union College Monthly_, Vol. 18, No. 3, 15 January 1931, p. 1.

40. See "Rabbi Wohl Replies to Dr. Morgenstern," _American Israelite_, 11 November 1943. "He (Morgenstern) has not pressed anti-Zionist views on the students or faculty, and it is evident that for many years the overwhelming majority of the H.U.C. student body were Zionists."

41. D. Max Eichorn, "Survey of the H.U.C. Student Body, 1900-1930," Hebrew Union College Library, Cincinnati. For the complete account of the survey data, see Appendix A.

42. _Ibid_., p. 14.

43. _Ibid_., p. 16.

44. See UAHC Commission on Social Action of Reform Judaism, _Where We Stand--Social Action Resolutions_, New York, 1960, p. 59. The Union declared that "conscious of the spiritual significance for the further development of Judaism implied in the establishment of a vigorous Jewish community in Palestine, and realizing the importance of the migration of many Jews from the lands of Eastern Europe to Palestine, this Convention urges all Israel to participate in the laudable efforts now underway for the reconstruction of that land."

45. The Committee recommended defeat of the measure by a vote of 12 to 4, but the assembled delegates over-ruled the adverse report and endorsed the resolution.

46. For a complete statement of the full text of the Pittsburgh Platform, the reader may consult, W. Gunther Plaut, *The Growth of Reform Judaism--American and European Sources Until 1948*. World Union for Progressive Judaism, New York, 1965, p. 32.

47. It should be recognized, of course, that despite their hostility, American German Jews established scores of philantrophic agencies to assist the East European immigrant in his adjustment to American life. Much of that generosity was prompted by a fear of embarrassment to their own social and economic status, but a good measure of it was also motivated by a genuine concern for other Jews in desperate need. See, for example, Salo Baron, *Steeled by Adversity*, Jewish Publication Society, Philadelphia, 1971; Nathan Glazer, ed., *The Social Characteristics of American Jews*, Jewish Education Committee Press, New York, 1965; C. Bezalel Sherman, *The Jew Within American Society*, Wayne State University Press, Detroit, 1965.

48. A few distinguished spokesmen of Reform Judaism, such as Felix Goldman, Prof. David Neumark, and Rabbi Bernard Felsenthal, dissented from the prevailing attitude toward Zionism almost from the outset, but they were a very distinct, albeit vocal, minority.

49. W. Gunther Plaut, *op. cit.*, pp. 34-36.

50. This was the major theme of Washington Gladden in his essay, *The Working People and Their Employers*, New York, Funk and Wagnalls, 1894. See also, *Applied Christianity* (1896), *Social Salvation* (1907). For additional perspectives on the Social Gospel, the reader may consult Paul H. Boase, *The Rhetoric of Christian Socialism* (1969); Robert T. Handy, *The Social Gospel in America, 1870-1920* (1966); George D. Herron, *The Christian Society* (1969); Charles H. Hopkins, *The Rise of the Social Gospel in American Protestantisim, 1865-1915* (1940); and Walter Rauschenbush, *Christianity and the Social Crisis* (1907), *Christianizing the Social Order* (1912) and *A Theology For the Social Gospel* (1918).

51. See John Robert Seeley, *Ecce Homo*, Boston, Roberts Bros., 1883.

52. "The Dawn" was a periodical published by the Society of Christian Socialists toward the end of the 19th century. Its principal personality, W. D. P. Bliss, was one of the most dynamic and effective of all Social Gospel leaders.

53. The Christian Commonwealth Colony was an experiment in socialist living founded by one of the most flamboyant and colorful 19th century Church liberals, George Herron, with the assistance of George Gates, President of Iowa College. The colony eventually failed in the early 20th century, but Herron was a decisive influence on Norman Thomas in the early formulation of his own socialist philosophy.

54. In 1892, the Rev. Charles Parkhurst produced a grand jury indictment against Tammany Hall in New York City which eventually led to the election of a reform administration and the beginning of a whole new era of reform politics in New York City.

55. See Irving Levitas, "Reform Jews and Zionism, 1919-1921," *American Jewish Archives Quarterly*, April, 1962, pp. 3-19.

56. *Central Conference of American Rabbis Yearbook*, Vol. 38, 1928, p. 140.

57. United Jewish Appeal, *The Rebuilding of Palestine*, New York, 1927, p. 6.

58. In much of his correspondence, Marshall denied any formal associations with Zionism. In a letter to Judah Magnes, as well as to many others, he wrote, "I have never been a Zionist and probably never shall be one." See Charles Reznikoff, *Louis Marshall: Champion of Liberty*, Jewish Publication Society, Philadelphia, 1957, Vol. II, p. 732.

59. *Ibid.*, p. 745, Letter to Rabbi Henry Cohen, 16 February 1925; p. 763, letter to Julius Rosenwald, 9 February 1927; p. 776, letter to Dr. Heinrich Stern, 2 February 1929.

60. See *CCAR Yearbook*, Vol. 41, 1931, pp. 115ff for discussion on the motion to approve the inclusion of *Hatikvah*.

61. *CCAR Yearbook*, Vol. 40, 1930, p. 99.

62. Pamphlet, "Rabbis of America to Labor Palestine," League for Labor Palestine, New York, 1935.

63. According to the *CCAR Yearbook* in 1935, the total membership of the Central Conference of American Rabbis numbered 401.

64. *CCAR Yearbook*, Vol. 45, 1935, p. 102; for the discussion that followed on the Neutrality Resolution, see pp. 110-112.

65. *Ibid.*, p. 112. In later years, the anti-Zionists would reject any further gestures of cooperation with Zionist objectives in the Conference as a violation and repudiation of the Neutrality Resolution which many of them never considered "neutral" from the very outset.

66. Abraham Franzblau, *Reform Judaism in the Large Cities--A Survey*, UAHC, Cincinnati, 1931.

67. *Ibid.*

68. *CCAR Yearbook*, Vol. 36, 1926, pp. 320-321.

69. Abraham Franzblau, *op. cit.*

70. See Samuel Halperin, *op. cit.*, Appendix 5, p. 327.

71. UAHC Commission on Social Action of Reform Judaism, *op. cit.*, pp. 60-61.

72. *Ibid.*, pp. 61-62.

73. *Ibid.*, p. 62, "Endorsing the Efforts of the Jewish Agency in Upbuilding Palestine."

74. *CCAR Yearbook*, Vol. 42, 1932, pp. 178ff.

75. *CCAR Yearbook*, Vol. 43, 1933, pp. 103-107.

76. *Ibid.*, p. 123.

77. *CCAR Yearbook*, Vol. 44, 1934, pp. 178-189.

78. *CCAR Yearbook*, Vol. 45, 1935, pp. 260ff, 309ff.

79. *CCAR Yearbook*, Vol. 46, 1936, p. 89ff.

80. CCAR Yearbook, Vol. 47, 1937, pp. 182, 188.

81. See Arthur J. Lelyveld, "The Conference View of the Position of the Jew in the Modern World," in Korn, Bertram, ed., Retrospect and Prospect--Essays in Commemoration of the 75th Anniversary of the Founding of the CCAR, 1889-1964, Central Conference of American Rabbis, New York, 1965, pp. 159-161. Lelyveld claims he encountered this state of affairs when he was sent out personally to recruit a quorum.

82. This appraisal of attitudes in the CCAR in 1937 was verified by the author in personal interviews with Rabbis Maurice N. Eisendrath, Abraham, J. Feldman, Arthur J. Lelyveld, Jacob R. Marcus and Samuel Silver.

83. See Larry Hexter, "Trends in Reform Judaism," The Congress Weekly, July 11, 1941, pp. 7-8. "If this year's convention (CCAR) is to be a test, there is hardly doubt that this drift is strongly to emphasis on Judaism rather than Reform . . . Even the talk of a Code of Practice . . . evidenced this feeling that in the abrupt severance from the moorings of traditional Judaism, important values were sacrificed, and it was now desired to recapture them . . ."

84. Ibid.

85. Philadelphia Jewish Exponent, 9 June 1939. In addition to his moderate statement in the Exponent, it should be noted that Morris Lazaron had also signed the statement of Reform Rabbis for Labor Zionism in 1935.

86. Philadelphia Jewish Exponent, 5 July 1940. See also Time Magazine, 28 December 1942 in which it reported that "the Jewish Army Committee claims 85,000 Palestinian and 100,000 stateless Jews of military age are waiting to volunteer. But the Jerusalem Haolam, a Zionist publication, recently placed the number available in Palestine at 34,000."

87. Philadelphia Jewish Exponent, 4 July 1941.

88. Jewish Press Service Bulletin, 11 May 1943.

89. Ibid.

90. New York Times, 31 October 1941.

91. Ibid., 14 November 1941.

92. See New York Times, 31 August 1943; Philadelphia Jewish Exponent, 2 January 1942; and Time Magazine, 28 December 1942.

93. CCAR Yearbook, Vol. 52, p. 169.

94. The Resolutions Committee included Rabbi Joseph L. Fink as Chairman, and the following rabbis as members: Solomon N. Bazell, Henry J. Berkowitz, Louis Binstock, Philip D. Bookstaber, Baruch Braunstein, Harry W. Ettelson, G. George Fox, Alan S. Green, Abraham Holtzberg, Isaac Landman, Samuel J. Levinson, Max Nussbaum and Max Reichler. This Resolutions Committee was composed of predominantly Zionist sympathizers, though not entirely so. Five of the fourteen Committee members eventually became founders of the American Council for Judaism.

95. Ibid., p. 170. The reworded resolution of the Committee also eliminated a paragraph in the preamble of the original resolution which stated, "And, whereas, despite its formal approval of

the plan, the Government of Great Britain has still failed to avail itself of the offer of the Jewish Agency for Palestine to establish a military unit based on Palestine, composed of Palestinian and stateless European Jews . . ."

96. Ibid., p. 174.

97. Ibid., p. 175.

98. Ibid., p. 177. Several of his colleagues recall that Eisendrath had recently reassessed his views of Zionism after a personal visit to Palestine. Eisendrath's transformation on this issue will be discussed in greater detail in another chapter.

99. Ibid., p. 180.

100. Ibid., p. 181.

101. Letter, William H. Fineschriber and Louis Wolsey to all members of the CCAR, 28 May 1942, American Council for Judaism File, American Jewish Archives, Cincinnati.

102. Letter, James G. Heller to all members of the CCAR, 18 March 1943, James G. Heller Collection, American Jewish Archives, Cincinnati.

103. Letter, Sidney L. Regner, Executive Vice-President, CCAR to the author, 22 January 1970, in which he stated, "I regret to say that we do not have documents for the period you are interested in. There was a hiatus of two years between the time that Rabbi Marcuson, who was administrative secretary of the Conference, and my appointment as executive vice-president and the opening of the central office. Unfortunately original material, such as minutes, correspondence, etc., disappeared in the meantime."

104. Minutes, Administrative Board of the UAHC, 1 March 1942, American Jewish Archives, Cincinnati.

105. Ibid.

106. The resolution read as follows: "We give our full and effectual support to the Government of the United States. We pledge ourselves to help keep our fair land free, and to help obtain for the world the right to life, liberty and the pursuit of happiness."

107. See also The Cincinnati Enquirer, 1 March 1942 and the American Israelite, 19 March 1942.

108. Sam Shankman, Mortimer May, Foot Soldier in Zion, Chapter 7, "Zionism and Reform Judaism," Bloch Publishing Company, New York, 1963.

109. Mr. Solomon's reference to 62 instead of 63 rabbis may stem from the source of his information. He had read "a little article" about this opposition in the Cleveland Plain Dealer, not the Exponent.

110. See Correspondence of Mr. Frank Solomon to Rabbi Barnett Brickner, 19 March 1942, American Jewish Archives, Cincinnati. Solomon wrote that "the immediate impression that this statement created among our non-Jewish citizens was that the Jews were afraid to fight and that the gentiles of the United Nations are having to fight the Jews' battles for them . . . I considered writing to some of my friends in Chicago suggesting their taking this matter up with

the Anti-Defamation League, as this was definitely an anti-Semitic utterance, but on thinking the matter over further, I decided not to stir things up."

111. The meeting was later changed to June 1-2.

112. The decision of Louis Wolsey to organize and lead this revolt was the culmination of many years of frustration and disappointment. It will be recalled that he warmly welcomed the realignment of the Jewish Agency to include non-Zionists as well as Zionists in 1929, a realignment which ultimately failed. He then wrote to Jacob Billikopf: "Everything that has taken place within recent weeks confirms me in my resistance to the propaganda of Zionism and to its gross misuse of the Agency and the Agency non-Zionist." He then voiced bitter indignation at Philip Bernstein for his remarks before the British section of the Jewish Agency in London. "What a joke," observed Wolsey, "that a Zionist should appear before the Agency and attack the non-Zionists of his native country before a British audience. What respect can any non-Zionist have for the Agency when it permits a thing of that sort to go by unchallenged? I thought we were allowed to have our own thoughts about the political solution of the Jewish problem, and yet give ourselves over wholeheartedly to the project in Palestine . . ." "The time is gone when we non-Zionists shall lie down and die. We are going to be very much alive this winter. It is a pity that the battle must be fought all over again, but it will be fought, and you are altogether too sage and well-informed an observer of Jewish life to know what the issue of that squabble is going to be." See letter, Louis Wolsey to Jacob Billikopf, 10 October 1930, Louis Wolsey Collection, American Jewish Archives, Cincinnati.

113. See Louis Wolsey, Introductory Address to Meeting of Non-Zionist Reform Rabbis, Atlantic City, 1 June 1942.

114. Ibid.

115. Heller later claimed that he had agreed to recommend such action to the Conference but that he could not possibly guarantee it. The Wolsey forces interpreted that position as a subterfuge, that Heller could have delivered on this issue if he had wanted to, but that he was simply unwilling and was camouflaging his true intent.

116. Letter, James G. Heller to all members of the CCAR, 18 March 1943, James G. Heller Collection, American Jewish Archives, Cincinnati. Heller's offer to propose another neutrality resolution was not well-received by either group. On May 13, 1942 he received a telegram from Stephen S. Wise regarding the forthcoming Atlantic City conference as a "wholly inadequate reason for adopting a by-law of Zionist neutrality at special or any other session . . . I earnestly object and would at extraordinary session of Conference if called for that purpose make desperate and surely successful fight against adoption of any such by-law or proposal."

117. Letter, William H. Fineshriber and Louis Wolsey to all members of the CCAR, 7 May 1942, and 21 May 1942, American Council for Judaism File, American Jewish Archives, Cincinnati.

118. Letter, James G. Heller to all members of the CCAR, 26 May 1942, James G. Heller Collection, American Jewish Archives, Cincinnati.

119. Letter, James G. Heller to all members of the CCAR, 26 May 1942, op. cit.

120. Letter, James G. Heller to all members of the CCAR, 11 February 1943, op. cit.

121. Letter, Executive Committee, American Council for Judaism to all members of the CCAR, 1 March 1943; Letter, Louis Wolsey and others to James G. Heller, 7 May 1942. American Council for Judaism File, American Jewish Archives, Cincinnati.

122. Letter, William H. Fineshriber and Louis Wolsey, op. cit.

123. Ibid.

124. Louis Wolsey Collection, American Jewish Archives, Cincinnati. The declaration was signed by 89 rabbis and eventually by 96. This declaration also makes it clear that at its inception, the American Council for Judaism was not so much anti-Zionist as it was a statement of disenchantment with the political priorities in the establishment of a Jewish state.

125. Edward Israel (1942) had served as rabbi of Har Sinai Congregation in Baltimore and later became President of the Union of American Hebrew Congregations. He was consistent in his support of Zionist activity. In a letter to Simon E. Sobeloff, a lay leader at Har Sinai, Stephen S. Wise wrote, "I cannot help saying to you . . . without wishing to be unpleasant, that I am terribly disappointed to think that Ed's successors should have joined the Lazarenes and Woolsey in the opposition to the Jewish military unit based on Palestine and again calling that 'Munich' conference at Atlantic City on June 2. I know that Shusterman cannot be expected to say 'Amen' to everything Ed said and believed, but I think it would be common decency on his part to refrain from public participation in a protest against the life or lifework of Ed. I do not say that he should have been for the Jewish Army, but I do say that he might have foregone to have added his name to the role of rabbinical dishonor . . ." 30 April 1942. Stephen S. Wise Collection, American Jewish Archives, Cincinnati.

126. Philadelphia Jewish Exponent, 18 December 1942. See also American Israelite, 24 December 1942.

127. Correspondence of Stephen S. Wise to CCAR on Zionism, American Jewish Archives, Cincinnati. See letter, Theodore N. Lewis to Stephen S. Wise, 28 December 1942.

128. The statement was released on 16 December 1942. See press clipping in American Israelite, 31 December 1942.

129. See the solicitation letter for support addressed to all American rabbis from the sponsors, 14 October 1942. The project originated out of the offices of the American Emergency Committee for Zionist Affairs and included the following signatories in addition to those cited: Israel Goldstein, Mordecai M. Kaplan, B. L. Levinthal, Israel H. Levinthal, Louis M. Levitsky, Joseph H. Lookstein, Jacob R. Marcus, Abraham A. Neuman, Louis I. Newman, David de Sola Pool and Milton Steinberg.

130. CCAR Yearbook, Vol. LII, pp. 188-189. Felix Levy, a past-President of the CCAR, supported Heller by stating "there is no need for the American Council for Judaism . . . Under any circumstances at a time when Jews can suffer no further sectarianisms and when the need for a united people for its own salvation as a people is paramount, the Council has no reason for existence. Its organization despite its assertion to the contrary is secession from the Conference, if not from Reform Jewry." See Felix Levy,

"Are Zionism and Reform Judaism Incompatible?" Cincinnati, CCAR, 1943, p. 33.

131. *Ibid*., pp. 92-93.

132. *Ibid*., p. 94. One final effort at compromise had been exhausted at a meeting in Baltimore on January 5, 1943 which involved representatives from both sides. Heller had offered to propose to the Conference a by-law on neutrality if the American Council for Judaism would agree to dissolve its organization, but the Anti-Zionists refused.

133. For evidence of the rapidly waning influence of the American Council for Judaism after its initial impact, see *Louis Wolsey Collection*, *Morris Lazaron Collection* and *William Fineshriber Collection*, American Jewish Archives, Cincinnati.

134. Samuel Goldenson, "Zionism, Jews and Judaism" (Sermon), December 30, 1942, Temple Emanuel File (New York), American Jewish Archives, Cincinnati.

135. Morris Lazaron, "Is This the Way?" (Sermon), April, 1942. William H. Fineshriber also declared that "all Jews worthy of the name, Zionists and non-Zionists alike have one common objective: The preservation of Judaism and the Jewish people . . . Palestine is uniquely precious to all Jews; Palestine must be rehabilitated so that it may be a place of refuge to the dispossessed Jews of Europe and a home for all Jews who wish to settle there. They differ as to the political organization of Palestine. Zionists are committed to the establishment of an independent Jewish State or Commonwealth of Palestine. Non-Zionists are opposed to it on both theoretical and practical grounds." See William H. Fineshriber, et al. "Are Zionism and Reform Judaism Incompatible?" Cincinnati, CCAR, 1943, pp. 1-3.

136. Leon Feuer, "The Gentlemen of the Opposition," *Hadassah Newsletter*, March, 1943, pp. 11-13. See also, Heller, A. M., "Fears vs. Convinctions," *Nashville Observer*, January 29, 1943. David Polish denied that the anti-Zionists ever even supported fully the concept of Jewish settlement in Palestine. He claimed that the record proved that "during Zionism's three most dangerous periods--at the end of the first World War, in 1929, and now--anti-Zionists, and in some instances, the same anti-Zionists, have selected a time of grief for Israel to lacerate the wound even more." See William H. Fineshriber, *op. cit*., p. 58.

137. Letter, Executive Committee, American Council for Judaism to all members of the CCAR, 1 March 1943.

138. *Ibid*. See also Letter, Norman Buckner to Stephen S. Wise, 19 May, 1944.

139. Alfred Segal, "Plain Talk," *American Israelite*, 11 February, 1943.

140. Interview with Rabbi Samuel Silver, Temple Sinai, Stamford, Connecticut, 23 June, 1971.

141. Minutes, Administrative Board, UAHC, 1 March, 1942.

142. Alfred Segal, "Plain Talk," *American Israelite*, 7 January, 1943.

143. Lessing Rosenwald as quoted by Alfred Segal, "Plain Talk," *American Israelite*, 15 July, 1943.

144. Leon Feuer, op. cit.

145. Statement of Principles by Non-Zionist Rabbis, op. cit.

146. Letter, William H. Fineshriber and Louis Wolsey to James Heller, 21 May, 1942, American Council for Judaism File, American Jewish Archives, Cincinnati.

147. Louis Wolsey, "Introductory Address to Meeting of Non-Zionist Reform Rabbis," Atlantic City, 1 June, 1942.

148. Alfred Segal, op. cit.

149. Samuel Goldenson, op. cit.

150. Letter, Morris Lazaron to Maurice Wertheim, President, American Jewish Committee, 18 January, 1942, Morris S. Lazaron Collection, American Jewish Archives, Cincinnati.

151. Heller, A. M., op. cit.

152. Letter, James Heller to all members of the CCAR, 26 May, 1942. James G. Heller Collection, American Jewish Archives, Cincinnati.

153. Rabbi William Fineshriber explained that non-Zionists saw no reason for despair over conditions in Europe, since "we Jews have survived many such storms and we shall weather this hurricane. This is a war against the very causes that have produced anti-Semitism, and if we win. . . . the future for us will be infinitely brighter than it has ever been. If world conditions will be as desperate as Zionists picture them, the little Jewish State in Palestine will not be able to protect itself and least of all the twelve to thirteen millions of Jews outside of that State." See William H. Fineshriber, "Are Zionism and Reform Incompatible?", Cincinnati, CCAR, 1943, p. 4.

154. While he was still in sympathy with Zionist aims, even Rabbis Morris Lazaron conceded that "the preservation of Israel is of equal importance with the preservation of Judaism. The two are inseparable? Neither can stand alone; each needs the other to give it substance and reality. This thought runs through the Torah from the very beginning." Morris S. Lazaron, "Reform Judaism and Jewish Nationalism," Baltimore Jewish Times, January 2, 1931.

155. The 38th Council of the UAHC passed a resolution in April, 1943 entitled, "Safeguarding Rights of Jews After World War II." The complete published text of the resolution stated that "God uses men and people at great moments in history as the instrument of revelation. The Four Freedoms, the Atlantic Charter, collective security, common responsibility for a just and enduring peace enunciated by our President and his advisors and the leaders of the United Nations have practical goals which may be measurably realized. To their achievement we pledge our unreserved devotion. While the Four Freedoms must be applied to all persons of whatever faith, the Union of American Hebrew Congregations is deeply concerned with the fate of Jews in all lands who are suffering special hardships and even loss of life simply because they are Jews. We call upon our government and, through it, on the United Nations, to see that in the post-war settlement adequate provision shall be made to safeguard their rights, as well as the rights of all people who have been persecuted because of race or religion. We urge that adequate provision be made for their rehabilitation in new homes and in Palestine. We ask that our government use its good offices to see that Palestine is opened as quickly as possible

for settlement of as many Jews as desire to go there and who can be taken care of." Note that this resolution omitted any reference to the restoration of European Jews to lands or origin as well as any references to Arab opposition to unlimited immigration of Jews.

156. See Henry Barnston, History of the Jew of Houston, pp. 3-21, and Henry Cohen, "The Settlement of the Jews of Texas," in American Jewish Historical Society Publication, No. 2, 1894. Both volumes investigate the beginnings and early development of the Jewish community in Houston. Also helpful is Helena Frentil Schlam, The Early Jews of Houston, Master's thesis, Library, Ohio State University, Columbus, 1971.

157. Anne Nathan Cohen, The Centenary History of Congregation Beth Israel of Houston, Texas, 1954, p. 10.

158. Ibid., p. 11.

159. Ibid., p. 12. See also The Occident, 15 March, 1860. "The Rev. Z. Emmich was engaged March 1 as Chazan, Schochet and Mohel of Congregation Beth Israel of Houston . . . His reputation . . . is very good, and he is well spoken of."

160. Anne Nathan Cohen, op. cit., p. 29.

161. Ibid.

162. Ibid., p. 30.

163. Report of Policy Formulation Committee, 1943, Beth Israel Congregation, Houston, Texas Collection, American Jewish Archives, Cincinnati.

164. Ibid.

165. Annual Report of Congregation Beth Israel, Houston, Texas, 30 May, 1944, p. 8ff.

166. Ibid.

167. Ibid. See also letter, Rabbi Robert Kahn to author, 25 January, 1972. According to Kahn, Leopold Meyer stated publicly at a later date that he had been primarily responsible for the wording of the Basic Principles.

168. Report of Policy Formulation Committee, op. cit.

169. Ibid.

170. Friedlander based this judgment upon certain considerations which he discussed more fully in the introduction to A Handbook of True Facts Concerning the Basic Principles of Congregation Beth Israel, Houston, Texas, November, 1943, American Jewish Archives, Cincinnati.

171. Annual Report, op. cit.

172. For additional evidence that the anti-Zionists would not accept any new interpretation of the role of Jewish nationalism in Reform Judaism, see Handbook, op. cit., p. 29.

173. See letter of "Committee Representing Petitioners Favoring 'The Basic Principles'," Simon Sakowitz, Chairman, to all members of Beth Israel, 16 November, 1943, Beth Israel of Houston, Texas Collection, American Jewish Archives, Cincinnati.

174. _Ibid_.

175. _Ibid_.

176. Letter, Rabbi Robert I, Kahn to Officers and Board Members of Congregation Beth Israel, 1 March, 1944, Congregation Beth Israel of Houston Collection, American Jewish Archives, Cincinnati.

177. Hyman Judah Schachtel, "Let There Be Light," released to Independent Jewish Press Service, 30 December, 1943, American Jewish Archives, Cincinnati. See also Minutes, _Informal Meeting of Rabbis_, 30 November, 1943. Schachtel probably stated his views on the subject most explicitly when he debated the question of Zionism and Reform Judaism with his colleagues at the CCAR Convention in 1943. He declared categorically then that "Reform Judaism and Political Zionism have never been and can never hope to be compatible. They are mutually irreconcilable, mutually antagonistic, mutually contradictory . . . This mutual hostility arises from differences within, from profound and basic disagreements . . . Zionism and Reform Judaism are incompatible, absolutely incompatible." See Hyman J. Schachtel, "Are Zionism and Reform Judaism Incompatible?", Cincinnati, CCAR, 1943, p. 36.

178. _Ibid_.

179. Telegram, Morris Lazaron to I. Friedlander, 23 November, 1943. See also letter to reply, I. Friedlander to Lazaron, 24 November, 1943, _Beth Israel of Houston, Collection_, American Jewish Archives, Cincinnati.

180. Letter, Lewis S. Goldberg to Solomon B. Freehof, April 2, 1944, CCAR Correspondence File, American Jewish Archives, Cincinnati.

181. Letter, David de Sola Pool to Abba Hillel Silver, December 18, 1943, _Abba Hillel Silver Collection_, American Jewish Archives, Cincinnati.

182. _Philadelphia Jewish Exponent_, 4 February, 1944, pp. 1, 8. See also _Jewish Telegraphic Agency Bulletin_, 21 March, 1944, p. 4.

183. _Philadelphia Jewish Exponent_, _op. cit_.

184. _Ibid_.

185. Minutes, Executive Board, UAHC, 18 January, 1944, Chicago, p. 37.

186. Alfred, Segal, "Let's Have Peace," _American Israelite_, 2 December, 1943.

187. James Heller, "The Houston Heresy," _Opinion_, April, 1944, pp. 110-12.

188. Editorial, _American Israelite_, _op. cit_.

189. _Ibid_.

190. Editorial, "Houston and Reform," _H.U.C. Monthly_, December, 1943, p. 4.

191. _Ibid_.

192. Editorial, "An Unwise Decision," *Liberal Judaism*, December, 1943, pp. 2-3.

193. *American Israelite*, 9 December, 1953, p. 1.

194. Minutes, UAHC Executive Board, *op. cit*.

195. *Ibid*.

196. See Minutes, Executive Committee, Zionist Organization of America, New York, 16 November, 1943.

197. *Ibid*.

198. Minutes, UAHC Executive Board, *op. cit.*, p. 38.

199. See *American Israelite*, 27 April, 1944, p. 1.

200. Letter, Solomon B. Freehof to Leopold Meyer, President, Beth Israel Congregation, 15 March, 1944. *CCAR Correspondence File*, American Jewish Archives, Cincinnati.

201. Letter, Solomon B. Freehof to all Reform rabbis, 15 March, 1944, *CCAR Correspondence File*, American Jewish Archives, Cincinnati.

202. See *American Israelite*, 15 June, 1944.

203. Maurice Eisendrath, "Answering Houston," *Liberal Judaism*, April, 1944.

204. Reply of the Executive Board of the UAHC to Congregation Beth Israel of Houston, Texas, 28 March, 1944, p. 2.

205. Maurice Eisendrath, *op. cit*., p. 58.

206. *Ibid*.

207. Minutes, Informal Meeting of Rabbis, *op. cit*. See also Minutes of Administrative Committee of UAHC, 4 March, 1945 and letter, Maurice N. Eisendrath to presidents of all Reform congregations, 1 May, 1945.

208. *CCAR Yearbook*, Vol. 54, p. 35.

209. *Ibid*., p. 39.

210. Letter, A. M. Weiss, President of Congregation B'nai Israel, Baton Rouge, La., to Maurice Eisendrath, April 26, 1945, *American Council for Judaism File*, American Jewish Archives, Cincinnati.

211. See letters of support and declaration of intent to emulate Houston: Norman Buckner, Pontiac, Michigan to Dr. Stephen S. Wise, 19 May, 1944; Edwin L. Levy, President, Congregation Beth Ahabah, Richmond, Va. to Rabbi Morris S. Lazaron, 9 May, 1944; Rabbi Walter G. Peiser, President A. M. Weiss and Secretary H. Louis Cohn, Congregation B'nai Israel, Baton Rouge, La. "to our good friends everywhere," 25 April, 1945, which may all be found in *American Council for Judaism File*, American Jewish Archives, Cincinnati.

212. Letter, Rabbi Hyman Judah Schachtel to author, 29 February, 1972. Rabbi Schachtel adds that with the establishment of the State of Israel in 1948, the Basic Principles were *de facto*

ignored. Mr. Leopold Meyer even became the city-wide chairman of the United Jewish Appeal shortly afterward. See also letter, Rabbi Robert A. Kahn to author, *op. cit*.

213. Mr. Melvin Lehman, 1973, Historian of Temple Israel, Dayton, Ohio and a member of the congregation for over 70 years, reported that by the mid-1940s, even the "classical" German Reform Jews contributed to the United Palestine Appeal and supported the establishment of a Jewish state because they thought their religious leaders "expected" them to do so in light of the catastrophe in Europe.

214. Letter, Solomon B. Freehof to Leopold Meyer, *op. cit*.

215. The source of material for this account of Morris S. Lazaron and his attitudes toward Zionism is based largely on a chapter on the subject in his yet unpublished autobiography. A copy of that manuscript is on file at the American Jewish Archives in Cincinnati. It shall be referred to hereafter as "Morris S. Lazaron, Autobiography."

216. Rabbi Stephen S. Wise once declared that "no American rabbi has built up a finer, stronger community than Dr. Lazaron. He has had a distinguished career in the ministry and is a man of notable pulpit powers." See *Weekly Bulletin*, Free Synagogue, New York, 22 April, 1930.

217. Morris S. Lazaron, *Autobiography*, p. 237.

218. *Ibid*., p. 238.

219. *Ibid*., p. 239.

220. For an excellent analysis of the distinction and confusion between Zionism and general philanthropic and moral support for settlement in Palestine, ("Palestinianism") see Yonathan Shapiro, *Leadership of the American Zionist Organization*, Chicago, Univ. of Illinois Press, 1971, pp. 195-214.

221. One of his favorite recollections as evidence of this concern for the Jewish people was a personal confrontation between him and Stephen S. Wise at the Congressional hearings before the House Foreign Relations Committee in February, 1944 on the subject of creating a Jewish Commonwealth in Palestine. Wise had recently written in his periodical, *Opinion*, a blistering editorial denouncing Lazaron for his leadership in the American Council for Judaism and proclaiming that no self-respecting Jewish congregation should allow Lazaron to be its rabbi. The two men had not seen each other since the appearance of Wise's denunciation. Lazaron recalls that "Wise was standing with Zionist leaders at the other end of Sol Bloom's office. We looked at each other. He smiled rather uncertainly. I was even then fond of him and though I believed his conduct, like his methods, were unworthy of the really great qualities of the man, what he had written did not really matter and the old friendliness welled up in my heart for him. He was definitely growing old and he had been a valiant warrior for many good causes. I returned his smile. We started across the room simultaneously. He held out his hand. I took it. There was considerable interest in the incident and all present turned to look as he said in his rich, deep voice, 'Morris, when are you coming back to your people?'

I could not resist the impulse to respond, consciously pitching my own voice several tones lower, in imitation of his and said, 'Stephen, I have never left my people . . .'". Lazaron also maintains he was the first in Reform circles to use the phrase "peoplehood of Israel" which he introduced at the Buffalo convention of the CCAR in 1917. *Ibid.*, p. 276.

222. Letter, Lazaron to Henrietta Szold, 13 October, 1922, *Morris S. Lazaron Collection*, American Jewish Archives, Cincinnati.

223. Lazaron, *op. cit.*, p. 240.

224. *Ibid.*, p. 241.

225. See letter, Paul Gordon, Chairman of Nominations Committee, to Lazaron, 14 September, 1933 and Lazaron to Gordon, 19 September, 1933, *Morris S. Lazaron Collection*, American Jewish Archives, Cincinnati.

226. From the very beginning, even in his "Zionist" period, Lazaron opposed the priority of a political state for Jews in Palestine. He conceded that "there are Jewish nationalists who put the hope of a Jewish state before everything--even Judaism itself. I have no sympathy with them," He proceeded to defend his position by citing Martin Buber's statement that "Zion is more than a piece of land in the Near East . . . . Zion is memory, admonition, promise. Zion is the new sanctuary in the image of the old; once again shall the law go forth from Zion. It is the foundation stone of the Messianic upbuilding of humanity. It is the unending task of the Jewish people." See Morris Lazaron, "Reform Judaism and Jewish Nationalism," *Baltimore Jewish Times*, 2 January, 1931, p. 5ff.

227. Lazaron, *op. cit.*, p. 244.

228. See the review of Lazaron's article, "Reform Judaism and Jewish Nationalism" by the Rev. L. Livingstone in the *London Jewish Guardian*, 27 March, 1931. *Morris S. Lazaron Collection*, American Jewish Archives.

229. Lazaron summoned Reform Judaism to "bravely re-emphasize the place of Israel . . . It must be courageous enough to say, 'We've made a mistake.' The Jewish people is more than a denominational group. We are a people. It will not preach a religious idea only and let the people die." Morris Lazaron, "Reform Judaism and Jewish Nationalism," *op. cit*.

230. See letter, Hyman Enelow to Lazaron, 8 January, 1931. *Morris S. Lazaron Collection*, American Jewish Archives, Cincinnati.

231. Morris S. Lazaron, *Autobiography*, p. 246.

232. Morris S. Lazaron, "Judaism, A Universal Religion" in *Christian Century*, 30 August, 1930.

233. *Ibid*. He concluded that Judaism therefore must become a universal religion, or it will remain a moribund, ethnic cult, self-conscious and uninviting. "We are indeed at the parting of the ways," he wrote. "Let us not repeat the tragic mistake of the centuries. It is not the Jew who preserves Judaism, but Judaism that preserves the Jew."

234. See Morris S. Lazaron, *Autobiography*, p. 249. The most heartbreaking event of all was probably his reaction to a performance of Verdi's *Nebuchadnezzar* presented by the Jewish Cultural Group in Berlin and attended by an attache of the Italian Embassy. Lazaron tells us that "it was Purim time, the spring of 1935, shades of Ahasuerus and Haman in the Book of Esther. The head of the Secret Police, Himmler, was in a box. He wore a Nazi

arm band. The production was based on the Haman-Mordecai-Esther theme, a suitable, daring parallel to the Nazi-Jewish situation. To produce it in Hitler's Germany required rare courage. The music, the dancing, the singing were heartbreaking in their beauty. Here were veritable heroes and heroines who in the black night of persecution were desperately trying to maintain some semblance of culture, determined not to let the spirit die."

235. See article, "Rabbi Lazaron Berates American Zionists," Baltimore Jewish Times, 5 June, 1942. "The resolutions of the Zionist Congress meetings reveal inconsistencies which are hard to reconcile. They proclaim unreserved support of the United Nations, yet continue to agitate for a Jewish Army. They declare for cooperation with the Arabs, but demand that the Jewish Agency have full control of immigration. They deny nationalism for the Jews, but demanding international status for the Jewish people, call upon Jews who are citizens of other countries to work for a political goal related to a land other than their own . . . While I understand the despair that breeds nationalism in Jewish life, it makes me sick at heart to contemplate that the people which gave the world its universal dream are urged to turn its back upon its greatest gift at the very moment in history when the free people of the world are united in an epic struggle to preserve that dream."

236. It is difficult to believe that Lazaron had traveled so far from his earlier conviction that Judah Maccabee would probably consider modern Palestine "your insurance . . . against the forces of death . . . How he would flag those who only see Arab numbers. How he would declare: Not by numbers - for when in all the centuries has the Jew conquered by numbers? . . . but by the spirit which comes from God Himself." Morris Lazaron, "If the Maccabees Lived Today," Baltimore Jewish Times, 26 December, 1930.

237. For the full text of the Resolution on Palestine, see Proceedings of the Biennial Assembly of the UAHC, Sixty-Third Annual Report, 1937, pp. 166-170.

238. Lazaron, op. cit., p. 266. Quoted from a letter from Lazaron to Maurice Wertheim, President of the American Jewish Committee, date unknown. In response to appeals like Lazaron's to favor the head over the heart, David Polish reminded anti-Zionists that "no Jew on the occupied continent now lives in the place which four years ago he called home. What shall we have them do? Shall we have them return some day to the place where they came, where the waters of terror and bitterness have swept away every memory of their presence? They are now in a howling wilderness, a no-man's land. If they are to go anywhere when peace comes, where is the wisdom in demanding that they return to a place which shall say, 'I know you not', while their kin in Palestine wait to receive them?" David Polish, "Are Zionism and Reform Judaism Incompatible?", Cincinnati, CCAR Yearbook, 1943, p. 62.

239. Ibid., p. 271.

240. Ibid., p. 277.

241. Ibid., p. 278. This particular rejection from the NCCJ was especially difficult for Lazaron to swallow. He remembers a certain "sadness" over it, "because I conceived of my work in the National Conference of Christians and Jews as one of the major functions of my ministry. It had brought me joy and inspiration and I cherished the thought I had made some small contribution to interfaith understanding and had built some bridges between

Christian and Jew." Lazaron, however, demonstrated no effort in opposing Nazism or alleviating Jewish homelessness through his associations with NCCJ.

242. See letter, Lazaron to Abba Hillel Silver, 4 October, 1937, Abba Hillel Silver Archives, Cleveland. "The reason we have never discussed our attitudes on basic Jewish matters is because up until now, I think there was basic agreement, the differences being perhaps only in emphasis . . . I do feel the need to maintain what has been done in Palestine; but matters of principle are certainly involved on the basic issue of a Jewish state . . . With reference to changing opinion, the issues have sufficiently changed to warrant it."

243. Letter, Lazaron to Silver, 30 November, 1939, Abba Hillel Silver Archives.

244. Address, "Talks On the Times," Message of Israel Hour, 2 December, 1939.

245. Letter, Silver to Lazaron, 14 December 1939, Abba Hillel Silver Archives, Cleveland.

246. Even during his period of Zionist sympathy, Lazaron declared that "it (Jewish Nationalism) has nothing to do with statehood. The political government of Palestine does not concern us. What does concern us is that in that land . . . we may once again develop our Jewish life." Morris Lazaron, "Reform Judaism and Jewish Nationalism," op. cit.

247. See letter, Julian Morgenstern to author, 17 July 1972. Also, Julian Morgenstern "What Are We Jews?", CCAR Journal, October, 1965.

248. Irving, Levitas, "Reform Jews and Zionism, 1919-1921", American Jewish Archives Quarterly, April, 1962, p. 12. Morgenstern was confident that "Zionist claims will receive scant consideration other than as a pure colonization scheme and . . . as a means to enable Great Britain to gain a diplomatic advantage over France."

249. Yonathan, Shapiro, Leadership of the American Zionist Organization, 1897-1930, University of Illinois Press, 1971, p. 256.

250. Report of mass protest meeting at Plum Street Temple, 29 August 1929, James G. Heller Papers, American Jewish Archives, Cincinnati.

251. Morgenstern, op. cit.

252. Julian Morgenstern, Address at the Opening Exercises of HUC, 29 September 1934, Julian Morgenstern Collection, American Jewish Archives, Cincinnati.

253. In reality, of course, the Zionists never permitted the debate to function at the level of an ideological conflict. The attack upon the anti-Zionists almost always centered on a suspicion of motives and loyalty to the Jewish people. Opposition to Zionism in light of religious considerations, such as peace, justice and brotherhood, was not impossible to substantiate; but that argument never received a full and fair hearing among American Reform Jews.

254. Julian Morgenstern, Address, "The Task of the Hebrew Union College," 7 October 1944, p. 8.

255. Ibid., p. 4. See also Morgenstern's address, "Unity In American Judaism, How and When?", 22 September 1945, p. 11.

256. Julian Morgenstern, "The Task of the Hebrew Union College," p. 10; also, p. 7. See also his address, "Assimilation, Isolation or Reform?", Contemporary Jewish Record, April, 1942. Morgenstern conceded the possible merits of Jewish nationalism in Palestine but certainly not in the United States where Jews will constitute exclusively a "Jewish religious community."

257. Ibid., pp. 134, 141.

258. Julian Morgenstern, "Unity in American Judaism," 22 September 1945, pp. 19-20. The Reconstructionists were a fourth segment of the American Jewish religious community (in addition to Orthodox, Conservative and Reform Judaism). It was founded by Mordecai Kaplan, emphasized Judaism as a religious civilization and redefined Jewish theology in terms of religious naturalism.

259. Ibid., p. 22.

260. Ibid., p. 24.

261. Julian Morgenstern, "Assimilation, Isolation or Reform?", p. 140. See also, Morgenstern, Julian, Address, "Judaism's Contribution to Post-War Religion," 26 September 1942, p. 17, American Jewish Archives, Cincinnati.

262. See Julian Morgenstern, "Unity in American Judaism," 22 September 1945, pp. 14-15.

263. Julian Morgenstern, "Nation, People, Religion - What Are We?", American Israelite, 21 October 1943, p. 1.

264. "Rabbi Wohl Replies to Dr. Morgenstern," American Israelite, 11 November 1943, p. 1.

265. Letter, Abba Hillel Silver to David A. Goldstein, 1 November 1943, Abba Hillel Silver Archives, Cleveland.

266. Letter, Goldstein to Silver, 18 October 1943, 26 October 1943, Abba Hillel Silver Collection, American Jewish Archives, Cincinnati.

267. Telegram, Joshua Loth Liebman to Abba Hillel Silver, 26 October 1943, Abba Hillel Silver Collection, American Jewish Archives, Cincinnati.

268. See letter, Joshua Loth Liebman to Abba Hillel Silver, 15 November 1943, Abba Hillel Silver Collection, American Jewish Archives, Cincinnati. Silver had suggested to Liebman that he lodge a formal protest with the Chairman of the HUC Board of Governors prior to its next meeting, to which Liebman replied that he could not spearhead such a personal rebuke, because Morgenstern "was not only a revered teacher of mine at the College but his kindness to me since graduation has been of such an unusual nature that I shall ever feel indebted to him."

269. Both Rabbi Wohl in his formal reply and the signatories to the telegram all cited Morgenstern's support for the CCAR action as evidence that the President's statements were wholly inconsistent with his earlier actions.

270. See Joshua Loth Liebman, "Kindler of Mental Light," Liberal Judaism, November, 1945, UAHC, Cincinnati, p. 22.

271. See Julian Morgenstern, "Opening Day Address" in Cincinnati Enquirer, 13 October 1946. See also, Morgenstern, "What Are We Jews?", CCAR Journal, October, 1965, p. 20. "We Jews, all over the world, we are a people, a people with a distinct and honored past."

272. Ibid.

273. Julian Morgenstern, "With History As Our Guide," CCAR Yearbook, Vol. LVII, 1947, pp. 257-287.

274. Ibid., p. 280.

275. Ibid., p. 283. See also letter from Morgenstern to the Editor of the Jewish Times in Baltimore, 2 January 1948, in which he repeated once more this statement from his Conference Lecture.

276. Maurice Eisendrath, Can Faith Survive?, McGraw-Hill, New York, 1964, pp. 49-50.

277. Maximilian Heller was the father of James Heller and one of the first Reform rabbis to endorse and labor actively on behalf of Jewish nationalism.

278. Maurice Eisendrath in personal interview with author, 21 November 1972.

279. Maurice Eisendrath in sermon delivered at Holy Blossom Temple, Toronto, 1934.

280. For his own recollections of these episodes, see Maurice Eisendrath, Chapter 3, op. cit.

281. See Maurice Eisendrath, "Building A Cooperative Commonwealth In Palestine," Holy Blossom Pulpit (collection of sermons), Vol. 6, No. 5, Toronto, 1935-36, p. 4. "The quest for righteous conduct, the search for absolute justice, emphasis on the inviolable personality of every child of God which had been the burden of the prophets' message, became the bulwark of a new life which the first pioneers of Zion were seeking to create." See also, pp. 15-16.

282. Ibid. David Polish echoed Eisendrath's enthusiasm in his judgment that "there is no other Jewish movement to rival the spiritual intensity of the Yishuv (Jewish settlement in Palestine) and its cohorts. No other Jewish community in the world has so heroically fulfilled the Mitzvah (commandment) of Pidyon Shevuyim (ransom of captives). No other Jewish community has more punctiliously lived the prophetic denunciation, Hoy magi vayis l' vayis sadeh v'sadeh yakrivu ad efes makom ("Woe to those who add house to house and join field to field until there is no room"). No other Jewish community has given not only of its increment but of its life blood to clothe the naked and feed the hungry. Nowhere else in Jewish life has the principle of man's responsibility to his fellowman been lived with greater integrity than in the Kibbutzim (communal agricultural settlements) and Moshave Ovdim (worker's settlements)." See David Polish, "Are Zionism and Reform Judaism Incompatible?". Cincinnati, CCAR Yearbook 1943, p. 57.

283. Op. cit., Vol. 6, No. 6.

284. Maurice Eisendrath in personal interview with author, 21 November 1972. Eisendrath agreed that passage of the Zionist statement was virtually a "coup d' etat," engineered by Zionist activists within the Conference.

285. Ibid.

286. The meeting of the Commission of Rabbis and Laymen was held at the Hotel New Yorker in New York City on 2 May 1943. Those present included Rabbis Barnett R. Brickner, Max C. Currick, William H. Fineshriber, James G. Heller, Morris S. Lazaron, Emil W. Leipziger, Felix A. Levy, Julian Morgenstern, and Messrs., Robert P. Goldman, Adolph Rosenberg, Joseph Proskauer, Meier Steinbrink, Horace Stern and Rabbis Maurice N. Eisendrath and Louis Egelson.

Those who expressed regrets for their absence included Jacob Aronson, Rabbi Solomon B. Freehof, Irving Lehman, Charles H. Simons, Rabbi Stephen S. Wise and Rabbi Louis Wolsey.

287. See letter, Maurice N. Eisendrath to Abba Hillel Silver, 23 April 1943, Abba Hillel Silver Archives. Eisendrath wrote "I do covet your presence at such a meeting and I pray that you may find some way of altering your opinion." Also in his personal interview with the author, Eisendrath recalled that "Silver would not sit down with those people (representatives of the American Council for Judaism)."

288. See minutes, Meeting of Commission of Rabbis and Laymen, 2 May 1943, New York, Abba Hillel Silver Archives, p. 4.

289. Those present at this meeting included Rabbis Abraham J. Feldman, Joseph L. Fink, James G. Heller, Felix A. Levy, Joshua L. Liebman, Jacob R. Marcus, Harry S. Margolis, Louis Binstock, Norman Gerstenfeld, B. Benedict Glazer, Morris S. Lazaron, Victor E. Reichert, Hyman J. Schachtel, Bernard J. Bamberger, Max C. Currick, Solomon B. Freehof, Julian Morgenstern, Abraham Shusterman, Maurice N. Eisendrath and Louis Engelson, the latter acting as secretary.

Those who expressed regrets for their absence included Rabbis Edgar F. Magnin, Abba Hillel Silver, Jacob J. Weinstein, Samuel Wohl, William H. Fineshriber, Samuel H. Goldenson, Samuel S. Mayerberg, Jonah B. Wise, Louis Wolsey and Louis Mann.

The following members of the Administrative Committee of the Union attended the meeting: Jesse Cohen, Solomon Eisner, Mrs. Hugo Hartmann, Lester A. Jaffe, Adolph Rosenberg and Melville S. Welt.

290. Minutes, Informal Meeting of Rabbis, 30 November 1943, Cincinnati. See Appendix B.

291. Letter, Abba Hillel Silver to Maurice N. Eisendrath, 23 September 1943, Abba Hillel Silver Archives.

292. Letter, Abba Hillel Silver to Solomon B. Freehof, 4 December 1943. Also, letter, Abba Hillel Silver to Felix A. Levy, 8 January 1944, Abba Hillel Silver Archives.

293. See letters, Edgar F. Magnin to Adolph Rosenberg, 8 November 1943; Jonah B. Wise to Maurice N. Eisendrath, 17 November 1943; Solomon B. Freehof to Adolph Rosenberg, 13 November 1943, Abba Hillel Silver Archives. See also Board Resolution on Zionism, Bulletin of Kenneseth Israel Congregation, Philadelphia, 3 December 1943.

294. See letters, Maurice N. Eisendrath to Abba Hillel Silver, 27 September 1943 and 19 November 1943 in which he declared that "I think that the whole future of our Reform movement is at stake." See also, Minutes, Informal Meeting of Rabbis, op. cit.

295. Maurice N. Eisendrath in personal interview with author, 21 November 1972.

296. Maurice Eisendrath, "For Such A Time As This" (Founders Day Address), 27 March 1943, Hebrew Union College, Cincinnati, pp. 9-10.

297. Ibid.

298. See Proceedings of the 39th Council of the UAHC, March 3-6, 1946, Cincinnati, pp. 105-109.

299. Liberal Judaism, UAHC, June, 1943, pp. 22-23.

300. Letter, Maurice N. Eisendrath to Morris S. Lazaron, 14 May 1945, Morris S. Lazaron Collection, American Jewish Archives.

301. It should be noted that Eisendrath's correspondence with Lazaron preceded the Biennial Council of 1946 which finally endorsed support for the American Jewish Conference.

302. Bulletin, Temple Emanu-El, New York, 17 January, 1930.

303. Ibid., 26 December, 1930.

304. Bulletin, Rodeph Shalom Congregation, Philadelphia, 14 March, 1928.

305. Ibid., 13 March, 1936.

306. Bulletin, Temple Israel, St. Louis, 24 December, 1933. The Round Table Discussion Group of the Temple Men's Club invited Rabbis Julius Gordon to speak on "Palestine".

307. Bulletin, The Temple, Cleveland, 25 October, 1936. The Zionist Society met at the Temple to hear Senator Royal S. Copeland of New York who had just returned from a tour of Palestine.

308. Bulletin, Holy Blossom Temple, Toronto, 31 December, 1933. The Bulletin article complained, "Thus far we must admit our disappointment that not more of our congregants and co-religionists have manifested interest in this specifically Jewish and most timely series of addresses. Whether in favor of or opposed to Zionism, no Jew can afford to be indifferent to Palestine today."

309. See Bulletin, The Temple, Cleveland, 20 December, 1936 and 24 January, 1937.

310. Franzblau, A., Reform Judaism in the Large Cities: A Survey, UAHC, U.S.A., 1931, p. 13.

311. See chapter above, "Prelude To Columbus," p. 15.

312. Kohanski, Alexander, ed., The American Jewish Conference: Its Organization and the Proceedings of the First Session, 29 August - 2 September, 1943, American Jewish Conference, New York, 1944, p. 15. See also letters and enclosures from James G. Heller to all members of the CCAR, 25 February, 1943, Abba Hillel Silver Archives, Cleveland; also, letters and enclosures from Henry Monsky to Adolph Rosenberg, Chairman of the UAHC, 6 January, 1943, Abba Hillel Silver Archives, Cleveland.

313. Henry Feingold, The Politics of Rescue, Rutgers University Press, New Brunswick, N. J., 1970, pp. 167-192. See also Arthur Morse, While Six Million Died, Random House, New York, 1967, pp. 3-36, and American Israelite, 10 December, 1942, Cincinnati: It is estimated that one million Jews - about one-third of the pre-War Jewish population of Poland - have been murdered since the Nazi occupation of Poland in 1939 . . . . The U.S. State Department has confirmed the existence of an official order by Adolph Hitler calling for the extermination of the 5,000,000 Jews in Nazi-occupied Europe by the end of 1942 . . ."

314. Henry Feingold, op. cit., p. 171.

315. Alexander Kohanski, op. cit., p. 44.

316. Henry Feingold, op. cit., p. 218. According to Kohanski, there were 379 delegates elected by 1,500,000 Jews.

317. Louis Wolsey, "My Impressions of the American Jewish Conference," Jewish Exponent, 1 October, 1943, Wolsey's major grievance was the failure of the Conference to discuss any other issue except Palestine and that no consideration whatever was given to such topics as "the problem of relief to the sufferers from Nazi barbarism, and their rescue from oppression, the rehabilitation of our suffering brethren in their original homes, the seeking of territories to which Jews might migrate, the study of anti-Semitism and how to combat it, the education of the world to considerations of decency and humanity, the establishment of equal rights for everybody throughout the world, the doctrine of the Four Freedoms - all this played no part in the oratory of the Conference."

318. American Hebrew, 11 June, 1943.

319. Minutes, Executive Board of UAHC, 1 April, 1943, pp. 17-18.

320. Quoted in Louis Wolsey, op. cit.

321. Minutes, Executive Board of UAHC, op. cit., p. 59.

322. Liberal Judaism, UAHC, June, 1943, pp. 3-4.

323. Underscored is that of the author.

324. Liberal Judaism, op. cit., p. 4.

325. Liberal Judaism, UAHC, September 1943, p. 35.

326. See Note 313.

327. See Minutes, UAHC Executive Board Meeting, Chicago, 18 January, 1944, p. 4. The Chairman of the UAHC Board reported numerous complaints from member congregations objecting to any postponement of the decision regarding participation in the American Jewish Conference.

328. Ibid., p. 6.

329. Letter, Abba Hillel Silver to Maurice N. Eisendrath, 26 November, 1943, Abba Hillel Silver Archives, Cleveland.

330. Maurice N. Eisendrath to Abba Hillel Silver, 1 December 1943 and 4 January, 1944, Abba Hillel Silver Archives, Cleveland.

Eisendrath confessed to Silver that "I do not exaggerate when I say that such a rift is well within the realm of possibility - even of probability."

331. See Note 8.

332. Liberal Judaism, UAHC, June 1943, p. 20.

333. Ibid.

334. See, for example, the declaration entitled, "The Common Purpose of Civilized Mankind," signed and passed by 68 Senators and 194 members of the House of Representatives on 2 November, 1942. Sen. Robert Wagner (N.Y.), Chairman of the American Palestine Committee, called it a "public declaration of such a constructive policy, aiming at the solution of the problem through the re-establishing of a Jewish Commonwealth in Palestine."

335. Liberal Judaism, op. cit., p. 11.

336. Minutes, UAHC Executive Board Meeting, Chicago, 18 January 1944, p. 9.

337. Ibid.

338. Ibid.

339. Letter, President of Har Sinai Congregation, Baltimore to Adolph Rosenberg, Chairman, UAHC, 10 February, 1944. See also letter, Adolph D. Cohn, President, Baltimore Hebrew Congregation to President, Executive Director and members of the Executive Board of UAHC, 11 May, 1944, Abba Hillel Silver Archives, Cleveland. Both letters rejected the endorsement of the resolution passed by the Executive Board 18 January, 1944.

340. Letter, Edwin L. Levy, President, Beth Ahabah Congregation, Richmond, Va., to Rabbi Morris Lazaron, 9 May, 1944, Morris S. Lazaron Collection, American Jewish Archives, Cincinnati.

341. Letter, Horace Stern to Maurice Eisendrath, 26 December, 1944, UAHC Correspondence File, American Jewish Archives, Cincinnati.

342. Letter, Lewis Strauss to Maurice Eisendrath, 5 January, 1945, UAHC Correspondence File, American Jewish Archives, Cincinnati.

343. Letter, I. Edward Tonkon to Maurice Eisendrath, 26 May, 1945, UAHC Correspondence File, American Jewish Archives, Cincinnati.

344. Ibid.

345. Liberal Judaism, UAHC, July, 1944, pp. 29-30.

346. The second assembly of the American Jewish Conference convened in Pittsburgh, 2-5 December, 1944.

347. Letter, Maurice N. Eisendrath and Adolph Rosenberg to Interim Committee, American Jewish Conference, 6 April, 1945, UAHC Correspondence File, American Jewish Archives, Cincinnati.

348. Ibid.

349. Telegram, American Jewish Conference to United States Secretary of State, 8 April, 1945, James C. Heller Collection, American Jewish Archives, Cincinnati.

350. _Proceedings of the Thirty-ninth Council of the UAHC_, March 3-6, 1946, UAHC Library, New York, p. 139.

351. _Ibid_., p. 181.

352. _Ibid_., p. 163.

353. _Ibid_., p. 168.

354. _Ibid_., p. 170.

355. _Ibid_., p. 239.

356. See chapter above on "The Inner Conflict - Advocates and Adversaries."

357. _Proceedings_, op. cit., p. 247.

358. Louis Rittenberg, "The Union Achieves Unity," _Liberal Judaism_, UAHC, April, 1946, p. 8.

359. See pp. 13-14 above. See also _Jewish Telegraphic Agency News_, _op. cit_.

360. Louis Rittenberg, _op. cit_., pp. 8-9.

361. _Jewish Telegraphic Agency News_, _op. cit_.

362. _Hebrew Union College Monthly_, March, 1946, p. 4.

363. See chapter above on "The Inner Conflict - Advocates and Adversaries." See also Maurice N. Eisendrath, _Can Faith Survive?_, McGraw-Hill, New York, 1964, Chapter 3, "The State of Israel - Is Nationhood Enough?"

364. This judgment was the result of personal interviews with Rabbis Abraham J. Feldman, Samuel Silver and Malcolm Stern. See also letter from Malcolm Stern to author, 26 January, 1972 in which Stern reports that "when Israel was born in 1948, I wrote to Fineshriber, 'We have been outvoted. It is time for the Council to go out of existence.'"

365. _CCAR Yearbook_, 1946, pp. 225-227.

366. _Ibid_., p. 246.

367. Editorial, "An Enheartening Council," _Liberal Judaism_ UAHC, April, 1946, pp. 6-7.

368. _CCAR Yearbook_, op. cit., p. 227.

369. See _Town Meeting-Bulletin of America's Town Meeting of the Air_, 8 November, 1945, Columbus, Ohio, p. 15.

370. _CCAR Yearbook_, _op. cit_., p. 213.

371. _Liberal Judaism_, UAHC, August, 1946, p. 10.

372. _CCAR Yearbook_, _op. cit_., p. 213.

373. _Ibid_., pp. 212-213 for full text of the resolution. The resolution had been submitted by Maurice N. Eisendrath, Julius Gordon, and C. George Fox, and received an overwhelming endorsement from the assembled rabbis. Some of them even joined Morton Berman in a picket line around the British Consulate in Chicago.

374. Letter, Isaac E. Marcuson, Administrative Secretary, CCAR to all members, 1 July, 1946, _CCAR Correspondence File_, American Jewish Archives, Cincinnati.

375. Letter to the Editor, _Liberal Judaism_, UAHC, February, 1948, p. 43.

376. _Ibid_.

377. Dean Alfange, "A Liberal Looks at the Jewish State." _The New Palestine_, Vol. XXXV, No. 9, p. 111.

378. _Ibid_., p. 119.

379. For the complete text of the resolution, see _CCAR Yearbook_, Vol. LVIII, 1948, pp. 27-28.

380. _Liberal Judaism_, U.A.H.C., May, 1947, p. 37.

381. _Liberal Judaism_, U.A.H.C., December, 1947, pp. 1-3.

382. _Liberal Judaism_, U.A.H.C., March, 1948, p. 2.

383. Official minutes, UAHC Fortieth General Assembly, Boston, 1948, p. 246.

384. _Ibid_.

385. _Ibid_., p. 262.

386. "President's Message," _CCAR Yearbook_, Vol. LVIII, 1948, p. 196.

387. The complete text on this lengthy resolution may be found in _CCAR Yearbook_, _op. cit_., pp. 93-95.

388. Editorial, "Israel Redivivus," _Liberal Judaism_, June-July, 1948, pp. 1-4.

BIBLIOGRAPHY

MANUSCRIPT COLLECTIONS AND UNPUBLISHED MATERIALS

I. Archival Materials

Hebrew Union College. American Jewish Archives. American Council for Judaism File.

Hebrew Union College. American Jewish Archives. Beth Israel of Houston, Texas Collection.

Hebrew Union College. American Jewish Archives. Barnett Brickner Collection.

Hebrew Union College. American Jewish Archives. CCAR Correspondence File.

Hebrew Union College. American Jewish Archives. William Fineshriber Collection.

Hebrew Union College. American Jewish Archives. James G. Heller Collection.

Hebrew Union College. American Jewish Archives. Morris S. Lazaron Collection.

Hebrew Union College. American Jewish Archives. Julian Morgenstern Collection.

Hebrew Union College. American Jewish Archives. Abba Hillel Silver Collection.

Hebrew Union College. American Jewish Archives. UAHC Correspondence File.

Hebrew Union College. American Jewish Archives. Correspondence of Stephen S. Wise to CCAR on Zionism.

Hebrew Union College. American Jewish Archives. Louis Wolsey Collection.

Lazaron, Morris S. Autobiography, Hebrew Union College. American Jewish Archives.

II. Papers and Addresses

Eichorn, D. Max. "Survey of the Hebrew Union College Student Body, 1900-1930." Library, Hebrew Union College, Cincinnati, 1931.

Eisendrath, Maurice N. "For Such A Time As This." Library, Hebrew Union College, 27 March 1943.

Fineshriber, W., Levy, F., Polish, D., Schachtel, H. "Are Zionism and Reform Judaism Incompatible?" Cincinnati: CCAR. 1943. American Jewish Archives.

Goldenson, Samuel. "Zionism, Jews and Judaism." 30 December 1942. Hebrew Union College, American Jewish Archives. Temple Emanuel File.

Lazaron, Morris S. "Is This The Way?". April 1942. Hebrew Union College.

American Jewish Archives. Morris S. Lazaron Collection. "Judaism A Universal Religion," (reprint) Christian Century, 30 August 1939.

American Jewish Archives. Morris S. Lazaron Collection. "Reform Judaism and Jewish Nationalism," (reprint) London Jewish Guardian, 27 March 1931, American Jewish Archives, Morris S. Lazaron Collection.

Tzafun, Hayyim. "Changing Attitudes Toward Zionsim As Reflected In The CCAR Yearbooks and UAHC Proceedings, 1897-1948." Term paper, Hebrew Union College, Cincinnati, 1967.

Morgenstern, Julian. "Judaism's Contribution to Post-War Religion" 26 September 1942. American Jewish Archives. Julian Morgenstern Collection. "Nation, People, Religion - What Are We?" 21 October 1943. American Jewish Archives. Julian Morgenstern Collection.

"The Task of the Hebrew Union College." 7 October 1944. American Jewish Archives. Julian Morgenstern Collection.

III. Correspondence

Bernstein, Philip S., Rabbi, Temple B'rith Kodesh, Rochester, N.Y. Letter to author, 23 January 1970.

Brooks, Sidney, Rabbi, Temple Israel, Omaha, Neb., Letter to author. 7 November 1972.

Feuer, Leon. Rabbi, Collingwood Ave. Temple, Toledo, Ohio. Letter to author. 26 January 1970.

Kahn, Robert. Rabbi, Temple Emanuel, Houston, Texas. Letter to author. 25 January 1972.

Lazaron, Morris S. Rabbi Emeritus, Baltimore Hebrew Congregation, Baltimore, Maryland. Letter to author. 25 May 1971.

Morgenstern, Julian. Past-President, Hebrew Union College, Cincinnati, Ohio. Letter to author. 27 July 1972.

Rudin, Jacob. Rabbi Emeritus, Temple Beth El, Great Neck, N.Y. Letter to author. 26 January 1970.

Schachtel, Hyman Judah. Rabbi, Beth Israel Congregation, Houston, Texas. Letter to author. 29 February 1972.

IV. Interviews and Tapes

Eisendrath, Maurice N. President, Union of American Hebrew Congregations, New York. Interview, 21 November 1972.

Feldman, Abraham J. Rabbi Emeritus, Beth Israel Congregation, Hartford, Conn. Interview, 23 June 1971.

Heller, James G. Rabbi Emeritus, Isaac M. Wise Temple, Cincinnati, Ohio. Interview, 26 October 1971.

Lelyveld, Arthur J. Rabbi, Fairmount Temple, Cleveland, Ohio. Interview, 29 December, 1970.

Marcus, Jacob R. Director, American Jewish Archives, Cincinnati, Ohio. Interview, 20 October 1970.

May, Mortimer. Temple Ahabei Sholom, Nashville, Tennessee. Interview, 9 November 1971.

NBC. "The Message of Israel," 2 December 1939, "Talks on the Times," Morris S. Lazaron.

"Town Meeting - Bulletin of America's Town Meeting of the Air," Columbus, Ohio, 8 November 1945.

Wohl, Samuel. Rabbi Emeritus, Isaac M. Wise Temple, Cincinnati, Ohio. Interview, 7 March 1971.

NEWSPAPERS

American Hebrew, 11 June 1943.

American Israelite, 24 January 1879, 14 July 1882, 19 March 1891, 23 January 1896, 19 August 1897, 2 September 1897, 30 September 1897, 7 July 1898, 8 September 1898, 19 January 1899, 19 March 1942, 24 December 1942, 31 December 1942, 21 October 1943, 11 November 1943, 9 December 1943, 27 April 1944, 15 June 1944.

Baltimore Jewish Times, 26 December 1930, 2 January 1931, 5 June 1942, 2 January 1948.

Cincinnati Enquirer, 1 March 1942, 13 October 1946.

Jewish Press Service Bulletin, 11 May 1943.

Jewish Telegraphic Agency Bulletin, 21 March 1944, 15 March 1946.

Milwaukee Wochenblatt, 1 August 1947.

New York Times, 31 October 1941, 31 August 1943.

The Occident, 15 March 1860.

Philadelphia Jewish Exponent, 9 June 1939, 5 July 1940, 4 July 1941, 2 January 1944, 10 December 1942, 1 October 1943, 4 February 1944.

Schachtel, Hyman Judah. "Let There Be Light." _Independent Jewish Press Service_, 30 December 1943.

Segal, Alfred. "Plain Talk." _American Israelite_, 3 January 1943, 11 February 1943, 15 July 1943, 2 December 1943.

PERIODICALS

Baltimore Hebrew Congregation. Baltimore. The Messenger (Temple Bulletin), 1930-1938.

Beth Israel Congregation. Houston. Temple Bulletins, 1930-1948.

Holy Blossom Temple. Toronto. Temple Bulletins, 1933-1937.

Kenneseth Israel Congregation. Philadelphia. Temple Bulletins, 1930-1948.

Rodeph Shalom Congregation. Philadelphia. Temple Bulletins, 1930-1948.

Stephen S. Wise Free Synagogue. New York. Temple Bulletin, 22 April 1930.

Temple Emanuel. New York. Temple Bulletins, 1930-1948.

Temple Israel. St. Louis. Temple Bulletins, 1933-1937.

The Temple. Cleveland. Temple Bulletins, 1930-1943.

Time Magazine, 28 December 1942.

OFFICIAL DOCUMENTS AND REPORTS

Annual Report of Congregation Beth Israel, Houston, Texas. Houston: By the Congregation, 1944.

Commission of Rabbis and Laymen. New York. Minutes of the meeting of 2 May 1943.

Handbook of True Facts Concerning the Basic Principles of Congregation Beth Israel, Houston, Texas. Houston: By the Congregation, 1944.

Hebrew Union College, Cincinnati. Board of Governors, Minutes of the meeting of 3 May 1905.

Report of the Policy Formulation Committee. American Jewish Archives, Beth Israel Congregation, Houston, Texas Collection.

UAHC Commission on Social Action of Reform Judaism. Where We Stand - Social Action Resolutions. New York: Union of American Hebrew Congregations, 1960.

Union of American Hebrew Congregations. New York. Proceedings of the Biennial Assembly of the UAHC, Sixty-Third Annual Report, 1937.

Proceedings of the 39th Council of the UAHC, 1946.

Proceedings of the 40th General Assembly of the UAHC, 1948.

Zionist Organization of America. New York. Executive Committee, Minutes of the meeting of 16 November 1943.

BOOKS AND PAMPHLETS

Barnston, Henry. History of the Jews of Houston.

Baron, Salo. Steeled by Adversity. Philadelphia: Jewish Publication Society. 1971.

Berger, Elmer. Judaism Or Jewish Nationalism?. New York: Bookman Associates. 1957.

Berman, Morton Mayer. For Zion's Sake: A Personal and Family Chronicle. Prescott, Arizona, Prescott Graphics. 1980.

Boase, Paul H. The Rhetoric of Christian Socialism. New York: Random House. 1969.

Central Conference of American Rabbis Yearbook, Vols. 36, 38, 40-47, 52-54, 56-58. Philadelphia: Jewish Publication Society.

Chertoff, Mordecai S. Zionism: A Basic Reader. New York: The Herzl Press. 1975.

Cohen, Anne Nathan. The Centenary History of Congregation Beth Israel of Houston, Texas. Houston: By the Congregation, 1954.

Davis, Moshe (ed.). Zionism In Transition. With forward by Ephraim Katzir, Fourth President of the State of Israel, New York: The Herzl Press. 1980.

Eisendrath, Maurice N. Can Faith Survive?. New York: McGraw-Hill. 1964.

Fackenheim, Emil. Encounters Between Judaism and Modern Philosophy. New York: Basic Books. 1973.

Fackenheim, Emil. The Jewish Return Into History. New York: Schocken. 1978.

Feingold, Henry. The Politics of Rescue. New Brunswick, New Jersey: Rutgers University Press. 1970.

Franzblau, Abraham N. A Quarter Century of Rabbinical Training at the Hebrew Union College. Cincinnati: Hebrew Union College. 1933.

Reform Judaism In The Large Cities - A Survey. Cincinnati: Union of American Hebrew Congregations. 1931.

Gladden, Washington. The Working People and Their Employers. New York: Funk and Wagnalls. 1894.

Glazer, Nathan, ed. The Social Characteristics of American Jews. New York: Jewish Education Committee Press. 1965.

Gottheil, Richard J. H. Zionism. Philadelphia: Jewish Publication Society of America. 1914.

Halperin, Samuel. The Political World of American Zionism. Detroit: Wayne State University Press. 1961.

Halpern, Ben. The Idea of the Jewish State. Cambridge: Harvard University Press. 1961.

Handy, Robert T. The Social Gospel In America, 1870-1920. New York: Oxford University Press. 1966.

Henson, George Davis. The Christian Society. New York: Johnson Reprint Corporation. 1969.

Hopkins, Charles Howard. The Rise of the Social Gospel in American Protestantism, 1865-1915. New Haven: Yale University Press. 1940.

Kallen, Horace. Zionism and World Politics. New York: Doubleday, Page and Co. 1921.

Knee, Stuart E. The Concept of Zionist Dissent in the American Mind, 1917-1941. New York, New York: Robert Speller & Sons, Publishers. 1979.

Kohanski, Alexander, ed. The American Jewish Conference: Its Organization and the Proceedings of the First Session, August 29-September 2, 1943. New York: American Jewish Conference. 1944.

Laqueur, Walter. A History of Zionism. New York: Holt, Rinehart and Winston. 1972.

Lilienthal, Alfred M. The Zionist Connection: What Price Peace?. New York: Dodd, Mead & Company. 1978.

Lucas, Noah. The Modern History of Israel. London: London, Weidenfeld and Nicolson. 1974.

Morse, Arthur. While Six Million Died. New York: Random House. 1967.

Plaut, W. Gunther. The Growth of Reform Judaism - American and European Sources Until 1948. New York: World Union for Progressive Judaism. 1965.

The Rise of Reform Judaism. New York: World Union for Progressive Judaism. 1963.

Polish, David. Renew Our Days: The Zionist Issue In Reform Judaism. Jerusalem: World Zionist Organization. 1976.

Rabbis of America To Labor Palestine (pamphlet). New York: League For Labor Palestine. 1935.

Rauschenbusch, Walter. A Theology For the Social Gospel. New York: MacMillan Company. 1918.

Reznikoff, Charles. Louis Marshall: Champion of Liberty. 2 vols. Philadelphia: Jewish Publication Society. 1957.

Safran, Nadav. The United States and Israel. Cambridge: Harvard University Press. 1963

Schechtman, Joseph B. The United States and the Jewish State Movement: The Crucial Decade 1939-1949. New York: Herzl Press. 1966.

Seely, John Robert. Ecce Homo. Boston: Roberts Brothers. 1883.

Selzer, Michael, ed. Zionism Reconsidered: The Rejection of Jewish Normalcy. New York: Macmillan. 1970.

Shankman, Sam. Mortimer May, Foot Soldier In Zion. New York: Bloch Publishing Co. 1963.

Shapiro, Yonathan. Leadership of the American Zionist Organization, 1897-1930. Chicago: University of Illinois Press. 1971.

Sherman, C. Bezalel. The Jew Within American Society. Detroit: Wayne State University Press. 1965.

Silver, Abba Hillel. The Democratic Impulse In Jewish History. New York: Bloch Publishing Co. 1928.

Simon, Leon. Ahad Ha'am. Philadelphia: Jewish Publication Society. 1960.

Stein, Leonard J. The Balfour Declaration. New York: Simon and Schuster. 1961.

Syrkin, Marie. The State of the Jews. New York: New Republic and Herzl Press. 1980.

United Jewish Appeal. The Building of Palestine (pamphlet). New York. 1927.

Urofsky, Melvin I. American Zionism from Herzl to the Holocaust. Garden City, New York. Doubleday. 1975.

Urofsky, Melvin I. ed. Essays in American Zionism, Herzl Year Book (Volume VIII -- 1978). New York: The Herzl Press. 1978.

Urofsky, Melvin I. We Are One. Garden City, New York. Doubleday. 1978.

ARTICLES

Alfange, Dean. "A Liberal Looks At The Jewish State." The New Palestine, Vol. 35, No. 11, pp. 111-112; 119.

Berman, Myron. "Rabbi Edward Nathan Cabisch and the Debate Over Zionism in Richmond, Virginia." American Jewish Historical Quarterly, March 1973, pp. 295-365.

Cohen, Henry. "The Settlement of the Jews in Texas." American Jewish Historical Society Publication, No. 2. 1894. pp. 3-14.

Cohon, Samuel. "A History of the Hebrew Union College." American Jewish Historical Quarterly, Vol. 50, No. 1, pp. 17-55.

Editorial. Hebrew Union College Monthly. #15, October 1929, p. 4.

Editorial. Hebrew Union College Monthly. 1 December 1929, p. 1.

Editorial. Hebrew Union College Monthly. 15 January 1930, p. 2.

Editorial. Hebrew Union College Monthly. 15 April 1930, p. 2.

Editorial. Hebrew Union College Monthly. 15 January 1931, p. 1.

Editorial. Hebrew Union College Monthly. December, 1943, p. 4.

Editorial. Hebrew Union College Monthly. March, 1946, p. 4.

Editorial. Liberal Judaism. September, 1943, p. 35.

Editorial. Liberal Judaism. December, 1943, pp. 2-3.

Editorial. Liberal Judaism. July, 1944, pp. 29-30.

Editorial. Liberal Judaism. November, 1945, p. 4.

Editorial. Liberal Judaism. April, 1946, pp. 6-7.

Editorial. Liberal Judaism. August, 1946, p. 10.

Editorial. Liberal Judaism. May, 1947, p. 37.

Editorial. Liberal Judaism. December, 1947, pp. 1-3.

Editorial. Liberal Judaism. February, 1948, p. 3.

Editorial. Liberal Judaism. March, 1948, p. 2.

Editorial. Liberal Judaism. June-July, 1948, pp. 1-4.

Editorial. Menorah Journal. October-November, 1926. (reprint) Hebrew Union College and Zionism File. American Jewish Archives, Cincinnati.

Eisendrath, Maurice N. "Answering Houston." Liberal Judaism. April 1944, pp. 20-25; 54-58.

Feuer, Leon. "The Gentlemen of the Opposition." Hadassah News-letter, March 1943, pp. 11-13.

Freehof, Solomon B. "Controversy Among Rabbis." Liberal Judaism. July, 1943, pp. 2-5.

"The War of Theories." Liberal Judaism. June 1943, pp. 19-26.

Heller, James G. "The Houston Heresy." Opinion. April 1944. pp. 10-12.

Hexter, Larry. "Trends in Reform Judaism." The Congress Weekly. 11 July 1941, pp. 7-8.

Kohler, Kaufman. "What the Hebrew Union College Stands For." Hebrew Union College Monthly. November, 1916, pp. 1-7.

Lelyveld, Arthur J. "The Conference View of the Position of the Jew in the Modern World" in Korn, Bertram, ed. Retrospect and Prospect - Essays in Commemoration of the 75th Anniversary of the Founding of the CCAR, 1889-1964. New York: Central: Conference of American Rabbis, 1965. pp. 129-180.

Levias, Caspar. "The Justification of Zionism." Hebrew Union College Journal, April, 1899. pp. 167-175.

Levitas, Irving. "Reform Jews and Zionism, 1919-1921." American Jewish Archives Quarterly. April, 1962, pp. 3-19.

Liebman, Joshua Loth. "Kindler of Mental Light." Liberal Judaism. November 1945.

"Assimilation, Isolation or Reform?" Contemporary Jewish Record, April 1942. pp. 131-144.

Morgenstern, Julian. "What Are We Jews?" CCAR Journal, October 1965. pp. 18-24.

"With History As Our Guide." CCAR Yearbook, 1947. pp. 257-287.

Oko, Adolph S. "Kaufman Kohler." Menorah Journal, Vol. 12, No. 5, pp. 513-521.

Philipson, David. "A History of the Hebrew Union College." H.U.C. Jubilee Volume. Cincinnati, 1925.

Rittenberg, Louis. "The Union Achieves Unity." Liberal Judaism, April 1946. p. 8-13.

Trachtenberg, Joshua. "Youth in the Temple." Hebrew Union College Monthly, 1 March 1930. pp. 16-18.

Wessel, Harvey E. "How I became A Zionist at the Hebrew Union College." Hebrew Union College Monthly, May-June 1920. pp. 186-191.

Wise, Isaac Mayer. "Zionism." Hebrew Union College Journal, December 1899. pp. 45-47.

Wolsey, Louis. "My Impressions of the American Jewish Conference." (reprint). Jewish Exponent, 1 October 1943. Louis Wolsey Collection, American Jewish Archives, Cincinnati.

UNPUBLISHED THESES AND DISSERTATIONS

Cohon, Naomi Wiener. "Reform Judaism In America and Zionism, 1897-1922." Master's thesis, Columbia University, New York, 1949.

Matz, Milton. "American Reform Judaism, 1890-1937." Rabbinic thesis, Hebrew Union College, Cincinnati, 1952.

Schlam, Helena Frenkil. "The Early Jews of Houston." Master's thesis, The Ohio State University, Columbus, 1971.

Weinman, Melvin. "The Attitude of Isaac M. Wise Toward Palestine and Zionism." Rabbinic thesis, Hebrew Union College, Cincinnati, 1947.

APPENDIX A

THE STUDENT BODY - TODAY AND YESTERDAY
(the results of a comparative study of the HUC student bodies of 1900 and 1930)

by D. Max Eichhorn

. . . This questionnaire was sent to 50 members of the 1900 student body and to 116 members of the 1930 student body. Twenty-four men or 48% of the first-named group, and 74 or 64% of the last-named responded. The percentage of returns was high and indicated that those who were asked to furnish information were deeply interested in the matter under consideration. These brief introductory remarks explain the purpose and methodology of this investigation. The figures, facts and fancies which follow are the result of a careful perusal of the answers received and a conscientious effort to give a true picture of the Hebrew Union College student body in 1900 and today.

SECTION I. BACKGROUND

A. Birthplace

	1900	1930
United States...	50%	79%
Eastern Europe..	29	8
Western Europe..	21	8
Canada.........	0	5

B. Parentage

1. Place of Origin

	1900	1930
United States...	9%	8%
Eastern Europe..	48	56
Western Europe..	39	14
Mixed..........	4	21
Canada.........	0	1

2. Financial Status

	1900	1930
Very poor.......	4%	1%
Poor............	52	19
Moderate........	44	81

3. Orthodox, Conservative or Reform?

	1900	1930
Orthodox........	52%	43%
Conservative....	0	27
Reform..........	48	30

4. Occupation of father

	1900	1930
Mercantile.......	50%	62%
Artisan..........	9	10
Professional.....	4	10
Jewish...........	37	18

5. Average number of children
1900 - 4 5/6 1930 - 3 9/10

6. Extent of Parent's Jewish education

Father	1900	1930
None.............	0%	3%
Poor.............	4	7
Fair.............	33	40
Excellent........	63	50

Mother	1900	1930
None.............	13%	7%
Poor.............	0	20
Fair.............	56	56
Excellent........	31	17

6a. Extent of Parents' Secular education

	1900	1930
Father		
None	5%	6%
Poor	19	21
Fair	62	53
Excellent	14	20
Mother		
None	5	7
Poor	18	20
Fair	68	59
Excellent	9	14

7. Was there rabbinical tradition in family?

	1900	1930
Yes	58%	56%
No	42	44

8. Did you contribute to family budget?

	1900	1930
Yes	29%	23%
No	71	77

C. Education Prior to Coming to HUC.

1. Jewish	1900	1930
None	0%	8%
Very little	10	7
Good	90	63
Excellent	0	22

2. Secular		
Public school	43%	4%
One year high school	19	0
Three years high school	5	0
High school graduate	29	47
One year university	0%	11%
Two years university	0%	14%
Three years university	0%	1%
B.A.	4	19
M.A.	0	4

SECTION II: COLLEGE ACTIVITIES

A. Scholastic

1. While at college, what was you major academic interest?

	1900	1930
Philosophy	23%	34%
History	27	21
Sociology	8	4
Hebrew	8	9
Other Jewish subjects	20	12
Other non-Jewish subjects	14	20

2. What was your major general reading interest?

	1900	1930
Philosophy	17%	24%
History	34	11
Sociology	14	9
English literature	21	12
Jewish literature	8	8
Miscellaneous	6	36

3. What languages did you speak?

	1900	1930
English	100%	100%
German	50	26
Yiddish	21	32
Hebrew	4	28
French	0	14
Spanish	0	3
Hungarian	0	1
Italian	0	1
Polish	0	1
Russian	0	1

4. What languages did you read?

	1900	1930
English	100%	100%
German	83	73
Hebrew	46	69
French	42	43
Yiddish	21	39
Latin	25	13
Greek	21	3
Italian	8	1
Russian	1	3
Spanish	0	7
Aramic	0	1
Arabic	0	1

B. Extra-curricular Activities

	1900	1930
Athletic	29%	32%
Dramatic	25	32
Forensic	42	24
Musical	13	30
Literary	71	49
Political	13	12
Religious	67	62
Scientific	4	8
Social	38	62
Zionist	8	39

C. Sources of Income

	1900	1930
Family aid	71%	59%
Loans	25	58
Scholarships	50	69
Salary from Religious Work	88%	55%
Salary from Secular Work	42	41
Prizes	8	8

SECTION III. ATTITUDES AND OPINIONS

A. Did you have any definite ideas about the rabbinate at the time of your entering the College? If so, what were they?

	1900	1930
No definite ideas	17%	13%
Vague	12	33
Definite	71	54

B. Your opinion of the mental calibre of your fellow-students.

	1900	1930
Average intelligence	44%	36%
Above average	56	60
Not willing to judge	0	4

Ba. All your fellow-students well-fitted for Rabbinate?

	1900	1930
No	57%	67%
Less than half	0	10
More than half	43	21
Yes	0	2

C. Attitudes

a. Zionism

	1900	1930
Unknown	4%	0%
Favorable	17	69
Neutral	33	22
Opposed	46	9

b. Yiddish

	1900	1930
Favorable	29%	46%
O.K. but doomed to die	8	24
Neutral	29	9
Opposed	34	21

c. Modern Hebrew

	1900	1930
Unknown	13%	0%
Favorable	57	77
O.K. but of no value to American Reform Rabbi	0	3
Neutral	26	13
Opposed	4	7

d. The East European Jew

	1900	1930
All Jews are brothers	8%	63%
Holder of destinies of Judaism	4	
Favorable	25	
Sympathetic	29	
Tolerant	4	

d. The East European Jew (Cont.)

	1900	1930
Needs to be Americanized	30%	
Most vital element in American Jewry	29	
Like him better than West European Jew	8	

e. The West European Jew

	1900
All Jews are brothers	8%
Never thought of him	21
Cultured gentleman	17
My nearest of kin	4
Favorable	25
Lax in Jewish feeling	17
Too apologetic to non-Jewish world	
Snob	4

	1930
All Jews are brothers	63%
Like him better than East European Jew	3
Superior to East European Jew in good breeding	4
Superior to East European Jew in secular culture	5
Adjusts more easily to American life	1
Social elite	2
Financial power	4
Arrogant	1
Lax in Jewish feeling	10
Superficial	4
Assimilationist	3

f. The Mission of Israel

	1900	1930
Non-existent	4%	38%
Undecided	13	4
Self-preservation and inner development	4	36
Teacher of religion to world	79	22

g. Ceremonialism

	1900	1930
We need more	0%	12%
Favorable	65	82
Up to individual	0	1
Neutral	4	0
Opposed	31	5

h. Intermarriage

	1900	1930
No problem	4%	4%
Impossible to generalize	0	16

h. Intermarriage (Cont.)

	1900	1930
Opposed..........	84%	77%
Unavoidable......	4	2
No objection.....	8	0
Favor it as solution of Jewish problem........	0	1

i. Place of Secular Activities in the Work of the Rabbi

	1900	1930
No attitude......	13%	0%
No distinction between religious and secular....	9%	1%
On par with religious work...........	4	9
Important........	52	43
Secondary to religious work.....	13	18
Depends on individual rabbi...	0	4
Depends on individual community	0	8
Very little importance.....	0	17
No place in rabbinical work...	9	0

D. What would be your definition of an ideal modern Reform Rabbi?

The student body of 1900 listed the qualities of an ideal rabbi in the following order:

1. Eloquent speaker
2. Good pedagogue
3. Jewish scholar
4. Communal leader
5. Spiritual personality
6. Teacher of prophetic Judaism
7. Cultured gentleman
8. Prophet of Israel

Today this same group of men has revised its opinion as follows:

1. Defender of Jewish interests
2. Good pedagogue
3. Harmonizer of Judaism with modern world
4. Spiritual personality
5. Jewish scholar
6. Eloquent speaker
7. Stresser of Jewish values
8. Teacher of prophetic Judaism

The student body of 1930 believes that an ideal modern Reform Rabbi must be:

1. Jewish scholar
2. Lover of all types of Jewry and Jewish problems
3. Eloquent speaker
4. Good secular education
5. Good pedagogue
6. Spiritual personality
7. Good pastor
8. Leader of Jewish community
9. Harmonizer of Judaism with modern world
10. Liberalizing influence in society

APPENDIX B

RESOLUTION ADOPTED AT INFORMAL MEETING OF RABBIS, 30 NOVEMBER 1943 AND APPROVED BY THE UAHC AT ITS BIENNIAL COUNCIL MEETING, 3-6 MARCH 1946

The Union declares that its function is to interpret, maintain and promote Reform Judaism and reaffirms its loyalty to its spiritual purposes.

The Union declares its sense of fellowship with all Israel and will associate itself with all worthy and practical efforts designed to ameliorate the tragic plight of world Jewry and therefore continues to be a member of the American Jewish Conference upon the conditions mentioned below.

Because in the congregations of the Union there are divergent opinions on the question of Zionism, the Union recognizes the right of each individual to determine his own attitude on this controversial question.

Therefore, the Union as an organization, is unable to associate itself with those parts of the Palestine Resolution of the American Jewish Conference which call for exclusive Jewish control of immigration into Palestine and the establishment of a Jewish Commonwealth.

The Union's position on Palestine has been stated and we herewith reaffirm the Resolution passed at the Committee meeting on May 30, 1943, whose recommendations were subsequently ratified by the Executive Board of the Union, as follows:

1. Provision shall be made for large-scale immigration into Palestine regulated in cooperation with the Jewish Agency for Palestine by such a concert of nations as shall be established after the war.

2. Palestine shall remain under the stewardship of this concert of nations until it shall become possible to establish self-government without jeopardizing the rights or status of any group in Palestine.

3. Such a government shall be democratic and nonsectarian, modelled upon the governments of the democratic nations. There shall be complete separation of Church and State. The inviolability of the Holy Places of the various religions shall be guaranteed.

We call upon our congregations and their members to rally loyally to the support of the Union.

We further resolve that a copy of this Resolution be forwarded to the American Jewish Conference with the request that they communicate it to the constituent members of the American Jewish Conference and make it known through their publications.

APPENDIX C

RESOLUTION ADOPTED BY THE EXECUTIVE BOARD OF THE UNION OF AMERICAN HEBREW CONGREGATIONS AT CHICAGO, SATURDAY, JUNE 5, 1948

"The Executive Board of the Union of American Hebrew Congregations has taken no stand on the problems of political Zionism, nor does it intend to cancel or to minimize this attitude. Nonetheless, this Executive Board feels that it represents the sentiment of its constituents in sending to the new State of Israel, to its officers and citizens the heartfelt salutation of the UAHC and its prayer that God may send it and them peace and tranquillity.

"We have always felt a deep and sincere interest in our brothers, in their stuggles and achievements. We follow their efforts now to defend themselves, to build up their life, and to bring in the maximum number of Jews from the DP camps and from lands of hatred and discrimination.

"We express our thanks to the President of the United States for prompt recognition of the de facto government of Israel. Be it resolved that this resolution be spread on the minutes, transmitted to the President of the United States, to the government of Israel, and that it be published."

APPENDIX D

REPLY TO RESOLUTION OF TRIBUTE TO THE STATE OF ISRAEL FROM THE EXECUTIVE BOARD OF THE UAHC

STATE OF ISRAEL

PROVISIONAL GOVERNMENT

Office of the Representative

2210 Massachusetts Avenue
Washington 8, D.C.

June 16, 1948

Adams 5411

Gentlemen:

Thank you for your letter of June 7 and for the good wishes you express for the future of Israel.

I have noted with great interest the resolution adopted on June 5, 1948 by the Executive Board of the Union of American Hebrew Congregations. On behalf of my Government I wish to acknowledge with gratitude the salutations of the State of Israel, its officers and citizens, which the resolution conveys from the constituency of your Union.

Very sincerely yours,

Eliahu Epstein
Special Representative

Dr. Maurice N. Eisendrath, President
Mr. Jacob Aronson, Chairman, Executive Board
The Union of American Hebrew Congregations
34 West Sixth Street
Cincinnati 2, Ohio

INDEX

Acharit hayamin, 97
Adler, Felix, 22
Ahad Ha'am, 5,76
Alfange, Dean, 122
American Council for Judaism, 30,34,40,42-45,47,49,62-63,68-69,74, 80-81,89,95,102,119-120,122,124,128,132
American Israelite, The, 70
American Jewish Committee, 105
American Jewish Conference, 70,80-81,89,95-96,98-99,101-125,129
American Unitarian Association, 122
Anti-semitism, 12,32,78,122
Anti-Zionists, 131-132
Arab nationalism, 48,79
Atlantic Charter, 110
Baeck, Leo, 98
Balfour Declaration, 14,21,32,66,75-76,83,107
Baltimore Hebrew Congregation, 74,81
Barnston, Henry, 52-53,62
Basic Principles of Congregation Beth Israel, 128. See also Houston Controversy
Ben-Gurion, David, 93
Berkowitz, Henry, 22,83
Berman, Morton, 119-120,122
Bernstein, Philip, 7,37,44,122
Bilu movement, 20
Bloomfield, Maurice, 22
B'nai B'rith, 103-115-116
B'nai Israel (Baton Rouge, Louisiana), 69
Bookstaber, Philip, 36
Brandeis, Louis D., 13,74
Brickner, Barnett, 27,37,39,44,88
Brooks, Sidney, 7
Buttenweiser, Moses, 92
Canadian Jewish Review, 93
Central Conference of American Rabbis, 9,23-26,33,35-36,38-39,41-42, 44-45,52,57,59-60,69-70,77-80,88-91,95,101-102,113,119-120,124, 127-128,131-132
Chovevay Zion movement, 20
Churchill, Winston, 109
Chyet, Stanley F., 7
Cohen, Anne Nathan, 51
Cohon, Samuel, 28
Columbus Platform, 23,28-30,33,57-58,68,81,95,102,119,127-128,131
Congregation Beth Ahabah (Richmond, Virginia), 112
Congregation Beth Israel (Houston, Texas), 51-57,89,128,131
Congregation Leshem Shomayim (Wheeling, West Virginia), 74
Conservative Judaism, 68
Covenant, 131
Cultural pluralism, 85-87
Dannenbaum, M. M., 114

Daud, Ibn, 98
de Haas, Jacob, 74-75
de Hirsch, Baron, 115
de Sola Pool, David, 63
Dewey, John, 20
Diaspora, 131
Dreyfus trial, 74-75
Eichorn, D. Max, 17
Eisendrath, Maurice N., 7,36,57,66-67,73,92-101,108,112-113,117,128, 132
Emancipation, 3
Emergency Committee for European Jewish Affairs, 103,122
Emmich, Zacharias (Rev.), 51
Enelow, Hyman, 77
Eretz Yisrael, 132. See also Israel, State of and Palestine
Feldman, Abraham J., 28,122,124
Feuer, Leon, 7
Feuerlicht, Morris, 77
Final solution, 103,108
Fineshriber, William, 40,116,122
Finkelstein, Louis, 66
Foster, Solomon, 68
Four Freedoms, 110
Freehof, Solomon B., 37,48,63,66,70,109-110,116
Freiberg, J. Walter, 22
Friedenwald, Henry, 74
Friedlander, I, 53,55,58,63
Galut, 1
Gilbert, Nathan, 115
Gittelsohn, Roland B., 6
Gladden, Washington, 20
Glueck, Nelson, 95
Goldberg, Louis, 63
Goldenson, Samuel, 28,40
Goldman, Robert, 95
Great Britain, 34
Gup, Samuel, 80
Hadassah, 26,76,102
Halutzim, 130
Harding, Warren G., 14
Hartman, Hugo (Mrs.), 105
Hatikvah Controversy, 24
Hebrew Union College-Jewish Institute of Religion, 9,52,60,64,69, 74-75,82-84,88,97,127-128,130
Hebrew Union College Journal, 10-11
Hebrew Union College Monthly, 15,65,117
Heller, Isaac, 114
Heller, James G., 7,13,28,31,33-34,37,40-45,49,64,66,79,88,114, 122,132
Heller, Max, 13,51,75,92
Herzl, Theodore, 3,75
Histadruth, 25,93
Holy Blossom Temple (Toronto, Canada), 92-93
Houston Controversy, 51-71,131. See also Basic Principles
Independent Jewish News Service, 43
Israel, Ed, 43
Israel, State of, 122-125,128. See also Eretz Yisrael and Palestine
James, William, 20
Jewish Agency for Palestine, 15,27
Jewish Army controversy, 33-50,80-81,102,114,127
Jewish Telegraphic Agency, 117
Joint Distribution Committee, 79
Judenstaat, 75
Kahn, Robert L., 7,52-54,61-62